Transatlantic Encounters

AMERICAN STUDIES AND MEDIA

Edited by Elżbieta H. Oleksy and Wiesław Oleksy

Volume 3

PETER LANG

Frankfurt am Main · Berlin · Bern · Bruxelles · New York · Oxford · Wien

Elżbieta H. Oleksy
Wiesław Oleksy
(eds.)

Transatlantic Encounters

Philosophy, Media, Politics

In Memory
of Mateusz Oleksy

PETER LANG
Internationaler Verlag der Wissenschaften

Bibliographic Information published by the Deutsche Nationalbibliothek
The Deutsche Nationalbibliothek lists this publication in the Deutsche Nationalbibliografie; detailed bibliographic data is available in the internet at http://dnb.d-nb.de.

Cover Design:
Olaf Gloeckler, Atelier Platen, Friedberg

Technical Editor: Evan Williams

Gratefully acknowledging the financial support
of the University of Łódź.

ISSN 1610-6814
ISBN 978-3-631-61728-1
© Peter Lang GmbH
Internationaler Verlag der Wissenschaften
Frankfurt am Main 2011
All rights reserved.

Contents

6

Acknowledgments

This collection grew in most part from the conference held at the University of Łódź, Poland, September 23-27, 2008. The conference created a forum to think and debate on transatlantic relations with the theme "Transatlantic Encounters: American Studies in the 21st Century." We would like to thank the Embassy of the United States in Poland, University of Łódź, Łódź City Council, and the Faculty of International and Political Studies, University of Łódź, for the funds that made the conference possible.

The volume *Transatlantic Encounters: Philosophy, Media, Politics* is also the outcome of an array of international collaborations that have developed over the years among individuals from the universities at different geographical sites. The perspectives they brought to this project from a wide variety of philosophical, historical, and political contexts, as well as those pertaining to contemporary mass media, have given this volume a particular richness. We thank all of them for representing the highest ideals of collegiality and cooperation. Sincere thanks are also due to Patrycja Chudzicka-Dudzik, Piotr Duchnowicz and Marta Kotwas for assisting to bring manuscript to production.

Elżbieta H. Oleksy and Wiesław Oleksy

Barbara Tuchańska
University of Łódź, Poland
Mateusz Oleksy – In Memoriam

Mateusz Wiesław Oleksy was born in Łódź in 1974 and brought up in Poland, blessed with loving parents, themselves academics. He graduated from Perry McCluer High School, Virginia, USA in 1991. Already he was an outstanding student, and in recognition of his achievements he was awarded President George Bush Academic Fitness Award. The same year he was admitted to Washington Lee University, Virginia, but decided to return to Poland and entered the Philosophy Program at the University of Łódź. In Virginia he polished his English by reading the works of Bertrand Russell and as a result his interest in philosophy was born. No wonder analytic philosophy became his first field of research. During the five year philosophy program Mateusz received scholarships to study at the University of Bochum (Germany) and the University of Utrecht (The Netherlands), as well as awards for scholarly achievements from the Minister of Education of Poland and the Rector of the University of Łódź. He graduated in Philosophy in 1996, having presented an MA thesis entitled *On the notion of indefiniteness in the philosophy of late Wittgenstein*. During his Ph.D. program in philosophy he received a scholarship to study at the University of Granada (Spain), and research grants at the University of Surrey (UK) and the University of Pittsburgh (USA). In 2001 he received his Ph.D. in Philosophy from the Faculty of History and Philosophy, University of Łódź, and joined the Department of Epistemology and Philosophy of Science at the University of Łódź.

Mateusz's dissertation *Language and Action. A Study in Radical Practical Philosophy* and a few other early publications belong to the field of analytic philosophy of language or even to a borderland between philosophy of language and linguistics. What attracted him to analytic philosophy were features of its craftsmanship: care for conceptual precision and clarity of exposition when presenting one's views, the demand for convincing arguments and correct reasoning, the conviction that reconstructions should be penetrating and exhaustive. Mateusz's attachment to solid tradecraft is present already in his master thesis. Philosophizing did not mean for him inventing beautiful metaphors and writing reader-friendly essays. On the contrary, it was to engage in solid conceptual work. This allows us to appreciate his respect for Ludwig Wittgenstein and Charles Sanders Peirce. In Mateusz's doctoral dissertation Wittgenstein, Peirce, and Aristotle are the main heroes and for good reasons. In the works of all three he found ideas on the relation between thinking and acting, philosophizing and practice. He wrote that practice is "a way of acting which decides who the person that acts is." Of utmost importance for Mateusz was a question: "Who am I?", "How can I understand myself and my actions philosophically?". His doc-

toral dissertation is an outstanding piece of philosophical analysis. Already at
this early stage in his career, Mateusz was able to combine detailed analysis with
daring synthesis to reveal certain tendencies in philosophy. In his dissertation he
also argued that "practice is a form of asceticism," which should allow us to
surpass ethnocentric closure, for example in language, and that it is "a form of
therapy that is supposed to restore confidence in the life world." This is an important idea. The problem of confidence and reliance on reality became one of
the issues in his next important project – a book *Realism and Individualism.
Charles S. Peirce and the Threat of Modern Nominalism*, which he submitted as
a "habilitation" in the tenure procedure and which was published by the University of Łódź Press (2008) in a limited edition.

This stage in Mateusz's academic career began when he received a Senior
Fulbright Grant and spent the academic year 2003-2004 at the University of California in Berkeley. The Fulbright Scholarship was followed by two research
grants from the Polish Science Foundation for especially talented young scholars. This support allowed him to write a book on Peirce, in which one of the
central issues became a discussion between realism and nominalistic rejections
of realism in reference to abstract terms and scientific theories.

Professor Wojciech Kalaga, who reviewed the book for the publisher, stated
that "the whole project of the dissertation is original and meriting a close
attention" and – for Kalaga – "the most original and boldest statement is the thesis, which the author admits Peirce might have rejected, that Peirce's pragmatic
realism is incompatible with scholastic realism and in fact replaces the latter at
some point." (p. 1, trans. by Marek Gensler). Indeed, in Peirce's philosophy Mateusz saw a way beyond skepticism and doubts about the solid empirical ground
of scientific knowledge. Peirce was also for Mateusz a thinker who helps us
overcome the individualist slant of modern philosophy. Professor Kalaga
emphasizes:

[Oleksy] presents a meticulous and convincing reconstruction of Peirce's perspective, from which modern nominalism is seen as a "real and historically significant
matrix of ideas cutting across the divisions of philosophical disciplines" and yet, despite its enormous influence, a nebular rather than monolithic system of ideas. ... his
brief (caption) version of that matrix, presented on pp. 86-87 and covering three divisions: (1) metaphysics, semantics and logic, (2) epistemology, methodology and
psychology, (3) social science and anthropology, is very well constructed, systematic and precise and thus helpful for the following discussions. (Kalaga, p. 2)

Also the last chapter, in which Mateusz reconstructs Peirce's assumptions
concerning the social, is undoubtedly a most crucial and original part. It contains
"a novel attempt at constructing Peirce's anthropology, even though Peirce himself apparently neglected that realm of inquiry" (Kalaga, p. 3). Peirce's organis-
tic social theory, which radically opposes an individualist and liberalist approach, has not been thoroughly studied. Mateusz asks "whether Peirce's quite

radical communal organicism, radical in its anti-individualism, is indispensable as a social counterpart to his PR [pragmatic realism – B.T.], or whether the latter could perhaps be successfully combined with a more moderate communitarian view, more open to liberal-individualistic concerns," for instance to "the minimal sense of individual autonomy, namely, the freedom to assent to a proposition." In reference to this question Mateusz said: "The particular problem provokes a much more general question – one of the questions I am presently prepared to pose, but not to answer" (Oleksy 2008, 20) and he left us with this unanswered question.

We have lost "an excellent interpreter of the philosopher's thought (at the same time 'archeological' and 'abductive'), "one of the most important Peirce specialists not only in Poland but also on the international scene" (Kalaga, p. 6). But we have also lost a convivial colleague and a dear friend.

Philosophy students at the University of Łódź have been deprived of an excellent teacher and an unforgettable tutor of their Philosophical Club. Mateusz greatly contributed to its transformation into a powerful organization which organized conferences, numerous talks, artistic events, and public presentations of the work of students. All of this was possible because Mateusz was a professional authority for both his students and his peers. No one who entered academic relations with him could doubt his professional knowledge and competence; no student with a passion for philosophy could fail to notice and appreciate his unceasing ability to discuss philosophical issues. He was an authority but not, like many prominent academics, one shut up in an ivory tower. In his encounters with students Mateusz was a frank, slightly older buddy, always ready for the sport of good company. Friendly attitudes toward students, such as authority, are not a warrant of pedagogic success. This requires care, and Mateusz did care for students, as well as for colleagues and friends, without being sentimental. He knew how to praise and blame, how to demand and bestow. This rare combination of characteristics made him a charismatic teacher, a great academic, an irreplaceable friend, and a beloved son.

Mateusz W. Oleksy's publications include a book, four book chapters, and over twenty articles published in Poland, Germany, and England. He also gave papers at numerous international conferences in Poland, Italy, and the USA.

References

Kalaga, Wojciech. 2008. Unpublished review of Mateusz Oleksy's manuscript "Realism and Individualism. Charles S. Peirce and the Threat of Modern Nominalism" for the University of Łódź Press.
Oleksy, Mateusz W. 2008. *Realism and Individualism. Charles S. Peirce and the Threat of Modern Nominalism*. Łódź: University of Łódź Press.

Part I – Philosophy

Pragmatic Humanism Forum. Transatlantic reverberations: prospects of Pragmatic Humanism

The term "humanism" has been used by F. C. S. Schiller to describe his own brand of pragmatism, and by William James to express the basic goal of pragmatist movement. This goal was to call attention to the richness and plurality of human experience, and to attack serious challenges facing civilization from a pragmatic perspective, free of the modern infatuation with certainty and abstract theory. Thus, classical pragmatists took up some of the intellectual goals of Renaissance humanists such as Erasmus and Montaigne.

Today the interest in Pragmatic Humanism is revived by eminent thinkers on both sides of the Atlantic Ocean who urge that we abandon modern interest in certainty, epistemic foundations, and purely theoretical problems and return to practical philosophizing sensitive to local problems facing particular communities in particular historical contexts. While these thinkers do not form a homogenous movement, they share several substantive and methodological interests: to study rationality and knowledge from the vantage point of pragmatics or rhetoric of discourse; to see intellectual activities as embodied in specific systems of beliefs, institutional settings, oral traditions, and cultural practices; to view basic philosophical problems in a social-historical context; and to revive interest in philosophy as a form of experience and an art of living.

Papers are invited from all fields of philosophy, especially these dealing with current philosophical problems from a pragmatist perspective and those that address the issue of rapprochement of American pragmatism (and neo-pragmatism) and various trends in contemporary European philosophy. Accepted papers will be presented at PRAGMATIC HUMANISM FORUM during the International American Studies Conference: University of Lodz, Poland: September 27-30, 2008.

Mateusz W. Oleksy

The above is Mateusz's Call for Papers in which he solicited contributions to the Pragmatic Humanism Forum, one of the sessions of the International American Studies Conference entitled "Transatlantic Encounters: American Studies in the 21st Century," Mateusz did not live to take part in. On July 23, 2008, he fell off the Khan Tengri glacier in Kirgizia.

Kacper Bartczak
University of Łódź, Poland

Richard Shusterman's complementary correction of Richard Rorty's model of reading literary texts

Richard Rorty's term "literary culture" is a description of a larger, temporally extended change within the Western intellectual culture. The term signifies a cluster of beliefs, spread among Western intellectuals, mainly those who have internalized findings and ideas coming from a variety of philosophers. The group of philosophical authors crucial for these beliefs could roughly be described as including such diverse names as Nietzsche, Dewey, Heidegger, Wittgenstein and Derrida. Even though this sounds like a rather loose set, Rorty's meta-philosophical narrative has been pointing to steady anti-representationalism and anti-foundationalism as the large-scale common denominators clasping these philosophers into messengers of a unified paradigm shift. In the new paradigm, the inquirer can no longer appeal to the idea of finding an overarching context, or frame, that would for ever stabilize the subjects of inquiry.

It is clear that for Rorty the inquirer is far from an innocent instrument. Inquirers themselves are texts, specific assortments of questions, goals, and methods. As such, they are open networks that will interact with their objects of inquiry, affecting them, and being affected in return. The inquirer is like a reader, who can, in some instances even should, be affected by the text he or she is coming in touch with. It is in the process of reading literary texts that the model of the most transformational inquiry may be found. Indeed, "literary culture" comes with a very specific understanding of the reading processes, capable of causing far reaching changes in critics and readers, contributing to the sense of flux and contingency of the readers' self.

Rorty's descriptions of these processes have created a picture that many critics have seen as implying and requiring models of the self that are too unstable, and thus unrealistic. One such critic is Rorty's fellow neo-pragmatist Richard Shusterman. In this paper I am going to, first, characterize Rorty's notion of "literary culture," with its attendant understanding of the potential inherent in the reading process. Second, I will consider what I believe to be a fruitful modification of Rorty's model offered by Richard Shusterman's understanding of the role of the bodily dimension in the formation of self, knowledge, and the aesthetic experience.

1. Richard Rorty's "literary culture"

The "literary culture" is the final offshoot in a longer series of cultural formations and it is preceded by religion and philosophy. These two earlier formations operated with the rich and promising ideas of constructing a permanent matrix that would constitute the final frame, ultimate reference structure, for all future descriptions of phenomena. Rorty labels these fabled destination ports of inquiry as "redemptive truth[s]," defining them in the following way:

> I shall use the term "redemptive truth" for a set of beliefs which would end, once and for all, the process of reflection on what to do with ourselves ... It would ... fulfill a need that religion and philosophy have attempted to satisfy. This is the need to fit everything – every thing, person, event, idea, and poem – into a single context. It would be the only context that would matter for purposes of shaping our lives, because it would be the only one in which those lives appear as they truly are. (Rorty 2007, 90)

Such an ultimate context would redeem human beings from their endless intellectual toil and uncertainty as to their basic nature and destiny. If found, both in religion and philosophy, the redemptive truth would function as a sphere of transcendence, in which the adept comes in touch with something big, sublime, definitely super-human. Rorty comments: "Monotheistic religion offers hope for redemption through entering into a new relation to a supremely powerful non-human person ... redemption by philosophy would consist in acquiring a set of beliefs that represent things as they truly are" (2007, 91). The first type of relation is "non-cognitive relation to a non-human person," while the other becomes "a cognitive relation to propositions" (2007, 93). Thus, for a religious and/or philosophical intellectual, to attain to "redemptive truth" was to undergo the sublime experience of entering a state of transport from the human state of eternal incompleteness and uncertainty.

Literature, on Rorty's account, cannot secure such transport. Here, the offer seems much more modest. The term "redemptive truth" ceases to obtain, as the "literary culture" gives up completely on the notion of the ultimate stabilizing context. Rorty's understanding of literature, primarily the novel, makes him think of this creative area as spawning endless descriptions of the clashes and interactions between characters whose variety and diversity are inexhaustible, rendering the dream of ever finding a stabilizing formula for the outcomes of these interactions an unrealistic, even unattractive, reverie. Thus the literary culture will no longer offer its members the good delivered earlier to the ardent religious believer and the devotee of the philosopher's cornerstone of knowledge: the "redemptive truth." However, while eliminating the notion of "truth" from the picture, Rorty does not give up on the very term "redemption." Even though the "literary culture" will not tempt its members with the notion of the ultimate end of inquiry into human variety, the close encounters with human variety, endless imaginative construction of human character, materializing amidst endless varieties of settings and interactions, will actually, with time, bring about some kind of "redemption" for the adept. In simplest terms, by making the reader an expert of the unclassifiable complexity of human behavior, "literature" will expand the consciousness of the reader, setting him or her free from the narrow wish of an ultimate context. The absence of such context will now be welcomed with relief, as a higher form of consciousness. Thus, "literature ... offers redemption through making the acquaintance of as great a variety of human beings as possible" (2007, 91). Such acquaintance is redeeming in the sense that it provides a greater flexibility, extent, and variety into the reader's personal awareness and development, making him or her able to maneuver much more skillfully in their real life encounters with other human types, amidst the endless display of the variety of these types. Consequently, here, "redemption" comes to mean "autonomy, in ... non-Kantian and [the] distinctively Bloomian sense" (Rorty 2007, 90). Harold Bloom claims that literature brings autonomy from "cant ... from pious platitudes, the peculiar vocabulary of a sect or a coven" (Bloom 2000, 23). The "redeemed" member of the literary culture has learnt to replace the hope of the final context with the thrill that comes with the enlarged consciousness, now able to weigh large numbers of alternative propositions of how to live one's life. Such ability also means the imaginative creations of possible futures. In this, Rorty returns to his Romantic roots: imaginative projection of the future is the only pathos and transcendence the intellectual should aspire to: "for members of the literary culture, redemption is to be achieved by getting in touch with the present limits of the human imagination" (2007, 94).

It is interesting to note at this point that Rorty's understanding of culture is deeply individualistic and has much to do with models of self-creation and self-shaping. The members of all three cultural formations – religious, philosophical, literary – strive after long term goals, which, if attained, signify their better selves, renewed and perfected versions of the self. However, while the adepts of religious and philosophical formations seek after some kind of stable, and higher unity of their selves – the avatars which would contain all movement and thus could remain motionless – the literary intellectuals' goals are the opposite: they dream of the ease of internal mobility, of flexibility, a talent for adapting to change, even a talent of instigating internal change and profiting from it. This idea of the self as an open-ended network of descriptions always busy reweaving itself was developed by Rorty in detail in *Contingency, Irony, and Solidarity*. It is the picture of the self as an artificial entity consisting of an accretion of descriptions, texts, perspectives, all of which serve as tools for making sense of the world. These descriptions come in historically bound "vocabularies" (Rorty's preferred term) which, internalized in more or less conscious manner, become the very stuff of self. Fed into the self's total set of sentential attitudes, "vocabularies" become the self's very identity. To put it bluntly, the self simply equals its vocabularies (Rorty 1989). Such model of the contingent self, fully aware of the re-describable quality of its beliefs, has far reaching reverberations for Rorty's version of the process of reading a literary text.

Rorty presents his understanding of what should be happening in the reading process at its most intense and fruitful in an essay called "The Pragmatist's Progress: Umberto Eco on Interpretation." The concept received further detailed development in later essays, notably "Redemption from Egotism: James and Proust as spiritual exercises," and "The Inspirational Value of Great Works of Literature" (the final chapter of *Achieving Our Country*). In "The Pragmatist's Progress," which starts as Rorty's argument against Umberto Eco's dualistic distinction between a valuable interpretation and the mere use of the text, Rorty goes on to distinguish two types of reading. This is his attempt to replace the Kantian aesthetic tenets of disinterestedness and distanced respect paid to the object of art, which Rorty sees behind Eco's interpretation/use distinction, with the model of reading as a conversational encounter with another person. This model of reading as an unpredictable personal engagement with the text also allows Rorty to point out the dryness of the highly formalistic and technical approaches to literature developed so successfully at American universities by such advanced, highly theoretical, critical formations as, for example, de Manian deconstruction. The success of such approaches produced, according to Rorty, a preference for readings that, although highly professional and expert, are in fact shallow by their guarded reliance on method, prefigured tools, results that can be predicted in advance. Here, the critic uses method as a shield, and remains untouched by his object of inquiry. Rorty is right to point out that methodical rigidity misses a crucial point about literature, which, after all, does not stem, and should not be contained, by academic categories and methods. Rorty complains:

> In an anthology of readings on Conrad's *Heart of Darkness* which I recently slogged through ... none of the readers had, as far as I could see, been enraptured or destabilized by *Heart of Darkness*. I got no sense that the book had made a big difference to them, that they cared much about Kurtz or Marlow ... These people, and that book, had no more changed these readers' purposes than the specimen under the microscope changes the purpose of the histologist. (1999, 145)

The hubris of methodical reading lies in its forgetfulness concerning the exceptionality of its own object of study; it reminds one of the professional blindness of a physician who forgets that the patient is a being that cannot be reduced to the condition of his or her organs. There is always an extra to literature: an emotional, psychological, aesthetic, cognitive extra. Does it mean that Rorty proposes his own method of capturing this excess? No. Here the answer is pragmatic: treat the afflatus offered by the literary work of art not as phenomenon calling for classification, but as a strong portion of energy needed for the internal change of the reader. In other words – follow the consequences. Thus Rorty reminds critics of the necessity of a non-methodical reading:

Unmethodical criticism of the sort which one occasionally wants to call "inspired" is the result of an encounter with an author, character, plot, stanza, line or archaic torso which has made a difference to the critic's conception of who she is, what she is good for, what she wants to do with herself: an encounter which has rearranged her priorities and purposes. Such criticism uses the author or text ... as an occasion for changing a previously accepted taxonomy. (1999, 145)

The key concept here is the capacity, in the reader, for a large scale change that is activated by reading. The literary text acts as a high voltage impulse which pushes the reader's network of beliefs and desires toward a new cycle of reweaving operations, which will result in a new balance grid created in the self, this, in turn, yielding new questions and thus new purposes. As such, the reading process is an opening toward a future: the future of the individual and his or her surroundings. The literary text itself is a richly arranged network of attitudes, which has no center, which will never yield its ultimate reading, as its meanings are context dependent. The reader himself is such a new context, and on Rorty's model the reader is himself read by the text, thus becoming this text's fresh chance for new meaning. What matters is an interaction between open-ended textual fabrics, whose encounter signals a chance for a new idea of a future. For Rorty, this seems the ultimate value and the only sublime. In "The Inspirational Value of Great Works of Literature" he treats literature as the locus of hope and hopeful mystery that, in quasi-religious fashion clearly reminiscent of William James's meliorism, is associated with the future: "When I attribute inspirational value to works of literature, I mean that these works make people think there is more to this life than they ever imagined" (Rorty 1998, 133).

It is here that we can appreciate the significance and centrality of Rorty's highly hopeful concept of the reading experience for the whole argument concerning the emergence of the "literary culture." Rorty sees the reader within the Emersonian module of self-reliance and self-creation. The crucial capacity of the individual is to always project new versions of the self, thus venturing on new versions of the private, but also communal, future. It is by such textual activation of the self-reweaving process that substance is given to Rorty's idea of "redemption" through literature, to the project of "getting in touch with the present limits of human imagination" (2007, 94). For the biggest mystery of the reading experience is its capacity of disclosing new purposes, earlier inaccessible to the reader.

2. Richard Shusterman's critique of Rorty's model of the self

Rorty's ideas of the structure of the self and the nature of the reading experience do not escape charges of weakness and inconsistency. Richard Shusterman points to a number of problems lurking in Rorty's idea of the contingent self that, as we have seen, is the necessary basis for the potential inherent in reading encounters. Simply put, Rorty's picture of the self as a self-regulating, freely floating conglomerate of texts and conversations, sounds far too fragile to Shusterman. Rorty sees the self as a web of descriptions, always capable of absorbing new pieces of text (new sentential attitudes, new beliefs), and then adjusting to the change. The reading process, as described above, would then be the apex of this capacity: a vast global change akin to religious conversion. For Shusterman this vision is unrealistic. Such centerlessness, claims Shusterman, goes too far, and poses a threat to stability. At one point of his critique Shusterman (2000b) refers to Rorty's attempt to rewrite Freud's hard divisions into separate regions of the self, always blocked off from each other, into a free and vibrant internal symposium of "quasi-persons," that is voices, or attitudes, residing within the vast web of the self. On Rorty's view (1991), such rewriting of Freud would allow us to see a new goal of moral life: keeping the internal conversation as open, flexible, and lively as possible. Needless to say, literature provides ample opportunity for the project. Shusterman, however, sees the danger of disintegration threatening the whole edifice of the freed, post-Freudian, internal debate advocated by Rorty. The contingent self is too volatile a being to be exposed to constant novelty. The pressures of such promiscuous transformational activity may burst the very notion of the self. Shusterman writes:

> If we abandon the aim of a unified, coherent self-narrative, for Rorty's chorus of inconsistent 'quasi-selves' constituted by alternative, constantly changing, often incommensurable narratives and vocabularies with no complex narrative able to make them all hang together, then the project of self enrichment becomes mythical and incoherent. (2000b, 249)

Yet this is not the end of the list of difficulties found in Rorty's idea of self-creation through reading. Another set of problems concerns the question of Rorty's rigid private/public split and his radically linguistic approach to meaning creation. Rorty has maintained at numerous places that aesthetic self-creation must be reserved for the individual's private sphere. Transformation through literature is of a non-cognitive and non-argumentative nature. The internal relocations caused within the network of beliefs and desires constituting the self are too vast to be closed or controlled by argumentation. The change Rorty describes is more of spiritual than argumentative kind, and it moves the self beyond the currently held criteria of discursive thought. Since for Rorty the public sphere is the area of argument, he wants his strong self-creators to care for the transformational processes in private seclusion:

> Although argumentation is essential for projects of social cooperation, redemption is an individual, private, matter ... This means acknowledging that private hopes for authenticity and autonomy should be left at home then the citizens of a democratic society foregather to deliberate what is to be done. (2007, 102)

For Shusterman such a split is too rigid, and, ultimately, unrealistic. Shusterman (2000b) has pointed out that the languages that will take part in aesthetic events of self-shaping will always already be a public creation.

I believe that these two criticisms of Rorty by Shusterman – concerning the instability of the contingent self and the rigidity of the private and public split – can be countered by Rorty's later views, expressed, for example, in such essays as "Redemption from Egotism." In that essay, the model of flexible self-creation through reading is shown to be continuous with the creation of self that integrates variety and plurality of reading experience into higher-level stable, psychological wholes, much as a skillful novelist is able to integrate a medley of characters and events into a coherent plot (Rorty 2001b). Incidentally, this newly created self is also much more sensitive to others and better in external dealings with diverse human types, which would also suggest, against Rorty's own consistent claims, that the private self-creation project does have a bearing on this self's public performance. However, Shusterman's most interesting and fruitful criticism of Rorty, finally amounting to what I take to be an important correction and modification of Rorty's project, concerns Rorty's radical and pervasive linguisticism.

For Rorty, consciousness is linguistic through and through, and the network of beliefs and desires, which constitutes the self and the area on which the change through aesthetic experience is effected, is a grid of sentential attitudes. Here, all meaning and significance are enclosed within linguistic productiveness and clashes between linguistically articulated attitudes. This, in turn, seems to suggest that meanings are always at hand, accessible to the linguistic consciousness, ready for interpretation and reinterpretation. For Shusterman, Rorty is part of "hermeneutic universalism," a vast tendency in philosophy in which radical anti-foundationalism results in the belief "that interpretation subsumes all meaningful experience and reality" (2000b, 116). Since "interpretation" is a conscious procedure, and because within the boundaries of hermeneutic universalism all linguistic exchange is interpretive, the global change in the sentential networks of the self that Rorty envisions would have to be eligible, at all points, for conscious and meaningful interpretation.

However, as we have seen, the very moment of the change occurring within the self on entering Rortian reading experience escapes argumentative discourse, and thus interpretation. The change engages areas of the self, but it does so through procedures that the self would not be able to reduce to argumentative, reflective, interpretation. There is a paradox functioning in Rorty's idea of transformation through reading. In "Pragmatist Progress," the very essay in which the transformational, or "inspired," reading experience is proposed against "methodical reading," Rorty (1999) makes clear that the reading process is activated by the questions that the reader has in himself and contributes to the reading encounter. Reading is triggered by the combination of goals and interests that the reader brings into the reading: "[The text's] coherence is no more than the fact that somebody has found something interesting to say about a group of marks or noises – some way of describing those marks and noises which relates them to some of the other things we are interested in talking about" (1999, 138). That "inspired" reading produces previously inaccessible questions and purposes may seem problematic then. We are dealing with the emergence of a new quality from the old set of beliefs, without any quantitative addition to the old set. In Rorty's description the text is not treated as, say, a new idea that is quantitatively added or superimposed on the group of beliefs the self possesses before reading. Rather, it is the self's grid that undergoes an internal reweaving out of its own openness to the text, and the new internal balance prompted by the text – the new set of goals and purposes – emerges from within the self. The literary text acts here not as carrier of cognitive content, but as an impulse causing the change. The text simply activates and puts to work a potential that must be inherent in the self, but screened from it, before the reading event. Thus, we are forced to conclude that there must be an area of the unknown and inaccessible in the initial grid of questions and purposes. Yet this suggests that there always is an area in the self that is meaningful, in the sense of constituting a potential for change, and yet not immediately accessible to meaningful and reflective interpretation. It is for the exploration of this sub-interpretive layer providing an active background of the capacity for change, that we can turn to Shusterman.

3. Richard Shusterman's aesthetic experience and somaesthetics

Shusterman has called this area simply "beneath interpretation." In *Pragmatist Aesthetics* he argued:

> Various camps of the ever-growing anti-foundationalist front seem united by the belief that interpretation subsumes all meaningful experience and reality ... I suggest the contrary idea that our intelligent and meaningful intercourse with the world includes non-interpretational experience, activity, and understanding, so that we should not think of interpretation as the only game in town. (2000b, 116-117)

The area "beneath interpretation" is non-discursive, pre-reflective, and thus non-interpretational. On this level action proceeds without recourse to interpretation, alongside habitual, and pre-reflective paths. And yet, the region "beneath interpretation" is meaningful, as it is in fact a ground from which meaningful action stems. "Beneath interpretation" is a form of "understanding": "Certainly there seem to be forms of ... awareness or understanding that are not linguistic in nature and that defy adequate linguistic characterization" (2000b, 117). Importantly, to make sure that he does not advocate any form of return to foundationalism, Shusterman assures the reader that the area of "beneath interpretation" is not the faculty or residue of the immediately given. Rather, it is an area of the previously acquired procedures, regularities, understandings and habits, which have now sunk to a background region. As such is fallible, but also accessible and corrigible: "if we abandon foundationalism by denying that any understanding is incorrigible, the idea of corrigible [pre-interpretive] understanding becomes possible and indeed necessary" (2000b, 121).

In Shusterman's discourse the distinguishing of the area "beneath interpretation" is a strategic clearing of the ground for his two central projects: the proper development and continuation of John Dewey's concept of aesthetic experience, and the philosophy of somatic mindfulness that Shusterman calls somaesthetics. The two arguments are interconnected. Shusterman reaches back to his greatest philosophical fascination, John Dewey, in order to continue the work of developing means by which to bring art and life closer together. "Aesthetic experience" is a crucial concept in this project. After Dewey, and against analytic aesthetics, Shusterman wants the aesthetic experience to be "evaluative, phenomenological, transformational," rather than just "purely descriptive, semantic one whose chief purpose is to explain and thus support the established demarcation of art from other human domains" (2000a, 21-22). Aesthetic experience is seen as a strongly defined moment of exhilarating and energetic sensation that enhances the liveliness and the live engagements of the human organism:

> From the humdrum flow of routine experience, aesthetic experience stands out … as a distinctly memorable, rewarding whole – not just experience, but 'an experience' – because in it we feel 'most alive' and fulfilled through the active, satisfying engagement of all our human faculties that contribute to this integrated whole. (Shusterman 2000a, 23)

Clearly, the concept of aesthetic experience signals Shusterman's holistic approach: the aesthetic effects comprise and influence the whole organism. The event of aesthetic experience is in fact an interface between the conscious and reflective and the sphere of the pre-reflective, non-discursive understanding, that is the region "beneath interpretation" described above. It is here, within the boundaries of the life enhancing encounters with aesthetic products that the crucial commerce takes place between the pre-reflective and the interpretive, and it is through aesthetic experience that the pre-reflective may in fact function as the background always keeping the project of interpretation alive.

These interactions between the pre-reflective and the interpretive, accelerated within the bounds of clearly delineated aesthetic experience, do not happen in any abstract sphere. Shusterman's holistic thinking recognizes a very palpable stage setting for them: the bodily. His "somaesthetics" is a large project for a new discipline, and I am unable within this essay to even start characterizing the whole undertaking. It is crucial for my purposes, however, to note at this point that Shusterman (2000a, 2000b, 2008) treats the body as the palpable reservoir of the pre-reflective habits constituting the self. It is the conscious care of the bodily sphere that facilitates the processes of interaction between the pre-reflective and the interpretive, at the same time enhancing, possibly even regulating, the aesthetic experiences of the organism. In his recent book *Body Consciousness*, Shusterman writes: "We can briefly describe somaesthetics as concerned with the critical study of how we experience and use the living body as a site of sensory appreciation and creative self-fashioning" (2008, 1). In fact, somatic consciousness is the ground and starting point for all aesthetic appreciation. Just as Dewey claimed that epistemological operations and structures may be traced to the human need for aesthetic creativity, so Shusterman transposes this argument onto the relation between our aesthetic life in general and the basic appreciation of the bodily being. At one point he argues: "There is the beautiful experience of one's own body from within – the endorphin enhanced glow of high level cardiovascular functioning, the slow savoring awareness of improved deeper breathing, the tingling thrill of feeling into new parts of one's spine" (2000b, 262). This is why, as noted earlier, somatic consciousness becomes a "site" for other projects and engagements, notably the project of self-creation through the arts, that Shusterman shares with his pragmatic predecessor Rorty.

Shusterman's holistic inquiry into the complex ways in which the bodily participates in the aesthetic transformations of the self, thus in aesthetic self-fashioning, expands the whole project, by providing it with important details, and solving some of the paradoxes lurking in Rorty's introductory outlining of these processes. The somatic attention allows us to conceive of more flexible and versatile models of the self. Importantly, Shusterman's description of how the self is necessarily connected to its environment through the bodily, helps us deal more comprehensively with the problems of the private/public split insisted on by Rorty. Even though one should agree with Rorty who says that the private self is a civilizational achievement, a privilege which we should be grateful for as it signals "responsibilities to ourselves," and that we should care for it as for a rare "hothouse flower" (2001a, 155), Shusterman's texts help us understand that the self-fashioning processes will always have a bearing on the public performance of the self, and that the private/public split is a very permeable membrane. Somaesthetics reminds us that each individual project participates, on some level, in the life of the species as a whole: "I contend that *any acutely attentive somatic self-consciousness will always be conscious of more than the body itself*" (Shusterman 2008, 8). In fact, there is a completely new version of the self, one that leaves behind for good the old problematic of solipsism, that could still be sensed, at least remotely, in Rorty's idea of the private creation. Shusterman envisions a new being that could be called "symbiotic self," and there is a chance for a new kind of spirituality inherent in this vision: "In our bodily actions, we are not self-sufficient agents but stewards and impresarios of larger powers that we organize to perform our tasks" (2008, 215).

However, most importantly for the reciprocity that I have been trying to establish between Rorty and Shusterman, Shustermanian inquiry into the bodily for the sake of aesthetic self-creation may be a chance to better understand the paradox that we noticed in Rorty's description of reading as a transformational experience. If the bodily is a locus of the pre-reflective, and if it also conditions our capacity for undergoing and participating in aesthetic experiences – which is one of the claims of somaesthetic – then the bodily sphere, as approached by Shusterman, becomes a candidate for the region of background otherness that we saw as implied in Rorty's "inspired reading." The bodily sphere is the locus of a certain capacity for the aesthetic enjoyment that can be activated by the aesthetic object. With Shusterman we not only enlarge our understanding of the constitution of the self, but we also begin to obtain a better picture, even a hold of, the complex exchanges between the conscious interpretive processes and those regions that are meaningful but not permanently present to consciousness. The bodily, as a locus of pre-conscious meanings, may in fact constitute the area of the potential for change, the area that the self is not constantly aware of. As it was noted earlier, such area must be posited to fully explain the transformational reading experience so valued by Rorty.

It might be stipulated, for instance, that interaction with artistic products both depends on, but also actively influences the rich, albeit sub-reflective, sphere in the self that is responsible for our capacity to feel pleasure. Pleasure-taking may be an art in itself, and may depend on the complex network of habits, predominantly non-reflective, that are responsible for forming aesthetic preferences, seeking their satisfaction, and including them in the difficult compositions of self-creation. If Shusterman is right, these habits are closely interwoven with a vast network of other habits: habits of thought, human interaction, self-care, but also bodily habits of movement, energy storing and expending. Such interweaving of different classes of habits, connected with Shusterman's Deweyan idea that the pre-reflective sphere is accessible and corrigible, provides us with a possible channel for a better maintenance of balance between the pre-reflective and the interpretive, the balance that may be responsible for the general quality of our activities, not only in the field of aesthetics.

The final conclusion is that Shusterman's philosophy calls for more work on developing a critical language of interaction with aesthetic objects that would give a fuller access to the now murky exchanges between the somatic care of the self and the interpretive meanings of the self's aesthetic engagements. Interaction with art should benefit from the chance of the better regulation of the aesthetic experience afforded by Shusterman.

28   Kacper Bartczak

References

Bloom, Harold. 2000. *How to Read and Why*. New York: Touchstone.
Rorty, Richard. 1989. *Contingency, Irony, and Solidarity*. Cambridge: Cambridge University Press.
------. 1991. *Essays on Heidegger and Others: Philosophical Papers volume 2*. Cambridge: Cambridge University Press.
------. 1998. The Inspirational Value of Great Works of Literature. In *Achieving our Country*. Cambridge, Mass.: Harvard University Press.
------. 1999. The Pragmatist's Progress: Umberto Eco on Interpretation. In *Philosophy as Social Hope*. New York: Penguin.
------. 2001a. Response to Richard Shusterman. In *Richard Rorty: Critical Dialogues*, ed. Matthew Festenstein and Simon Thompson, 153-57. Blackwell: Molden, MA.
------. 2001b. Redemption from Egotism: James and Proust as Spiritual Exercises. *Telos* 3: 243-63.
------. 2007. *Philosophy as Cultural Politics: Philosophical Papers, volume 4*. Cambridge: Cambridge University Press.
Shusterman, Richard. 2000a. *Performing Live: Aesthetic Alternatives for the Ends of Art*. Ithaca: Cornell University Press.
------. 2000b. *Pragmatist Aesthetics: Living Beauty, Rethinking Art*. 2nd edition. Lanham, New York: Rowman & Littlefield.
------. 2008. *Body Consciousness: a Philosophy of Mindfulness and Somaesthetics*. Cambridge: Cambridge University Press.

Katarzyna Dąbrowska
University of Łódź, Poland
A utopia or a solution? The Deweyan project of participatory democracy and the public sphere

1. Introduction

Although more than 50 years have passed since the death of John Dewey, many of the problems raised in his writings are still current and – what is more – a lot of his concepts apply to the present time. One of the problems examined in his writings is that of democracy and liberalism. Nowadays liberalism has many enemies, just in Dewey's times. These enemies are recruited not only from the circles reluctant to social change, but also from circles of revolutionaries, who demand immediate change, irrespective of the costs that society might pay for such rapidity. The latter group justifies the use of drastic measures in order to carry these changes into effect. In comparison to the two aforementioned extremes and because of its mediatory character, liberalism can be seen as a diluted, milk-and-water doctrine for opportunists. There are a lot of people today using the word *liberal* as an insult and proffer it as an adequate epithet for indecisive people of mutable views, who pride themselves on being able to adapt to all kinds of conditions. In my opinion such usage of the adjective "liberal" is unfair, yet I am aware that there must be some reasons for this situation.

Being a true-born social reformer, Dewey projected his own, revised liberal creed in response to this critique. He thoroughly reconsidered and reformulated the notion and the office of liberalism, which is the reason why some critics question whether he can be called a liberal at all (Gamwell 1984). His project of democracy is innovative and intriguing and it would be easy to discuss it, were it not so controversial. One way to examine the controversy is by asking the question whether Dewey's contrivance is an ingenious, but reasonable plan for social betterment or a fascinating but naïve utopia. It is exactly this dilemma that will be the core of my paper. In the course of my considerations I will try to prove that the above-mentioned problem can be solved to the advantage of Dewey. Thus, this paper is a defense of the thesis that Dewey's project is thoroughly innovative and that Deweyan postulates provide reasonable answers to some current social problems.

In this paper I will consider two problems, which are essential to an analysis of Deweyan democracy. First, Dewey's views on democracy and liberalism will be analyzed from two perspectives: (a) a negative perspective, by which I mean Dewey's opinions on the history of traditional liberalism and his critique of this doctrine and; (b) a positive perspective that is Dewey's own project of democracy. Second, I will analyze the feasibility of the Deweyan conception of liberalism and try to defend the aforementioned thesis of this paper.

2. The history of liberalism

For the purposes of this paper it is necessary to review the history of liberalism. The reader should be warned that it will be the history described by Dewey in his writings on political philosophy, for the most part in *Liberalism and Social Action*, that I will discuss. I am constrained to abridge his reasoning, since it is not the main topic of my essay and any simplifications and imperfections in this part are the result of indispensable shortening.

Classical liberalism arose in seventeenth century Europe and it is John Locke who we call its founding father. The character of the Lockean version of liberalism was highly individualistic and its influence was political. His project was aimed "against levies on property made by rulers without authorization from the representatives of the people" (Dewey 2000, 16). Locke claimed the supremacy of an individual over the state and set individualism against organized social action. The opposition was emphasized by the doctrine of natural rights constituting the inherent endowment of an individual. These rights included liberties of thought and action; reason was also something that individuals possessed by their distinctive nature. The sole role of government was to protect these rights, but in the times of Locke the situation differed from this ideal. This is why Locke saw a natural antagonism between organized society and the individual and characterized them as two different spheres. One of the Lockean natural rights was the right of property. This idea inspired the later economic version of liberalism. Actually, Locke was interested in property already possessed, by which he understood properties and estates. Thus his version of economic liberalism was evidently static (Dewey 2000, 15-18).

The next stage in the evolution of liberalism was the dynamic concept connected with *laissez faire* liberalism. This idea of liberalism was interested in *production* of wealth and its main aim was to enhance productivity and trade through fewer legal restrictions. The shift from the earlier to the later form of economic liberalism was significant. What changed was the practical meaning of liberty and the influence of liberal thought. The later liberalism granted priority to purely economic activity. The rights of production and trade were included to the doctrine of natural laws. The leader of this movement – Adam Smith, who was not a follower of *laissez-fairism* – claimed that the unrestricted activity of individuals is the main source of progress and social welfare. Individuals are inherently inclined to improve their conditions and satisfy their needs; the efforts to enhance one's situation contribute to the improvement of social conditions, as described in Smith's doctrine of the invisible hand. As a consequence, a view developed among *laissez faire* liberals that every organized social action is an attack delivered against social progress (Dewey 2000, 18-21).

The doctrine of *laissez faire* liberalism identified freedom with the "absence of governmental action, conceived as an interference with natural liberty" (Dewey 2000, 22). It is not a surprise – says Dewey – that this doctrine arose in Great Britain, where the legal and political systems were not divided. British common law favored not the economical activity of individuals, but of landed property owners. According to Dewey, this system could be improved thanks to Jeremy Bentham, who demanded radical changes.

In the United Kingdom the influence of Bentham and his school was far greater than that of Locke. Yet, the ideas of the latter lasted in the United States. In that country social conditions were much different than those in the United Kingdom and hence these two liberalisms are completely different. To the time of the Civil War, the United States were mostly agrarian. The concepts of Locke met pioneer and frontier conditions. Self-help and individual initiative were practiced spontaneously and did not need intellectual support. The influence of romanticism caused a change of meaning of liberalism. It was – in Dewey's words – "disassociated from the *laissez faire* creed and ... associated with the use of governmental action for aid to those at economic disadvantage and for alleviation of their conditions" (Dewey 2000, 30).

3. Dewey's critique of traditional liberalism

Dewey clearly indicates the cause of the crisis of liberalism and its growing impotency. For him a split among liberal thinkers was the source of accusing the doctrine of political lukewarmness (Dewey 2000, 35). Different views on the relationship between the individual and the social (and – accordingly – distinct concepts of freedom) were the bone of contention for liberals. In Dewey's opinion, there were two groups of liberals. The first group regards the individual and the social in opposition to each other. They understand liberty as a freedom from political pressure and from external (i.e. governmental) limitations and restrictions. Any action of a state is justified only in times of a crisis, when special measures are needed. Except for sporadic occurrences, any governmental action is highly unwelcome, not to say harmful. The second faction claims that organized society can (and should) support initiatives and efforts of its members and create conditions under which individuals can gain their actual, and not only legal liberty. Thus liberalism should be a comprehensive program of social reforms aiming at this goal, namely the liberation of individuals. Yet – says Dewey – both of these groups fall short of this requirement: the former entirely negates all reformative projects, the latter reduces the functions of a state to a protective nature (Dewey 2000, 35-36).

Dewey admits that all the social changes brought about in the nineteenth century were due to the active struggle of his predecessors. Yet in spite of all the successes, new liberalism has to realize the defects of its earlier versions. The method of sole analysis is no longer effective for liberalism and does not meet the requirements of the present. Furthermore, it is no longer a sufficient response to current social problems (Dewey 2000, 37). As will be shown later, the philosopher's own idea of liberalism provides an innovatory solution to some of these problems.

For Dewey the first considerable defect of traditional liberalism was the lack of historic sense and interest (Dewey 2000, 40-41). This shortcoming was an excellent instrument in the struggle against early liberals' enemies, who they saw as being opposed to social change. By appealing to history the opponents of liberalism sanctified existing social abuses. Nevertheless, this negation of historic relativity was also a weapon against liberals themselves. They could not notice that their interpretation of the three key notions of liberalism – *liberty*, *individuality* and *intelligence* – was historically conditioned and relative.[1] Their ideas were intended to abolish the *status quo* sanctified by social customs. Yet, in the middle of the nineteenth century this situation had transformed entirely since to a large degree the aims for which they fought had been achieved. By then they were the force that protected the status quo. They became as absolutist as their enemies, for they believed that social welfare can be achieved only by the measures of the *laissez faire* liberalism that they professed.

Dewey gives us a good example of early liberals' historic nearsightedness (Dewey 2000, 44). For instance, Benthamites were aware that the private interests of rulers must be controlled by society. Otherwise a situation would develop which condoned abuses and finally lead to the suppression of the liberty of individuals. Yet they omitted the fact that the same rule applies to economics. Economic self-interest, not checked socially, leads to consequences similar to those of private control of political power. They opted for new legal institutions in order to limit governmental arbitrary actions and achieve political liberty and equality of people, but they did not see that a socially controlled economy is *conditio sine qua non* of obtaining economical freedom for the masses.

Liberals assumed that economic liberty would automatically bring social transformations. The history of the twentieth century is proof that the era of affluence did not actually come and as a consequence of their tenets came an era of private, not common wealth. They overlooked the fact that economic liberty is not enough. What about – to give an example – cultural liberty? It seemed like the virtues of initiative, independence, choice and responsibility – treated as in-

---

[1] It has to be noted that Dewey understood these terms in an axiological sense, i.e. he conceived them not as ideas but as values. This fact is pointed out by Włodzimierz Kaczocha in his book on, inter alia, the philosophy of John Dewey (see: Kaczocha 2008, 101).

herent elements of individuals' natures – only related to the material sphere of life (Dewey 2000, 46).

Here we can understand the way their concept of individuality proceeded from their idea of liberty. They regarded individuality as something given, "ready-made, already possessed, needing only the removal of certain legal restrictions to come into full play" (Dewey 2000, 46). Because of their inherent nature, individuals have the same opportunities of action. The only thing that needs to be done is the removal of external limitations and the application of equal rights for all. Under these conditions the innate freedom of individuals can flourish. In regard to society, individuals were seen as Newtonian atoms, the only relationships connecting them with other atoms being time and space (Dewey 1935, 226). Yet, the truth is that individuals from their day of birth are constantly changed by their interaction and interrelationships. Thus the natural laws are not psychological, but are "laws of individuals in associations" (Dewey 2000, 48).

The problem of the third central value of liberalism – intelligence – is analogous to the previous two. Dewey argues that "the doctrine of *laissez faire* was applied to intelligence as well as to economic action" (Dewey 2000, 50). Liberals conceived the human mind in the same way as they conceived society, namely as a set of external relations between atomistic elements, each of them being characterized by its fixed nature. Their conception did not allow anything like collective social planning or far-reaching social experiments. For the author of *Liberalism and Social Action* liberalism should provide an idea of intelligence that gives direction to social transformations (Dewey 2000, 51). This is also the task of new, reconstructed liberalism: to mediate between these transformations (Dewey 2000, 54-55). The problem of new social organization, of democracy, can be solved only by reversal of the methods to which early liberalism was committed (Dewey 2000, 60). Later in this paper I will try to prove that the Deweyan project is a noteworthy response to the problem of the new social order.

There are three burning questions, which new liberalism has to solve. These are: (1) the problem of achieving freedom, (2) the problem of science and (3) the problem of democracy. Freedom cannot be characterized as a conflict between an organized society and an individual. Science is not only a measure of increasing material productivity but should contribute to the development of society. Universal suffrage and representative government have been established, but these are only elements of democracy so bringing them into effect does not instantly make one country democratic (Dewey 2000, 39). As a confirmation of this thesis Dewey quotes Havelock Ellis: "We see now that the vote and the ballot-box do not make the voter free from even external pressure; and, which is of much more consequence, they do not necessarily free him from his own slavish instincts" (Dewey 2000, 39-40).

4. The Deweyan project

Now it is essential to present the Deweyan project of democracy and his plan of healing traditional liberalism. Obviously, it is impossible to discuss this subject exhaustively, therefore I am constrained to focus only on the most important issues and to present them in brief.

First of all, Dewey as an antiabsolutist emphasizes the role of historical, cultural and temporal relativity. He points out that every social inquiry is a part of a social process itself and cannot be conducted apart from it (Dewey 2000, 51). The aims of liberals should correspond with actual social conditions. Hence, for Dewey one of these goals is "the liberation of individuals so that realization of their capacities may be the law of their life" (Dewey 2000, 61). Such an aim can be attained only by "a social organization that will make possible effective liberty and opportunity for personal growth in mind and spirit in all individuals" (Dewey 2000, 62). To meet this requirement liberalism should become radical (Dewey 2000, 66). The word "radical" is not usually connected with the doctrine of liberalism, but in Dewey's grasp of this issue liberalism is radical when theories to which it is committed lead to radical and not just partial transitions. To quote Dewey's words: the term radical means "perception of the necessity of thoroughgoing changes in the set-up of institutions and corresponding activity to bring the changes to pass" (Dewey 2000, 66). One may wonder why Dewey characterizes the main concern of liberalism in terms of radicalism. The philosopher's response to this question is that the gap between the actual state of affairs and the state that is possible to achieve is so substantial, that liberalism has to become a constructive, complete and concrete program of profound social reforms. What distinguishes Deweyan liberalism from other radical movements is its experimental method: using freed intelligence in order to direct and initiate changes. As opposed to liberalism, other radicalisms often use violence and coercion to achieve their ends. However, for Dewey using force is not a solution and sooner or later it will result the same method being used by those against whom this force was initially directed (Dewey 2000, 67, 87).

Dewey gives an entirely new interpretation of the three liberal values: liberty, individuality and intelligence. These values stay in a close union and come out of each other. I shall begin with the concept of individuality, for it is impossible to comprehend the other two without a glimpse of Deweyan anthropology.

4.1. Individuality

The philosopher constructed his idea of an individual in opposition to traditional liberal approaches. For him an individual is not a given, fixed entity, but – using his words – "[a] *distinctive* way of behaving in conjunction and *connection* with other distinctive ways of acting, not a self-enclosed way of acting, independent of everything else" (Dewey 1991, 188). Hence, individuals are not separate atoms, which can be understood and defined apart from their connections with others. Individuality can also be characterized as a connection of freedom and self-realization (Shusterman 1994, 6). According to Dewey, we can achieve this by means of constant growth, without being separated from other individuals, but should be directed by deliberated social regulations and institutions. What is more, growth and consequently the realization of the individual self are attainable only by an active life in a community. It is thesis which makes the pragmatist's concept both attractive and controversial. Dewey points out that nowadays an individual left to himself is helpless and cannot realize his own capabilities (Dewey 2000, 65). What has been said so far does not result in the subordination of individuals to society, since the relationship between these two spheres is reciprocal. As an individual can be understood only with reference to society, thus society can be interpreted only with reference to the individual. It follows that societal development cannot be achieved without the individual growth of its members. Individuals should be seen as "sustaining and sustained members of a social whole" (Dewey 1962, 56). This relationship can be compared with the relationship of letters in the alphabet with the alphabet. As Dewey puts it, "[a]n alphabet *is* letters, and 'society' is individuals in their connections with one another" (Dewey 1991, 69).

4.2. Freedom

As it now appears, such defined individuality thoroughly changes the understanding of the second liberal value – freedom. It cannot be characterized only as a lack of external limitations, for it is not an element of individuals' natural make-up. Dewey distinguished legal and purely formal liberty from actual, virtual liberty of thought, speech and action (Dewey 2000, 42-43). The latter is not an automatic result of legal acts; it is something to be achieved and aimed at:

> No man and no mind was ever emancipated merely by being left alone. Removal of formal limitations is but a negative condition; positive freedom is not a state but an act which involves methods and instrumentalities for control of conditions (Dewey 1991, 168).

What is more, freedom is not a characteristic of merely the economic sphere of life, but has its cultural and spiritual dimension. The *go-as-you-please* rule (Dewey 2000, 50), applied to cultural activity, has the same harmful effects as applied to the material sphere of life: it leads to oligarchy and inequality.

The practical meaning of freedom is historically conditioned. It is connected with forces that at a given time and place are felt to be oppressive and is characterized as a release from the influence of these forces. It is a concrete good dependent on a given community, not an inherent feature of individuals (Dewey 2000, 54).

While presenting the concept of freedom, it is essential to discuss the notion of equality. It has been said that liberals – similarly to other liberal values – regarded it as an element of individual's inherent nature and as an abstract term that is not related to social practice. Individuals were seen as equal by nature, since they were supposed to have the same set of features; considering that they had the same opportunities of action and development. The only requirement that has to be met in order to actualize this equality was the removal of external limitations.

Dewey rejects the doctrine of natural laws and consequently he claims that individuals do not have the same opportunities in bettering their conditions. Since individuals are not equal by nature, their growth is diverse and unequal. A progressive liberal must be aware of the influence of institutions upon the actions of individuals. For this reason, liberalism should establish social organization that promotes individual progress and that helps individuals to achieve their freedom.

4.3. Intelligence

Regarding the third value, namely intelligence, Dewey claims that it is a social asset (Dewey 2000, 70). Thus he refers to the Lockean doctrine of natural laws. We cannot treat intelligence as an individual possession and right, since understanding intelligence in this way will always contribute only to private, not social welfare. The method of organized, cooperative intelligence (and not – as I have already mentioned – the method of coercion) should be the method of democracy. Why should we apply the method of freed and organized intelligence to social inquiry? First of all, Dewey states, there is a huge gap between the results of the physical and social sciences. The former applied the experimental method, while the latter is still based on uncontrolled speculation (Dewey 1991, 3, 5-7). What is more, social and legal systems consent to the use of force in the form of coercion. In support of this thesis Dewey gives an example of the competitive system which theoretically should help individuals to develop their abilities. Practically, it sanctifies the domination of one social group upon the rest of society (Dewey 2000, 67-68). To bring democracy into being we should use an alternative to the use of force, namely the use of intelligence. Hence the method of intelligence is the method of science which consists in observing particular facts, formulating hypotheses regarding their explanation and testing the latter by experimentation (Gamwell 1984, 92-93). An incalculable help in applying the new method is education, which is also one of the key subjects of renascent liberalism. Its role lies in forming intellectual and moral patterns in individuals so that democracy could become "a *personal* way of individual life" (Dewey 1951, 391).

4.4. Democracy

Finally, there remains the last concern of renascent liberalism, namely the problem of democracy. Dewey distinguishes "between democracy as a social idea and political democracy as a system of government" (Dewey 1991, 143). These notions are connected, but the former is wider and fuller than the latter. Democracy as a social idea is an axiological notion. It is of primary character: firstly because it is a moral good, and secondly because democracy as a system of government can be derived from this social concept. It is democracy in a moral sense, an idea of communal life that can be analyzed from two perspectives:

> [f]rom the standpoint of the individual, it consists in having a responsible share according to capacity in forming and directing the activities of the groups to which one belongs and in participating according to need in the values which the groups sustain. From the standpoint of the groups, it demands liberation of the potentialities of members of a group in harmony with the interests and goods which are common. (Dewey 1991, 147)

Political democracy is, on the contrary, an axiologically neutral notion of a purely formal character. It is simply a set of historically conditioned mechanisms and instruments; in Dewey's opinion this form of government met contemporary social needs. Yet, only democracy in an axiological sense can become the goal of one's life.

It is impossible to give one complete definition of democracy as an idea, for it has a lot of meanings. One can call it "the idea of community life itself" (Dewey 1991, 148), "a fighting faith" (Dewey 2000, 91), "a *personal* way of individual life" (Dewey 1951, 391), it is forming one's character, using certain attitudes. Thus understood, democracy relates to all spheres of individual and social life. It starts here and now, in the closest community of neighbors, on the street corner or in the shop. Its heart lies in free, unprejudiced discussion with other people, for it actualizes in communication, in constant exchange of experience and opinions (Dewey 2004, 118-119, Dewey 1991, 151-2).

5. Critique

Now it is indispensable to recapitulate what has been said so far. One may notice that the Deweyan program is highly controversial and as such it is exposed to certain allegations. I will express some of these possible objections.

First of all, the Deweyan project is encumbered with one problematic assumption, namely the idea that individuals want to grow, progress and develop their capabilities. The concept is based on positive anthropology, which is evident in his characteristic of freed intelligence, and a presumption that in human nature there are certain dispositions to diligence, cooperation, brotherhood, that individuals want to self-realize and actively control social organization, that they want to make democracy their way of life. However, maybe individuals just prefer to be left alone, to anesthetize and go-as-they-please? To what extent can we require continuous growth from individuals? What kind of means should we use if they do not wish to cooperate? Furthermore, social regulations will be based on coercion to a high degree, if individuals do not wish to achieve and develop their positive liberty. This concept of liberty is quite ambiguous, because without effective cooperation of the whole society desired social changes may just as well be imposed by some group or class. In such a case will there be changes desired by the *whole* society?

Dewey would not of course advocate any form of coercion and he would reply that the shape of democracy, government and state, depends on many cultural, social and historical conditions. No society is ideal or exemplary. In fact, no society would probably ever satisfy Dewey's requirements – he was a utopian to a certain degree, but he was also quite reasonable in his observations of politics, realizing that his ideas were only propositions, not a priori truths. Therefore, if one state is not as advanced as one would like it to be, all that can be done is to change it through a reformed educational system, through various public institutions promoting democracy, etc. No violation of individual rights is permitted and if an individual wishes to be left alone all we can do is show him why it is good to cooperate.

One can argue that the Deweyan concept is utopic, very attractive and tempting, but unfeasible and inapplicable. It can be pointed out that living in a Deweyan society would probably be wonderful. However one can question if it is altogether feasible, at least in this world and in this life.

Dewey's advocate would possibly reply that we cannot speak of the feasibility of a theory that has not been tested by observation. In other words – we should apply it and verify in practice, for wondering how it would work without knowing the real consequences of this project is but futile speculation. Dewey himself never spoke of his concept as a set of *a priori* rules – he only suggested the possible ways of transformations. Some similar critiques derive from the controversy of human nature – Dewey's philosophy is based on positive anthropology, his opponents' attitude (e.g. Walter Lippmann's) was not so optimistic. Other objections include the offshoot dispute between determinists and indeterminists; Dewey's opponents would claim that in the process of forming a state there are certain mechanisms and forces (naturally they are beyond our control), whose role is so great that they cannot be omitted. Dewey – to the contrary – believed in human capacities and abilities to change social and individual conditions.

6. Conclusions

It is not my intention to either discuss or settle all these controversies; as long as we work in the field of theory these problems will probably remain unsolved. My purpose is to assert that the undeniable advantage of Deweyan democracy is its innovatory character. What is more, Dewey's observations are still up-to-date and provide a reasonable answer to some current social problems. His postulates of a reform of education, his remarks on the processes of forming public opinion, his claims for active participation in community life and in public debate apply to the actual state of affairs. Last but not least – and let it be a conclusion – showing that democracy starts here and now, in the closest community of neighbors, is Dewey's undeniable contribution.

References

Dewey, John. 1935. The Future of Liberalism. *The Journal of Philosophy* 32.9: 225-30.

------ 1951. Creative Democracy – The Task Before Us. In *Classic American Philosophers*, ed. Max H. Fish, 389-94. New York: Appleton-Century-Crofts.

------ 1962. *Individualism Old and New*. New York: Capricorn Books.

------ 1991. *The Public and its Problems*. Athens: Swallow Press, Ohio University Press.

------ 2000. *Liberalism and Social Action*. Amherst: Prometheus Books.

------ 2004. *Reconstruction in Philosophy*. Mineola: Dover Publications.

Gamwell, Franklin I. 1984. *Beyond Preference. Liberal Theories of Independent Associations*. Chicago: The University of Chicago Press.

Kaczocha, Włodzimierz. 2008. *Studia z filozofii XX wieku [Studies on the Philosophy of the 20th Century]*. Poznań: Wydawnictwo Fundacji Humaniora.

Shusterman, Richard. 1994. Pragmatism and Liberalism between Dewey and Rorty. *Political Theory* 22.3: 391-413.

Luis E. Echarte
University of Navarra, Spain
Neuromythology and the dilemma of 'dangerous truths.' Could pragmatism make scientific and social progress compatible?

To the memory of Mateusz Oleksy

1. The selfish gene and memes

In *The Selfish Gene*, Richard Dawkins assumes one of the most important principles of Evolutionism: to find the adaptive processes associated with living things is to find the explanation for their conservation and propagation, and ultimately, to understand their nature. For Dawkins (1989), the identity of such phenomena is based on their unique ability to keep in time and according to evolutionistic patterns. However, as a means to justify the presence of "altruism" in animal behavior, that is, conducts of sacrifice for the sake of the group or the species, Dawkins proposes to distinguish two elements: the vehicle and the replicator.[1] The first is the survival machine, a biological apparatus that is set to serve the second, i.e. the genes, the real protagonists in the function of conservation and propagation.

The idea of the replicator supposes a revolution in biology because the shift from the "basic unit" of the body to a gene, implies a very particular reinterpretation of relations between the elements that make up an ecosystem, i.e. of the effectiveness and direction of the adaptive processes that occur therein. What seems to be particularly interesting is the fact that Dawkins uses the theory of the "selfish gene" to explain not only the physical dimension of the interactions, but also the psychological. The characteristic aspects of the replicator is its casual and formal nature, that is, the appearance of random phenomena in systems, shaped by forces that favor the selection and enable the auto-replication of its elements. For Dawkins, the cultural dynamics typical for human beings are susceptible to mentioned description. He identifies replicators inside it, naming them *memes*, i.e. units of cultural ideas, whose origins and activity can be explained analogically to the genes.[2] The presence of the memes is justified, according to Dawkins, in the common fact that human minds, now seen as ve-

---

[1] For Dawkins, a sacrifice of an individual for the sake of a group is nothing else but a perfect manifestation of the primacy of a gene (as a code) over the individuals (elements in which the code is implemented).

[2] Dawkins creates the acronym *meme* combining phonetically two terms: *gene*, for obvious reasons, and *mímesis*, in relation to the human capacity of retaining information by imitation.

hicles for memes, are frequently and "altruistically" sacrificed for the preservation of an idea or a set of them (Dawkins 1989, 352).

Dawkins's hypothesis was widely echoed, not only in the experimental sciences, but also outside this area, particularly in the philosophy of mind. One of its most important diffusers, Daniel Dennett, defines human consciousness as a vast web of memes, a result of archaic invasion similar to that which occurred, as the author compares, in human mitochondria: primitive bacteria that were colonizing and gradually integrating with the functioning of the cells of modern human being. That is the reason why, in Dennett's words, "scholar is just a library's way of making another library" (Dennett 1991, 202). Other authors, however, are more pessimistic with regard to such supposed symbiotic relation. Susan Blackmore, for example, who defends the closest position to the current line of Dawkins' thinking, believes that this integration has not occurred yet, and may never occur. The brain is, in this sense, a place of a never-ending process of cultivation of memes that compete with each other, a situation that impedes a harmonious relation with the carrier or even harms the other type of replicators that share the vehicle, i.e. genes (Blackmore 1999, 22).

In the works of Dawkins it is not clearly stated whether the science and its products are part of the events marked by processes of natural selection. On the one hand, he evokes the example of a rapid spread of the theory of the "selfish gene" as a sign of mimetic dynamics, which is at least partly true. The criteria of acceptance, handled by the various communities and dimensions that integrate and form a society (scientists, politicians, clergy, etc.), would represent selective forces that may cause disappearance, growth or transformation of scientific theories. On the other hand, however, in relating to the scientific community itself, he adopts scientific postulates. This last perspective may be inferred from the fact that, for Dawkins, genetics is situated above *memetics* (science that studies memes), because the former can easily identify and work with independent units of human actions, and therefore is completely objective, whereas, the latter, is a diffused field and is necessarily contaminated by the observer's perspective. Indeed, for Dawkins, the certainty of the genetic theory is supported by its experimental validity, unlike *memetics*, in which case it is more difficult to verify hypotheses. Deriving from this naïve foundationalism, the dynamics of scientific statements is based, according to Dawkins, on the laws of coherence and rationality. In other words, here we find the only refuge of objectivity in a blind universe.

The evolutionism of Dawkins implies not only granting the experimental science primacy over the other intellectual disciplines, but also arguing that its promotion is the best protection against harmful intellectual output. In *The Extended Phenotype*, the author advances another of his most famous theses about the relation between vehicles and replicators: not always does the adaptive advantage of a determined phenotypic trait necessarily lead to its carrier. Dawkins establishes the Theorem of Central Extended Phenotype as follows: "an animal's behavior tends to maximize the survival of the genes 'for' that behavior, whether or not those genes happen to be in the body of the particular animal performing it" (Dawkins 1982, 233). In order to show the nature of this accidental relation, Dawkins uses, again, the example of altruistic behavior, the cases of men who sacrifice themselves for ideals. Dennett and Dawkins share the idea that the toxicity of a meme is proportional to the number of conducts that involves the acceptance, and inversely proportional to the amount of science that supports it, or at least, that accompanies it. In the same manner, science is revealed as the condition of possibility of any rebellion of (living) machines. The conclusion is clear: experimental methodology is the real pillar of human autonomy, the main tool against the tyranny of genes and memes.

The development of this approach leads both authors to classify religious beliefs as potentially dangerous,[3] as not only do they chiefly consist of unquestionable truths and dogmas, but also because they are presented as a taboo territory to science. Therefore a person is completely unprotected against these types of memes, the ones that evolve towards fully parasitic relations with their vehicles. In brief, the proposal of Dawkins and Dennett, consistent with this approach, is defending and promoting the idea that one of the most important obligations of scientists is to assume the colonization of the prohibited land of religion and other ideologies of the taboo.[4]

2. Evolutionist pragmatism and the disenchantment of Nature

The proposal of the urgent need to scientifically address religious facts is developed in Daniel Dennett's book *Breaking the Spell*. This work also challenges the original Darwinian idea that all attributes or functions preserved by a species, as a result of natural selection, necessarily have to be advantageous. For Dennett this argument is flawed in two aspects. Firstly, it can be the case that the advantages of a particular ancient evolutionary trait might have disappeared due to the modification of the organism or its environment. But it is also possible that the benefits of this evolutionary trait have never been focused on the carrier. To support this idea, which follows Dawkins's line of thinking, Dennett draws on

---

[3] Later on, I will make a distinction between what is a "potentially dangerous idea" in the context used by Dawkins and Dennett, and what is a "dangerous idea," one of the key issues of this article.

[4] The approach of Dawkins about the potential risks of taboo beliefs is true for many believers, at least, for those who accept a dialogue between science, reason, and faith. Dawkins does not conceal doubts about the ability of science to show the fictitious nature of God. However, this is not contradictory to the dialogue itself. It does not necessarily preclude nor invalidate it: to debate it is not necessary to adopt a neutral position as far as the subject of debate is concerned.

his now famous example of *Dicrocelium dentriticim*. Certain ants climb constantly to the apex of grass blades, a behavior that brings no benefits to them but instead to the parasite, the *Dicrocelium*, that lives in their brains (Dennett 2006, 186).[5] The point is that facing the consequences of both possibilities implies refusing the optimistic attitude with which we have historically tried to understand human traits.

Within the evolutionary framework, there are, however, several objections related to the aim of science in revealing the "false illusion of God," or better, in reinterpreting "religion as a natural phenomenon." There are many writers who, throughout history, have justified religious fictions as key elements in the progress of the individual and society. Among the most important ones in the last century, it is of interest here to mention three: Émile Durkheim, one of the founders of modern sociology, for whom religion is crucial in promoting social cohesion; Gordon W. Allport, a pioneer in the psychological study of personality, who identifies religion as a matter of inspiring and unifying scientific framework; and Erik Erikson, one of the most representative figures in developmental psychology, for whom this kind of existential fiction is essential in the development of personal identity. Also in the field of philosophy there are many figures who advocate the same line of thought. Jürgen Habermas, one of the best known among them, encourages scientists and philosophers to appreciate and take charge of spiritual and human heritage through translation of the mythic-religious imagery into scientific discourse, so that the value of their schemes and practices can be accepted by any rational community (Habermas 2001, 101-115). However, all of these perspectives lead to a crucial question: What are the implications for the approach to the disenchantment of nature which assumes that the belief in God, being false, can be more or less useful?

Neither Dawkins nor Dennett deny that existential fictions may be advantageous for certain aspects of human life, however, considering the problem globally, and especially the growing conflict between religions, both consider it necessary to take the risk of disappearance. "Many of us saw religion as harmless nonsense. Beliefs might lack all supporting evidence but, we thought, if people needed a crutch for consolation, where's the harm? September 11th changed all that" (Dawkins 2001, 10-11).[6] Leaving aside the debate on public space that may or may not occupy the existential beliefs of a particular group or community, it is interesting to note here how, from the pragmatic point of view

---

[5] This worm needs to be ingested by a sheep or a cow to fill the reproductive cycle in its stomach.

[6] The preventive attitude that governments should maintain towards religions is undoubtedly one of the most controversial theses of Dawkins. In part because, as Dennett himself acknowledges, what science knows about the religion is very little. Furthermore, this position does not help in promoting dialogue between science and faith, to which the author of *The Selfish Gene* alluded previously.

of Evolutionism, social and scientific progress are balanced. The human capacity for objective knowledge is recognized as a unique feature that gives an unusual position in the dynamics of natural selection, but on the other hand, it is not claimed that science is the main guide of lifestyles. A scientific truth does not lead necessarily to social progress, nor has the pursuit of reality to be the main aspiration of human beings. Science is, ultimately, just like hospitals, useful only when and where it is needed. And a good example of this, confirms Dawkins, is prevention and elimination of dangerous genes/memes. However, there is no strictly scientific argument to promote the rejection of all false memes. Dawkins acknowledges, in this regard, that the memes can adopt their behavior based primarily on objective knowledge. Even more, he has no difficulty in admitting other lifestyles different from his own.[7] It cannot be otherwise since, from an evolutionary interpretation, the universe does not necessarily prevail as rational.

The pragmatism of the evolutionary position, presented as paradigmatic in the thinking of Dawkins, on the one hand, defends the objectivity of scientific statements, and, secondly, denies that an increase in knowledge is followed always by a greater ability to survive. Moreover, this perspective is being currently strengthened in John A. Teske's works. This researcher, professor of Psychology at Elizabethtown College Pennsylvania, studies the role of myths in human neurological and psychological development. For Teske any storyline, whether fictional or not, has a positive effect on brain development and the formation of personal identity. The only condition is that such fictions bring narrative unity and logical consistency to the conscious experience of the perceived stimulus (Teske 2000, 192-193, and 2005, 16). According to the author, logical consistency is essential for the construction of a theoretical framework from which the subject can not only understand the surrounding world, but also himself. And indeed, there are neuropsychological evidences about the link between the emergences of the "I" and the ability to produce a strong autobiographical narrative, i.e. to integrate the experiences into a single network of connections. Specifically, Teske highlights some particularly significant facts related on the one hand, to how events that become part of long-term memory are processed mainly in narrative form, and, on the other, to proofs about how brain reaches a more stable configuration when the individual manages to integrate and explain a large number of significant events using a single theory (Teske 2001, 665-676).

Among Teske's conclusions stand out those related to the importance of myths in neural and psychological development. They are useful to the integration of information under patterns of continuity and coherence. The explanation

---

[7] "If the demise of God will leave a gap, different people will fill it in different ways. My way includes a good dose of science, the honest and systematic endeavour to find out the truth about the real world" (Dawkins 2006, 361).

is simple: science is not usually the main source that provides paradigms for the maturation and stability of the subject. For example, during childhood, a story sufficiently plausible and attractive is more accessible and beneficial to the mind of a child than a scientific theory, often honest, but always difficult, partial and imprecise. And although to a lesser extent, fictions are useful also for adults, especially when philosophical and scientific paradigms are not received with sufficient conviction to replace the effective myths of childhood or tradition.[8] Like Dawkins, Teske believes that scientific access is essential to the religious phenomenon, although for contrary reasons: not because of its potential danger to individual and social progress, but because of the role of religion in the development of human beings. Of course, for Teske, the research should not be called *Neurotheology*, a term commonly used to label experimental research on religion, but *Neuromythology*, a concept which is more in unison with the very nature of the existential beliefs deal with by such studies.

However, if Teske's hypothesis concerning the *Neuromythology* is correct, there are strong arguments for preventing the disappearance of existential fiction, at least as long as science fails to offer objective paradigms of equal scope. Francisco Mora, professor of Physiology and Biophysics at the Universidad Complutense of Madrid, understands the problem in this way.

> Knowing that biological evolution selects functions or circuits of the brain (or other parts of the body) which are eventually useful for biological survival: what final utility, what function of survival gives the human being the sense of the supernaturalism, the religiousness ..., God, as definitive? Would not it be one's own destruction to decode irrational mechanisms (that means, to emerge in consciousness), the primal, motivational, emotional force, that has kept him alive, precisely at the expense of the lack of conscience? (Mora 2000, 199-200, translation from Spanish by M. Biskupski)

Indeed, natural selection could have provided human beings with one of the greatest evolutionistic tools for the adaptation of living organisms, i.e. rationality, but this claim does not legitimize extrapolating its effectiveness to any possible ecosystem. Even more, the advantage of carrying any biological trait could vary in the same environment. That is the idea that Aldous Huxley (whose approach will be discussed in further detail below) has in mind when he writes: "Nothing fails like success; and creatures which have proved eminently successful in specializing themselves to perform one sort of task and to live in one sort of environment are by that very fact foredoomed to ultimate failure" (Huxley

---

[8] This interpretation of the role of fiction in human identity sheds light, in addition, on theories about the social dynamics of the relationship between mythology and science. The hypothesis could be stated as follows: the degree of acceptance of the mythical explanations in a society will depend, among other factors, on the degree of inadequacy of the existing scientific paradigm.

1941, 263). The neuromythological hypothesis of the role of fiction in human identity is a good example of Huxley's warning, that is to say, of how the development of science can turn against our own species.

3. Towards a practical relativism

For Erikson, the downfall of idols, Gods who found the system of beliefs of a group or society, would weaken the "sense of identity" of its members, and would cause the disappearance of a way of "being in the world" that prevents the archaic fear of an unstructured existence (Erikson 1962, 56-58). Is this risk greater than that deriving from the enchantment of nature? If the answer is affirmative, and the works of Teske head in that direction, what should be the attitude of science towards religion, and generally towards all "dangerous truth"?

At this point it is important to establish a distinction between "potentially dangerous knowledge" and "dangerous knowledge." The risk of the first depends on the human capacity to handle it more or less adequately: for instance, that associated with "Nuclear Physics" and the construction of more or less safe nuclear plants. By contrast, I am going to call here "dangerous knowledge" that whose harmful effects appear with its very acquisition. Existential beliefs fall into this second kind of knowledge, at least, as already mentioned, while science was unable to provide a solid enough scientific paradigm, one comprehensive and accessible to each society and culture.

Coming back to the previous question and being consistent with Dawkins's position, the problems stemming from religious *taboo* would represent a lesser evil. However, this has a significant cost, which is intertwined with two of the principle assumptions of my article: first, as already partly discussed, there is a reason to predict that the Evolutionistic Pragmatism will end up defending a position similar to the Neo-pragmatism of Richard Rorty, namely, renouncing the quest for objective truths, and their replacement by fiction; and secondly, there are serious difficulties, from both perspectives, in reconciling social and scientific progress.

Evolutionistic Pragmatism and Neo-pragmatism, following different paths, end up agreeing on some important findings, especially those related to managing knowledge. We have seen how pragmatic evolutionism, accepting the possibility of "dangerous truths" and, because of that, subordinating social progress to science, has to be enforced to impose taboo areas on researchers and to promote holistic fictions in unwanted situations of "accidental disenchantment." Similarly, Neo-pragmatism pleads for managing information also separated from any value of objectivity, even though now the reasons are not related to the survival of the species, but to the inability of human mind to act as a "mirror of nature," i.e., as a means to know reality. At the first glance, the renunciation of

Neo-pragmatism could seem much greater than that of Evolutionistic Pragmatism, since, in the latter, not all parts of reality are disavowed. However ultimately, as I will argue below, this distinction is artificial because Evolutionistic Pragmatism ends up necessarily in a "practical relativism" (relativism of practical origin), with similar consequences to the "theoretical relativism" of Neopragmatism. To explain this statement I need to first present, in short, some of the features of Neo-pragmatism, and second, the background of Evolutionistic Pragmatism.

The origins of pragmatism are related to a rejection of both dualism and epistemological foundationalism, and to the recovery of the *embodied knowledge* interpretation, that is, one closely linked to human activity. In this perspective, the connection to the pragmatic (subfield of linguistics) study of language and understanding is particularly important. However, Neo-pragmatism takes the "linguistic turn" to the most radical positions: knowledge is always dependent on webs of interpretation or "vocabularies," and therefore, any statement, theory or conceptual scheme only has meaning as a useful tool for a particular environment. Consequently, it is absurd to question the connection of a theory with reality, as much as asking about the relation between a hammer and truth. For the same reason, and because of impossibility of finding rational principles, metaphysical or meta-linguistic (the only way to rank or translate different levels or webs of interpretation), Rorty proposes the "democratization" of all the "vocabularies" managed by humans, i.e. the cessation of privileges based on a greater or lesser proximity to reality. The conclusions are not trivial: Ptolemaic astronomy, Christianity, Darwinism, or feminist poetry are nothing but different linguistic, contemporary or archaic contexts. This argument, on the one hand, leads Rorty to name their position as "Pragmatism without method," and on the other, to define a new attitude to reality: the rejection of any theory, scientific, philosophical or ideological, whose main value was the achievement of objectivity (Rorty 1991, 63-77).

Simultaneously, it is possible to trace the roots of Evolutionistic Pragmatism, widespread in the American experimental field, by analyzing John Dewey's works.[9] The philosopher from Vermont upholds the "metaphysics of experience," in which the experimental sciences are given hegemony over the rest. In other words, they are the reservoir in which we are able to find all the principles necessary for translation. The notion of principle is understood here as an idea that has withstood the scrutiny of the experience (in its broadest sense) throughout the history of mankind (Dewey and Tufts 1932, 304). However, Dewey does not strictly defend a scientificist perspective. He does not present foundationalistic statements, as he considers all theory and formula only as tentative human

---

[9]   Dewey's influence in the experimental field is still present, unlike in the philosophical one. In philosophy, from the second half of the 20th century, the interest in pragmatism was first replaced with logical positivism, then with analytic philosophy.

constructions. Particularly speaking, neither does he assume the tenets of classical pragmatism. For Dewey, experimental claims are not connected more or less fallibly with reality, but with the human way of interacting with it. In this instrumentalism, subsequently renamed as Dewey's *operationism*, the value of the truth in a theory is limited to its application, i.e. its ability to predict, not phenomena, but achievements. As heir of this tradition, Evolutionistic Pragmatism recognizes the primacy of experimental statements, which does not imply the exclusion of fiction, when benefits can be proved. Of course, there is no full identification between instrumentalism and Evolutionistic Pragmatism. The second is closer to the scientificist theories, even though it preserves the notion, not of truth, but utility. For that reason, science is understood as the field of facts and fictions. In other words, using Dawkins' terminology, the purpose of any researcher has to be putting memes in the service of humanity, a task for which experimental method happens to be the best help in anticipating the expected results.

It is here that we find the problem. If Evolutionistic Pragmatism, recognizing the possibility of dangerous truths and imposing taboo areas of knowledge, restricts the ability to predict events, then the principles that gave hegemony to scientific statements are also undermined. Because a principle, in Dewey's context, is only a principle if it can be taken to formulate, validate and translate any entire interpretive web. To identify some contexts useful but out of reach, means inevitably to relativize all of them – using Rorty's expression, to democratize them. Ultimately, to notice the possibility of dangerous memes means to commence treating knowledge as a mere mimetic product, i.e. a phenomenon governed by mechanisms of natural selection. From that moment on, we have to assume that forces of nature do not explain science but the appropriateness of the ideas to the current scientific paradigms, and are always explicitly partial. This way, we may find the main difference between the post-evolutionistic scientism and Neo-pragmatism: in the first, relativism is chosen for the sake of the species, while in the second, relativism is a logical necessity. Nevertheless, this difference is inessential, as we shall see below, to the way that both perspectives face the challenge of making scientific and social progress compatible.

4. Postmodernity and Posthumanism

While Evolutionistic Pragmatism is still in the process of transition to what I called a practical relativism, Neo-pragmatism has been developing its assumptions for the past thirty years. It is understandable therefore that, in the second, we may encounter more sophisticated and widespread theses about the changing role of the intellectuals in social progress after the disenchantment of nature and science, a phenomenon that many authors understand as the turning point towards postmodernity. The best known are, undoubtedly, those of Rorty, who, apart from maintaining the rejection of the last foundationalist dreams (the primary obligation of any philosopher) pleads for social development based on the construction of new metaphors about human activities, i.e. more original descriptions capable of persuading (in the rhetorical sense of the word) the diverse communities of a society about the need for changes in their paradigms or "vocabularies" (shared or not) in order to resolve their differences. "The method is to redescribe lots and lots of things in new ways, until you have created a pattern of linguistic behavior which will tempt the rising generation to adopt it'' (Rorty 1989, 9). Intellectuals must, eventually, facilitate the emergence of aesthetic discourse to elicit different emotional responses. In other words, their role is to pave the way for new social prophets, be they poets, politicians or biologists.

Liberal democracies are, in the neo-pragmatist context, the best grounds for social progress, because they recognize a citizen's right to choose the "vocabulary" for one's self-realization, a goal that should be considered a cornerstone of any society (Rorty 1998, 33). Obviously, Rorty notices the absurdity of, on the other hand, justifying his confidence in liberal values, i.e. tolerance and solidarity, and, at the same time, maintaining skepticism about the objectivity of these values. "Irony" is his way of cohering both postulates, an activity that implies not taking too seriously any argument. This attitude leads, according to the author, to a meta-stable situation, because within it intellectuals avoid endless and futile discussions that alienate humans from their most important and immediate problems and aspirations (Rorty 1989, 74). Irony, however, is not present as a remedy to any dispute arising from social interests or different vocabularies, but only as the best available tool. Of course, there are also "intra-societal tensions" that cannot be solved by any kind of persuasive attitude, but such situations should not preoccupy the intellectual, since, as Rorty "ironically" states, they also end up being solved by the "anecdote," i.e. a random balance of social forces (Rorty 1991, 201).

Transition from Evolutionistic Pragmatism to a practical relativism will depend on the grade of communication between scientificists and neo-pragmatists. This convergence requires, however, the increase in bridges of thought on both sides of the ocean. The point is that evolutionist pragmatism is predominantly based on the American continent, while Neo-pragmatism has been better received in old Europe.[10] Some significant events have already helped in catalyzing their mutual transformation. One of the most notorious, in my opinion, was

---

[10] I have in mind a comment made by Professor Mateusz Oleksy in a conversation with Richard Rorty during our stay at the University of Berkeley (California) in 2003. According to Oleksy, Rorty conveyed his disappointment at the limited reception of Neo-pragmatism in the USA, in contrast to its good welcome at European universities. Oleksy was well aware of the latter, as a vast part of his research was aimed at the refutation of the new nominalisms, like that of Rorty, that threaten any possible realistic interpretation of the fruits of science and philosophy (Oleksy 2004, 227-238, and 2005).

the participation of Steve Fuller as expert witness in the case *Kitzmiller vs. Dover Area School District*. In this double trial, first, on what should and should not be taught in American classrooms and, second, about the alleged scientific nature of "Intelligent Design," Fuller testified in favor of teaching this theory in schools. His argument was motivated not by the supposed validity of Intelligent Design Theory, but because, according to him, science itself is a human construction, and, therefore no more or less legitimate than other narratives[11] (Fuller 2005). Even more important that his testimony is the ruling in favor of freedom of education in which the most relevant of Fuller's arguments were cited. Indeed, Fuller's social constructionism, which follows guidelines set by Rorty (in this case aimed at fostering a full liberal education system) has been one of the most serious confrontations between Evolutionistic Pragmatism and Neopragmatism.[12]

The transatlantic interaction of ideas does not only involve the transformation of Pragmatic Evolutionism into relativist attitudes, but the dilemma of the "dangerous truths" of evolutionism also implies changes in Neo-pragmatism. Can societies allow ironic attitudes in the development of science, i.e. uses of myth in the education system? Can they give up objectivity as a means of social progress without serious and alienating harms to personal and cultural identity? If the hypothesis of neuromythology is correct, Neopragmatism has to choose between social and scientific progress. The first option implies, leaving relativistic theory and its dissemination, and, at the same time, promoting, artificially and voluntarily, the re-enchantment of science and nature. These "new" intellectuals would induce "sympathetic" existential fictions in society, a deception that should reach, as far as possible, and for its own sake, at such a "forger of beliefs." However, this alternative, given its paternalistic and manipulative character, is nothing "persuasive," at least in our contemporary emotional culture. The second option is, nevertheless, irresponsible. What arguments can be made, from the evolutionary or neo-pragmatist point of view, to justify that the knowledge of any truth (even the most fragile, partial and uncertain) is valuable enough to sacrifice mental and social stability? Moreover, this last option will not enjoy

---

[11] It is illuminating to note that, on the one hand, Fuller is currently working at the University of Warwick (England), and secondly, that his testimony was fiercely criticized by both, American scientists and creationists.

[12] Another example of this kind of interocean *collision*, though of a much less significant impact, emerged in the workshop "Metaphysics, Ontology and the Science-Religion Debate." In this workshop, held in May of 2009 at the *Thomas More Institute* in London, in which Fuller and I participated, there was a particular controversy during the presentation of my thesis on the relativistic approach; that evolutionism seems inevitably ending. The presentation and subsequent discussion can be found in "http://www.thomasmoreinstitute.org.uk/artigas".

a good reception in an occidental culture, where people are educated, at least affectively, to appreciate and purse truth.

There is also a third way of solving the dilemma of the dangerous truths, which to some extent is already present in postmodern societies: changing the rules that shape human identity. For if one of the problems arising from the absence of existential beliefs is the harmful emotions that evoke such failures, why not amend human emotional responses? In fact, quite a few authors think that this scenario is related to the increasing consumption of psychotropic drugs in the second half of the twentieth century. For example, according to Berger and Chodoff, it represents the beginning of a new and dangerous era primarily marked by strong social demands (Berger 1978, 979; Chodoff 2002, 627-628). But not all psychiatrists and psychologists criticize such medical change. The couch of many psychotherapists has become a new area of inspiration in the search for consistency in life. There, reality is less esteemed than the important experiences caused by emotional (albeit false) narratives. This line of thinking is assumed, among others, by the Italian neuropsychiatrist Vittorio Guidano, one of the best proponents of the new constructivist and post-rationalist psychotherapy (Guidano 1987, 1995, 89-102).[13]

The emotional solution to the dilemma of dangerous truths brings us into the debate on the handling of human identity (also known as the problem of a posthuman future), that seems to address both Neo-pragmatism and Practical Relativism. First of all, will maintaining a positive emotional response to an unstructured and irrational existence be sufficient to promote the healthy development of human identity? Second, what will represent such an affective change in terms of the scientific progress? In other words, will we still be bodies adapted to our environment, if the new state of mind dents the main human evolutionary advantage, i.e. rationality? And third, will the post-human future be sufficiently persuasive to voluntarily change our species? Would the only other alternative be an "anecdotal" evolution? These questions do not deal with mere futurists' speculations; on the contrary, they represent one of the emerging issues that cause concern and interest in interdisciplinary areas of experimental science. Bioethics, for example, is today one of the main promoters of discussion forums on posthumanism.[14]

---

[13] This movement is deeply influenced by the social constructivism of Michel Foucault.

[14] A proof of the bioethical interest in issues related to the enhancement of Posthumanism is the fact that one of its most prestigious journals, *The American Journal of Bioethics*, has dedicated five issues to it in the past three years (volume 7, No.1 and No.10; volume 8, No.9; volume 9, No.1 and No.9).

5. Dangerous truths and non-relativistic pragmatisms

Finally, I find it interesting to analyze how other philosophical and scientific currents that defend the pursuit of objectivity may be more or less affected by the neuromythological argument about the risks concerning the disenchantment of nature. In order to shed some light on this, I would like to draw attention to statements of Charles S. Peirce, not only because the founder of pragmatism is arousing a renewed interest in anti-foundationalist and antirelativist approaches, but also for his honest interest in reconciling science and society, or more specifically, science and religion.

One of the primary aims of his work is to show how recognizing the fact that shortcomings and limitations of a concept or theory do not necessarily imply rejecting it or assigning it a mere utilitarian value of truth. On the contrary, it is possible to attach objectivity to such assertions, although not in the very concepts but in the experimental attitude of the researcher, i.e. the intention of including them within a special research program: one in which all statement could be continuously and publicly reviewed (Peirce 1898, CP 6.3). Along with *fallibilism* (coined by Peirce), the objectivity of science is safeguarded in "the desire to learn," that is, in the natural human desire to integrate all the necessary assumptions for formulating and solving a problem. Of course, that means "do not block the path of inquiry" (1899, CP 1135), which is just reflecting the recognition of the "dangerous truths" possibility. The important point to consider here is that Peirce's *pragmaticism* avoids any sort of practical relativism, not because he thought that truths were more relevant than human survival, but because he assumes an ontological cosmology in which knowledge could never be harmful.

The works of Peirce reveal explicitly and implicitly a *cosmological* interpretation of reality, namely the belief in a bright universe ruled by love, the main regulator of an infinite and harmonious development process. As in evolutionary tenets, this classic interpretation offers a world where many of the phenotypic traits of living beings require explanation, taking into account factors external to the carrier. It is intrinsic in the entire harmonious balance, that the benefits of a particular fact may be exploited by others. But there is one major difference that attacks the main thesis on dangerous truths: the benefits of a phenotypic trait can transcend but never be independent of the carrier.

Secondly, for Peirce, human beings participate in this Logos or light of reason: through abduction we can incarnate it. As Peirce stated: "the ideal of conduct will be to execute our little function in the operation of the creation by giving a hand toward rendering world more reasonable whenever, as the slang is, it is "up to us" to do so" (Peirce 1903, CP 1.615). And despite the little attention paid by most experts to the theism of Peirce's thought, this is intimately united, as Jaime Nubiola points out, with his theories concerning the experimental method and scientific progress. Very briefly, the connection is as follows. For Peirce, the great number of scientific discoveries, the obvious human capacity (of abduction) that generates hypotheses and helps to explain surprising facts, is not the result of coincidence but of the capacity of human mind to be "in tune with the truth of things." Indeed, according to Peirce "It is the very bedrock of logical truth" (Peirce 1908, CP 6.476). In other words, "In Peirce's view, the creatural nature of matter and the continuity between matter and mind explain the surprising success of the sciences" (Nubiola 2004, 99).

Peirce's theory of unity between science and religion is an example of how a realist theory of nature saves, with a benevolent interpretation of Universe, the dilemma of dangerous truths.[15] Knowledge, any knowledge, necessarily improves our understanding of universal harmony, a quality that brings only advantages. The most important is optimizing the power of human beings to assist in the natural order of things. In this sense, science and religion should not be afraid of one another. The researcher can look without fear on any matter. There is no need to be prudent in the pursuit of truth, let alone establish taboo areas for the sake of social progress. Even more, that possibility becomes a scientific obligation in topics significantly committed to human existence. Conversely, science and society can move freely and cooperatively because the purpose of knowledge is also the goal of human beings. The only requirement for any good researcher is honesty, a minimum common factor for a scientific realist community, one whose members are joined not by greater or lesser consensus on the proposed models, but by the desire for objectivity. As Nubiola argues, "the truth is not the result of consensus, but rather the consensus is the fruit of truth" (Nubiola 2002, 23-65).

Neither should religions, at least those who identify knowledge with apprehension of the benevolent order of nature, fear the scientific progress. In The Marriage of Religion and Science, Peirce writes about such religious attitudes:

> It becomes animated by the scientific spirit, confident that all the conquests of science will be triumphs of its own, and accepting all the results of science, as scientific men themselves accept them, as steps toward the truth, which may appear for a time to be in conflict with other truths, but which in such cases merely await adjustments which time is sure to effect. This attitude, be it observed, is one which religion will assume not at the dictate of science, still less by way of a compromise, but simply and solely out of a bolder confidence in herself and in her own destiny. (Peirce 1893, CP 6.433)

The honesty should be, according to Peirce, the most cohesive element in this kind of community, for believers long for the same reality. There is no room

---

[15] For Peirce, "Science, without emotive and experiential forms of religion, would be mere scientificism, an inefficient and without inspiration theory, and religion without science would turn into a blind faith incapable of growing up" (Barrena and Nubiola 2007).

for taboos; there is no excuse to encourage the ignorance of their followers. This kind of existential belief is not part of that main breeding ground, as Dennett recognizes, for all subsequent "unsavory miasma of hypocrisy, lies, and frantic but fruitless attempts at distraction" (Dennett 2006, 288).

The framework-theory of Peirce also provides an excellent approximation of the problem of negative affective states associated with the "times of crisis" caused by the absence (or simple inadequacy) of a given scientific or existential paradigm. In his opinion, more psychological than scientific or philosophical, Peirce points out that the problem is not about the scope of a theory (otherwise anguish would have killed moderns a long time ago) but its significance for the quantity and quality of responses related to the human concerns in each histori-cal moment and in every society. Peirce refuses both those defending the "me-thodical doubt" as the most valuable quality of the researcher, and those seeking *panacea* for all scientific models, namely, the unifying theory of all human *vocabularies*. Intellectuals should not waste their time engaging in "paper doubts" as Peirce calls them, or barren investigations outside the deepest human wishes, but to reintegrate science and philosophy in the humanities, because it is not the certainty of knowledge but the confidence and hope in the scientific project which provides real peace to researchers, and to human beings in general (Peirce 1868, CP 5.265 and 1905, CP 5.445).

Of course, Peirce's approach is not, strictly speaking, a solution to the di-lemma of dangerous truths but a change of premises in which it is dissolved. However, from the purely sociological approach of pragmatism, and beyond the validity of the argument on which Peirce founded his cosmology, we must rec-ognize that his intellectual attitude fosters and makes compatible social and scientific development. At this point of the discussion and as a way of analyzing more specifically this sort of cosmological model of interaction between expe-rimental and existential beliefs, I turn to the works of Aldous Huxley. Not coin-cidentally, he is the creator of the neologism "*Neurotheology*."

Huxley, like Peirce, identifies the goals of humanity and science: "the know-ledge of the immanent and transcendent Ground of all being" (Huxley 1970, vii). The achievement of this goal, what he calls "enlightenment," represents the richness of human beings but also of reality in its entirety. Indeed, the universe is understood by the British novelist and philosopher in cosmological terms (bright order staying in matter), although now, in contrast to Peirce, the connec-tion between human beings and reality is purely pantheistic. On the other hand, psychology will be considered the field which studies the connections between mind and matter, action and thought. In this frame, Huxley defines the brain as the organ of consciousness, and this last as the "divine element" inherent to hu-manity and other pluralities. Actually, in Huxley's thought, it is simply because we share part of the nature of the Universe that we can understand: "something of what lies beyond our experience by considering analogous cases lying within our experience" (Huxley 1947, 34). Peirce's thesis also resonates here.

Similarly to Peirce's, Huxley does not rely on the naive realism of intuitionism. In fact, part of his work is devoted to seeking ways to reveal the false aura of objectivity inherent to any states of consciousness, always shaped by the scientific and cultural patterns prevailing in each society and time. The knowledge of such subjectivity or, as he calls it, the deontologization of the limits, is one of the most important preparatory steps in entering the real objective[16] (Huxley, 1971, 47 and 100). In fact, this is one of the two reasons Huxley prioritizes the neuropsychological approach of religion in what is the set of possible relationships between science and existential beliefs. First, because humans perceive reality through the brain, and second, because the brain itself is, more than culture, the main inductor of false experiences of certainty. In this context, Huxley defines Neurotheology as the study of the neural bases of the human spiritual dimension, a field that provides the best means for humans to reach, through the manipulation of the body, not only physiological and psychological completeness but also harmony with the cosmos.[17]

It is fair to say that Huxley's vision of how science should have access to religion is extremely focused on the neurological correlates of religious experiences. There are many other prospects for experimental analysis. All the same, in the next and final section of this paper, I want to focus the discussion on how the ideal of humanistic pragmatism is embodied in Huxley's approach, and how it resolves the postmodern dilemma of dangerous truths.

6. The challenge to reconcile scientific and social progress

Several unique features characterize Huxley's Neurotheology. First of all, it does not require an existential commitment of its researchers to any particular belief, at least in regard to the objectives of "practical" and "transcendental" operationism, two of the three types of projects that conform, according to Huxley, this new interdisciplinary area. The first, the investigations of the *practical operationism*, are geared to the experimental study of religious experiences and spiritual practices, looking for objective profits (or losses) independently of his system of underlying beliefs. Probably, this is the kind of neurotheological study more currently in vogue. The most notorious example is how prestigious scientific institutions are investing time and money to develop research on the sup-

---

[16] The latter steps are linked to the exercise of a series of human virtues, among which charity will be the largest of all (Huxley 1947, 98, 103, 107).

[17] While the neologism "neurotheology" appears only in his last novel, *Island*, the question of the relation between science and religion is recurring in many of his works. A good collection of essays with this orientation was made by himself in *Huxley and God* (1947).

posed therapeutic benefits of meditative practices (Davidson, Kabat, et al. 2003, 564-570).

Nevertheless, Neurotheology, as Huxley claims, is not limited only to scrutiny of religion, but also to science. In the *transcendental operationism*, he includes all the important projects related to how objective and subjective experiences are induced in mind. An example of research covered by this group would be related to what he calls "visionary experiences," i.e. fictions valuable in themselves because they help subjects to reveal the false objectivity of most human beliefs. According to Huxley, altered states of consciousness remind us that "the real word is very different from the misshapen universe they have created for themselves by means of their culture-conditioned prejudices" (Huxley 1960, 68). This does not mean that Huxley denies natural or traditional knowledge, he simply wants to show the always accompanying mental limits, a vital step in achieving objectivity. On the contrary, ignorance of the subjective human knowledge is, according to the author of *A Brave New World*, responsible at the great extent for scientism and its consequent anti-utopias. In summary, Huxley advocated promoting, in all possible fields, "science as a defense against sciences."

Huxley's Neurotheology is not all about natural aims. Studies of *practical* and *transcendental operationism* can be held in psychological terms, and based on a total agnosticism. However, very different things are those concerning *mystical operationism*, the third pillar of Neurotheology: to use scientific findings in the development of different religious ideas and practices. Science, according to Huxley, can, from its empirical point of view, help to understand the most intangible truth, and help to optimize the material part of any mysterious and supernatural ritual.

In summary, Huxley's Neurotheology is a prime example of how a pragmatic perspective can build humanistic fields that encourage the development of a wide range of interdisciplinary projects, scientific and social. It supports a great meeting place between believers and non-believers, provided that they all support a benevolent concept of reality. Furthermore, this approach is very interesting in the pragmatist debate because of the social predictions that Huxley used to present it. *A Brave New World* is a very intuitive picture of what could be the postmodern future. This anti-utopian novel displays a model of a society, not governed by science and/or love but by makers of tales and psycho-engineers, a place where natural human desire to know reality is appeased with fictions and psychotropic substances. In such a technocracy, the main aim pursued is the emergence of positive emotive experiences, i.e. "revivalist sermons, impressive ceremonials, or the deliberate efforts of one's own imagination." The problem, according to the author, is that these emotions are more related to the isolation of the individual than with their opening (Huxley 1947, 293). He disdains this type of belief as "pseudo-religion" or "pseudo-belief" because its purpose is not to face reality, but to assimilate fictions first through emotional drunkenness, or second, in an even more Gnostic manner, through exaltation of affection itself. It is meaningful how Huxley identifies evolutionism as cause of both excesses. "The general acceptance of a doctrine that denies meaning and value to the world as a whole, while assigning them in a supreme degree to certain arbitrarily selected parts of the totality, can have only evil and disastrous results. All that we are (and consequently all that we do) is the result of what we have thought" (Huxley 1941, 274). In this context, he points out, the current idolatry of feeling is a particularly damaging social phenomenon for liberal societies. It promotes policies that justify the provision of "vital lies" to the masses, in order to give those who accept them, not only happiness, but also good behavior (Huxley 1947, 287-291).

Nevertheless, despite admonishing of the risks of posthumanism claims, Huxley is optimistic about the future. The complete implementation of "artificial paradises" does not seem possible. "Some people, it is true, can live contentedly with a philosophy of meaninglessness for a very long time. But in most cases it will be found that these people possess some talent or accomplishment that permits them to live a life which, to a limited extent, is profoundly meaningful and valuable" (Huxley 1941, 275). On the basis of the inability of psychotropic to reach the deepest mystery of the human heart, he predicts the invariable defeat of materialistic utopias and the eternal revival of the "Perennial Philosophy," the return of those seeking a confident and hopeful reality. In fact, his novel *Island* reflects an alternative to such a disgusting (now called post-humanistic culture) one in which Neurotheology plays a relevant role.

The cosmological perspective not only makes scientific progress compatible with the social, but identifies the objective of both. As Mariano Artigas writes, "the meaning of science is twofold: pursuit of truth and service to humankind" (Artigas 2006, 16). Nevertheless, one must recognize that the cosmological arguments presented here do not avoid entirely some obscure and intuitionistic thesis. Peirce, for example, does not believe that God can be reached by mere reasoning, but that this also requires the opening of the heart, and the vitality of experience (Nubiola 2004, 5). As far as Huxley is concerned, his approach does not establish objective criteria for distinguishing visionary experiences from genuine mystical ones, namely, objective states of consciousness (also called "illumination").

To conclude, I would like to mention two questions that arise here. First, do pragmatic realists perceive argumentative shortcomings as inherent to the problem or, on the contrary, do they want to assume it as an intellectual project for the new century? This is an important question, since intuitionism and emotivism are separated by a thin red line. And second, is it possible to avoid or resolve the dilemma of dangerous truths without having to refer to cosmological approaches? The interaction of pragmatisms, both relativistic as realistic, will shape the future of the society, in the task of assuming such questions.

References

Artigas, M. 2006. *The Mind of Universe. Understanding Science and Religion.* London: Templeton Foundation Press.

Barrena, S., and J. Nubiola. 2007. Charles Sanders Peirce. In *Philosophica: Enciclopedia filosófica on line*, ed. F. Fernández Labastida and J.A. Mercado.
http://www.philosophica.info/archivo/2007/voces/peirce/Peirce.html

Berger, P.A. 1978. Medical Treatment of Mental Illness. *Science* 200: 974-981.

Blackmore, S. 1999. *The Meme Machine.* Oxford: Oxford University Press.

Chodoff, P.C. 2002. The Medicalization of the Human Condition. *Psychiatric Services* 53: 627-628.

Davidson, R.J., J. Kabat-Zinn, J. Schumacher, M. Rosenkranz, D. Muller, S.F. Santorelli, F. Urbanowski, A. Harrington, K. Bonus, and J.F. Sheridan. 2003. Alterations in Brain and Immune Function Produced by Mindfulness Meditation. *Psychosomatic Medicine* 6(4): 564-70.

Dawkins, R. 1982. *The Extended Phenotype. The Gene as the Unit of Selection.* Oxford: Oxford University Press.

------. 1989. *The Selfish Gene.* Oxford: Oxford University Press.

------. 2001. Has the World Changed? *The Guardian*, October 11.

------. 2006. *The God Delusion.* Boston: Houghton Mifflin.

Dennett, D. 1991. *Consciousness Explained.* Boston, MA: Little Brown & Co.

------. 2006. *Breaking the Spell. Religions as a Natural Phenomenon.* London: Penguin.

Dewey, J., and J. Tufts. 1932. *Ethics.* New York: Henry Holt.

Erikson, E. 1962. *Young Man Luther: A study in Psychoanalysis and History.* New York: Norton.

Fuller, S. 2005. Schools for the Enlightenment or Epiphany? *The Times Higher Education Supplement*, December 25.

Guidano, V.F. 1987. *Complexity of the Self.* New York: Guilford Press.

------. 1995. A Constructivist Outline of Human Knowing Processes. In *Cognitive and Constructive Psychotherapies*, ed. M.J. Mahoney, 89-102. New York: Springer.

Habermas, J. 2001. *The Future of Human Nature.* Cambridge: Polity Press.

Huxley, A. 1941. *Ends and Means. An Enquiry into the Nature of Ideals and into the Methods Employed for their Realization.* London: Chatto & Windus.

------. 1947. *The Perennial Philosophy.* London: Chatto & Windus.

------. 1960. The Art of Fiction. *The Paris Review* 23 (spring): 66-69.

------. 1962. *Island*. New York: Harper and Row.

------. 1971. *The Doors of Perception. Heaven and Hell*. Middlessex: Penguin Books.

Mora, F. 2000. Cerebro, emoción y naturaleza humana. In *El cerebro sintiente*, 189-201. Barcelona: Ariel Neurociencia.

Nubiola, J. 2002. La búsqueda de la verdad. *Humanidades. Revista de la Universidad de Montevideo*, 2(1): 23-65.

------. 2004. Il Lume Naturale: Abduction and God. *Semiotiche*, I/2: 91-102.

Oleksy, M. 2004. An Almost Lost Cause of a Battle Against Metaphysics. Deconstruction and Deflation on the Common Track. In *Deconstruction and Reconstruction. The Central European Pragmatist Forum*, Vol. 2, ed. J. Ryder & K. Wilkoszewska, 227-238. Amsterdam/New York: Rodopi.

------. 2005. C. S. Peirce y su cruzada contra el nominalismo moderno. Paper presented at *Conferencia impartida en la Universidad de Navarra para el Grupo de Estudios Peirceanos*, June 9, Navarra, Spain.

Peirce, C.S. 1998. *Collected Papers*, 8 vols. Ed. C. Hartshorne, P. Weiss and A. Burks A. Bristol: Thoemmes Press.

Rorty R. 1989. *Contingency, Irony, and Solidarity*. Cambridge: Cambridge University Press.

------. 1991. *Objectivity, Relativism and Truth: Philosophical Papers*. Cambridge: Cambridge University Press.

------. 1998. Pragmatism as Romantic Polytheism. In *The Revival of Pragmatism: New Essays on Social Thought, Law, and Culture*, ed. M. M. Dickstein. Durham: Duke University Press.

Teske, J.A. 2000. The Social Construction of the Human Spirit. In *The Human Person in Science and Theology*, ed. N.H. Gregersen, W.B. Drees, U. Gorman, 189-211. Edinburgh: T&T Clark; Grand Rapids: Eerdmans.

------. 2001. Cognitive Neuroscience, Temporal Ordering, and the Human Spirit. Zygon. *Journal of Religion and Science* 36: 665-676.

------. 2005. Neuromythology: Brain and Stories. Paper presented at the conference *Science and Religion: Global Perspectives*, June 4-8, in Philadelphia, USA.

Ahti-Veikko Pietarinen
University of Helsinki, Finland
Remarks on the Peirce-Schiller correspondence

"We can only know [the] human aspect [of things]. But that is all the universe is for us."
(Peirce's letter to Welby, SS: 141).

I.

Charles Peirce and Ferdinand C.S. Schiller exchanged a series of letters from 1905 to 1906, of which nine have survived, some of them as draft versions. The correspondence is of considerable interest in drawing the philosophies of the two men into sharper focus and wider perspective. In this paper, my aim is to outline some of the most salient issues and ideas featured in those letters.[1] Understanding the intellectual relationship between the two is pivotal to understanding the key connections and divergences between Schiller's so-called *humanistic pragmatism* and Peirce's recasting of his own philosophical method as *pragmaticism*. In the year 1905, pragmaticism had just been secured from kidnappers, including, as Peirce recounts, Schiller himself as one of those 'literary' rogues.

Pinpointing the main topics of discussion in the correspondence also helps us to understand both of the two philosophers in their own right. The letters reveal that the two gentlemen were very candid with each other yet respectful. The common perception concerning the relationship between Peirce and Schiller is that Peirce accused Schiller, just as he accused William James, of carrying pragmatism too far, into directions that he himself would not have been ready to go. It is also routinely held that, as a consequence, Peirce did not accept Schiller's pragmatism at all. The reasons for these claims have not been made reasonably clear, however. It is only part of the truth to state that Peirce did not accept Schiller's philosophy. Peirce held Schiller in high regard, calling him in print an "admirably clear and brilliant thinker" (CP 5.414, *What Pragmatism* is, 1905) and "the brilliant and marvelously human thinker" (CP 5.466, *A Survey of Pragmaticism*, 1907). The correspondence furthermore reveals that, as a matter of fact, Peirce largely agrees with the anthropomorphic nature of metaphysics. I would like to point out that his anthropomorphism could be seen as meaning something similar to what has much later been labeled as the 'descriptive' approach to metaphysics: the idea that the study of the structures of the world must

---

[1] Scott (1973) contains transcriptions of most of the Peirce-Schiller correspondence, together with commentary on the origins and background of the letters. The topics considered in the present essay are not taken up in Scott's paper.

go through the study of the structures of the mind. In studying the structures of the mind we are at once studying the structures of the world.

Such an unexpected alignment of Peirce and Schiller becomes much easier to appreciate as soon as we recognize that at the time the two men shared a common enemy. As presented in his 1903 *The Principles of Mathematics*, Bertrand Russell had just begun propagating his notion of an uninterpreted, purely formal conception of logic. Peirce acknowledged Russell's book in passing in a little book notice published in the *Nation* in October 1903. The main focus of that review was Victoria Welby's *What is Meaning?*, which was published in the same year. Right after the review had appeared in print, Schiller revealed privately to Welby how furious and "hugely annoyed" Russell had been after having read Peirce's criticism in the Nation (*Schiller to Welby*, 26 November 1903).[2] From that point, Welby began her correspondence with Peirce.

In his 1905 letter to Schiller, Peirce accused James of misleadingly taking Schiller's philosophy to be closer to James himself than to Peirce. What Peirce tells Schiller is that he in fact perceives himself to be much closer to Schiller's ideas than to James's. This view – even if somewhat exaggerated – is expressed in Peirce's statement that Schiller's philosophy is "at any rate in its conclusions nearer my own than does any other man's" (*Peirce to Schiller*, 12 May 1905).

Pihlström (2004: 46) accepts the standard interpretation in stating that "it seems that Peirce was more critical of Schiller than of James." It is, however, more accurate to restate the matter in terms of Peirce being equally critical of both James and Schiller, in the sense of taking their presuppositions of constructing pragmatic philosophy to be equally mistaken, yet keeping in mind that with Schiller, Peirce felt that they shared some common goals. James, on the other hand, was in Peirce's opinion a bystander rather than an earnest contestant in the early debates over the nature of pragmatism.

Backed up by evidence from the letters, my aim is thus to correct the common perception: the view according to which Peirce's dismissal of both Schiller's and James' versions of pragmatism were constructed on similar grounds and largely for the same reasons. This said, I do not aim to reproach Peirce's and Schiller's thoughts, since I believe that cannot be done. In fact, I will argue that the sharp severance of pragmaticism from Schiller's humanistic or personal pragmatism has an irresistible explanation. The two thoughts are, I shall maintain, separated by one of the deepest presuppositions that can underlie any rational philosophical design. That presupposition concerns *one* vs. *many world* philosophies. These terms will become clearer as we proceed. Nevertheless, this absolute presupposition, to borrow a term from R. G. Collingwood, offers the grounds for the fundamental disparity in Peirce's and Schiller's thoughts.

---

[2] Letters are deposited at the Welby Fonds, York University Archives, Toronto.

In brief, it is the conception of reality that Peirce and Schiller are seen to seize in two fundamentally different senses.

II.

The correspondence between the two men took off after Peirce had sent his work "What Pragmatism Is" to Schiller in April 1905, the same month the paper appeared in the *Monist*. Earlier, Peirce had kept a close eye on Schiller's work. He commented on Schiller's 1902 "Axioms as Postulates," a paper published in the collection *Personal Idealism* and which Peirce later tagged to be Schiller's "most remarkable paper" (*What Pragmatism Is*, 1905, EP), with the famous gloss that "Mr. Schiller does not believe there are any hard facts which remain true independently of what we may think about them" (Peirce, *Review of Personal Idealism, The Nation*, 4 June 1903, 462-463; in CN 3:127).

It is obvious that Schiller's conception clashes with Peirce's objective notion of facts. Humanism takes human experience, human interests, and human acts, such as wishes, hopes, desires, and expectations, to be constitutive of knowledge. It is such interests and acts, Schiller holds, that determine the hard facts that enter the field of human cognition. Because Schiller accepted logic in its broad sense as a form of human action, his conception of facts is not far removed from Ernst Mach's *phenomenalism*, which takes physical objects to be logical constructions from sense-data. Phenomenalism, in turn, gave rise to the positivistic philosophy of science around the turn of the century. Another closely related upshot is that Schiller is committed to an extreme form of *empiricism* concerning the verificationistic postulate. These two implications from Schiller's position, phenomenalism and early logical positivism, are likely to be something that a casual Schiller aficionado may find had to swallow.

To James, Peirce explains how his and Schiller's "humanistic element of pragmatism is very true and important and impressive," but that he did "not think that the doctrine can be *proved* in that way." Peirce writes: "The present generation likes to skip proofs ... You and Schiller carry pragmatism too far for me. I don't want to exaggerate it but keep it within the bounds to which the evidences of it are limited. The most important consequence of it, by far, on which I have always insisted ... is that under that conception of reality we must abandon nominalism" (*Peirce to James*, CP 8.258, 7 March 1904). Peirce takes James and Schiller to be *nominalists*, who do not believe in the real nature of general laws, habits of action, or universals. Peirce's remark was written during the time when he had embarked on his grand project of trying to actually prove, by valid and rigorous argumentation, that his pragmaticism is a correct and true method of doing philosophy. Whether and how he succeeded in this is another matter not to be taken up here (see Pietarinen & Snellman 2006; Pietarinen 2011).

Peirce's conception of reality was *scholastic realism*: that there are real possibilities as constituents of reality. This is the crucial departure. In Schiller's writings there are precious few references to possibilities or to any other modal concepts for that matter. He is a hard-headed actualist and as an actualist is a one-world philosopher: he thinks that matters of philosophy can be resolved here and now, referring only to the world we inhabit, within the context of actual human affairs, and with no recourse to the futile technicalities provided by possibilities and the vain contemplations of 'how things might have been'.

To support this point, let me arrange the key snippets from Schiller's and Peirce's correspondence in the form of the following dialogue:

> *Schiller*: I am ashamed to say that I have not yet been able to grasp wherein the specific peculiarity of 'pragmaticism' consists as compared with other pragmatisms (30 April 1905).

> *Peirce*: I am not sure of understanding you; for there is one word whose meaning in your mouth I cannot guess. It is *reality*. I should be particularly obliged to you if you would send me a definition of it (23 May 1905). But while I seem to agree with your philosophical opinions, we are separated by two differences much deeper (23 May 1905). [One is that] the word *real* was introduced as a technical term (first of law and then of logic) and was so little used before Scotus & so continually by him that it ought to be regarded as his word; and my ethics of terminology will not permit me to give it any other meaning than that it is that whose characters do not at all depend upon what any man or men think that they are (12 May 1905). Another difference seems to be that I think the very first application that should be made of pragmatism of any stripe is to define words (June 1905 or later). From what you say about me, I infer that you have never read any philosophical or logical paper of mine unless perhaps this last one [*What Pragmatism Is*] (23 May 1905).

> *Schiller*: Dear Mr. Peirce. I fear that my unfortunate misapprehension as to the relation of James's account of pragmatism to your authentic doctrine (which I was first enabled to realize by your first letter), must have rendered my article in Mind unsatisfactory reading to you. [However,] James and I both agree that if there are real alternatives anywhere, the whole course of things might have been different, and so that the acceptance of human freedom carries with it the assertion of an indefinite 'plasticity' of the 'real' (5 June 1905).

> *Peirce*: As to the plasticity of the real, I am, on one side, entirely with you. ... The power of self-control is certainly not a power over what one is doing at the very instant the operation of self-control is commenced. It consists (to mention only the leading constituents), first, in comparing one's past deeds with standards, second, in rational deliberation concerning how one will act in the future, in itself a highly complicated operation, third, in the formation of a resolve, fourth, in the creation, on the basis of the resolve, of a strong determination, or modification of habit. [Therefore,] the most important and far-reaching difference is in regard to scholastic realism (Late June or later 1905; partly in CP 8.320).

After their correspondence ceased, Peirce complained on Schiller's blindness to the important tenet of scholastic realism in defining pragmatism in his

1907 book Studies in Humanism. Peirce remarks how "Mr. Schiller seems habitually to use the word 'actual' in some peculiar sense" (CP 5.494, *A Survey of Pragmatism*, 1907). This is an acute observation, not least because Schiller did not follow Peirce's suggestion for the first and foremost application of pragmatism to be to "define words." Schiller subscribes to the view that all propositions must be actually verified to be true. Here is an example of what he has to say:

> On its entry into the world of existence, a truth claim has merely commended itself (perhaps provisionally) to its maker. To become really true it has to be tested, and it is tested by being *applied*. Only when this is done, only, that is, when it is *used*, can it be determined what it really means, and what conditions it must fulfill to be really true. Hence all real truths must have shown themselves to be useful; they must have been applied to some problem of *actual* knowing (Schiller 1966: 61, *The Definition of Pragmatism and Humanism*, in *Studies in Humanism*, last emphasis added).

Note the profusion with which Schiller appeals to a "truth claim" to be "really" true, to be a "real" truth, and to "really" mean something. A great deal thus hinges on Schiller's conception of reality and it is this conception with which Peirce has the key disagreement in their correspondence. Furthermore, by "applying" and "using" a "truth claim" Schiller means actual application and actual use that has to take place in this world and nowhere else. He notes how pragmatism "essays to trace out the actual 'making of truth'" (Schiller 1907: 4). Undeniably, Schiller portrays himself as a prime example of a 'one-world' philosopher.

What follows from a one-world philosophy, and therefore from dispensing with the philosophical inquiry that aims at ascertaining the truth with reference to what *would* be the case, is conceptual relativism. Personal interests are singular and not general phenomena, and for that reason leave the case open as to which ends and purposes "real" truths are ultimately aimed at. As for Schiller, they certainly are not truths 'in the limit', as those would go beyond individual and personal human interests. How Peirce describes the situation is that "Schiller informs us that he and James [*Pragmatism*, 1907] have made up their minds that the true is simply the satisfactory." He continues, "No doubt; but to say 'satisfactory' is not to complete any predicate whatever. Satisfactory to what end?" (CP 5.552, *Truth*, 1907).

About a year later, in one of his last publications, Peirce continues this line of criticism: "[I]f Truth consists in satisfaction, it cannot be any actual satisfaction, but must be the satisfaction which would ultimately be found if the inquiry were pushed to its ultimate and indefeasible issue. This, I beg to point out, is a very different position from that of Mr. Schiller and the pragmatists of today" (CP 6.485, *A Neglected Argument for the Reality of God*, 1908).

That such relativism is bound to follow from the one-world assumption is also seen from the fact that Schiller equates the meaning of propositions with the "making" of truth claims. Yet no matter what the precise meaning of the making here turns out to be, as noted earlier, the whole idea presupposes a heavily empiricist rendering of verificationism, with its identical presupposition that it is the one, actual world that is the source of all meaning.

As far as Schiller's criticism of formal logic is concerned, his object of ridicule was the logical notion of truth, a study of "valid inferences" (Schiller 1912: 14). We can appreciate Schiller's criticism from the point of view that such a narrow conception of logic that was becoming an all too commonplace those years did not, as Schiller remarks, take into account the "problem of material truth" (Schiller 1912: 6). It was only much later with Tarski's semantic conception of truth in the 1930s that the latter problem came to be framed and studied in an equal precision as logical truth. Peirce, too, was studying the problem of material truth in his logic after 1885 (Pietarinen 2006). Schiller certainly was not aware of those traits of an early theory of semantics in Peirce's thought.

III.

Let me summarize three key points of contest in the Peirce-Schiller correspondence and the main conclusions from them:

(1) In his hasty reaction to Peirce's essay *What Pragmatism Is* (*Schiller to Peirce*, 30 April 1905), Schiller misinterprets pragmaticism as a "generic" and "sweeping" term that agrees with his "plurality of pragmatisms." Peirce's reply is that, unlike Schiller, he does not want "philosophy to embody the whole man" (*Peirce to Schiller*, 12 May 1905). Peirce does largely agree with anthropomorphism, though he gives it his own bent towards the descriptive methodology of metaphysics. In brief, he accepts that (i) the needs of life asseverate philosophical perspectives, that (ii) ideals take human shape, and that (iii) human instincts ought to be trusted in the main (*Peirce to Schiller*, undated, draft, apparently 23 May 1905). The first point refers to the Kantian "*pragmatisch*," the second follows from all knowledge being anthropological, and the third from all knowledge being derived from "inborn animal instincts." However, while anthropomorphism may be present in the metaphysical part of Peirce's architectonic philosophy, he dismisses Schiller's idea of the "plurality of pragmatisms" with no hesitation. He holds such self-avowed pluralism, which has nothing to do with the pluralism of methods that Peirce endorses, to be an expression of an unacceptably restrictive approach in all inquiry, philosophy included. My interpretation of these remarks is that it is Peirce's original version, pragmaticism, that ought to be seen as appropriately pluralistic in the sense in which Schiller's pragmatic humanism is not, namely in the range and application of methodologies that are available in philosophical inquiry.

The explanation for Peirce's radically different view on what pluralism means is in my view that a one-world philosopher is bound to be a *universalist* concerning the meaning of language. He cannot use meta-systematic approaches, for example meta-linguistic methods, in tackling important philosophical questions and problems. Thus he cannot assert conceptual truths in language. We might see such a vantage point from which to consider philosophy, and something which Schiller and James are in the end both committed to, as a roadblock to the progress of scientific inquiry.

(2) Peirce agrees, surprisingly enough, that Schiller's pragmatism nevertheless comes "in its conclusions nearer my own than does any other man's" (*Peirce to Schiller*, 12 May 1905). This statement becomes much more understandable as soon as we recognize the aforementioned fact that Peirce and Schiller both agreed to defend a wider concept of logic against the soon-to-be-prevailing formal, uninterpreted notion of logic that Russell was promulgating (see Schiller's 1912 book *Formal Logic* and its follow-up from 1929 *Logic for Use*). In *Formal Logic*, which was Schiller's attack not on logic as such but on the idea of solely resorting to uninterpreted languages of logic, he states that "It is not possible to abstract from the actual use of the logical material and to consider 'forms of thought' in themselves, without incurring thereby a total loss, not only of truth but also meaning" (Schiller 1912: ix). Schiller accuses those who wish to sever logic from metaphysics or psychology to act "in a wholly illogical manner" when drawing "the line between the 'logical' and 'extra-logical'" (*ibid.*: ix). This line of criticism was continued, together with some positive suggestions, in *Logic for Use*. Peirce would certainly have agreed that "the use of the logical material" is the key here, but that it must not be confined to "actual use," precisely because of its consequence of conceptual relativism, which in the end risks making all genuine communication impossible.

Another difference between Peirce and Schiller over the nature of logic concerns psychologism. Schiller aligned the appearance of logical assertions with "the jungle of wishes, desires, emotions, questions, commands, imaginations, hopes and fears," which "in real life" are the contexts in which logical assertions arise as either "the answer to or the raising of a question" (Schiller 1912: 9). Peirce, who did not agree that the criteria for the validity of logical postulates could be in the individual psychic lives of living persons, had written earlier that "when you say that logical consequences cannot be separated from psychological effects, etc. in my opinion you are merely adopting a mode of expression highly inconvenient which cannot help, but can only confuse, any sound argumentation. It is a part of nominalism which is utterly antipragmatistic, as I think, and mere refusal to make use of valuable forms of thought" (*Peirce to Schiller*, draft, 10 September 1906; CP 8.326).

Apparently this letter, which contains the last surviving material Peirce intended for Schiller, was never sent, however. That it was not is an unfortunate accident of history, because consequently, Schiller did not take up Peirce's charge of adopting an uncritical stance towards psychologism in his *Formal Logic* nor in any of its sequels. Schiller keeps on insisting that by disentangling "the nature of logical assertion from various psychological processes with which it is bound up in its actual occurrence," the field of logic as a purely formal study of assertion is seriously "incapacitated" (Schiller 1912: 8).

Not having received Peirce's last weighty letter and therefore failing to critically re-evaluate his avowed psychologism is in fact doubly unfortunate because of the dire consequences that follow from the association of the study of logical assertions with concrete human thought processes. Yet such an association seems to have been one of the main causes of misinterpretations of both the original meaning of pragmatism as well as of letting those interpretations roam free in the later discourse. This is evident already from Schiller's ill-conceived 1911 *Encyclopedia Britannica* entry on "pragmatism" as well as from Russell's equally misplaced reactions to James's version of pragmatism (Russell 1910).

(3) I take the reasonable conclusion from the Peirce-Schiller correspondence to be that Peirce sees no way of reconciling Schiller's view with pragmaticism. An explanation of this can, as remarked, be cast in terms of their conception of reality and Schiller being a 'one-world' philosopher and Peirce as a 'many-world' one. I have discussed in Pietarinen (2008) in more detail the more precise senses in which these two labels can be applied to other pragmatistically inclined thinkers besides Peirce and Schiller.

It is, therefore, an error to see Peirce's pragmaticism as a narrower form of philosophy than humanism. In the methodological sense, pragmaticism is the more admissible and pluralistic one, and for these reasons a wider and "much less ambitious" (*Peirce to Schiller*, 23 May 1905) method for philosophy than Schiller's anthropomorphic humanism – and we need no mention of what Schiller's soi-disant neo-pragmatist followers came to suggest much later. One-world philosophy is tied to actual human action and the idea of singular human interests guiding actions. It authorizes pragmatism to fantasize on the nearly unlimited applicability of its core pragmatist tenets. At face value, this might sound like an open-minded pluralism, but in reality it yields one-world relativism. Humanism is limited to using the concept of applicability here from a methodologically monistic vantage point.

In the light of my observations, I pose in closing an open question: If one-world philosophies, such as Schiller's pragmatic humanism, are methodologically more restricted forms of pragmatism, how are they expected to cope with increasingly complex and acute contemporary questions and problems facing us in the world today? I must surely forego any attempts to answer this question, so let me just set this question up as a theoretical challenge. It is a challenge that needs to be tackled by anyone who sees pragmatic humanism as a valuable and defendable alternative to mainstream philosophy.

References

Abel, Reuben. 1955. *The Pragmatic Humanism of F. C. S. Schiller*. New York: King's Crown Press.

Peirce, Charles S. 1931-58. (CP) *Collected Papers of Charles Sanders Peirce*. Ed. Charles Hartshorne, Paul Weiss and Arthur W. Burks. Cambridge, Mass.: Harvard University Press.

------. 1967. (MS) Manuscripts. In the Houghton Library of Harvard University, as identified by Richard Robin, *Annotated Catalogue of the Papers of Charles S. Peirce* (Amherst: University of Massachusetts Press, 1967), and in The Peirce Papers: A supplementary catalogue, *Transactions of the C. S. Peirce Society* 7 (1971): 37-57.

-----. 1975-87. (CN) *Charles Sanders Peirce: Contributions to The Nation*. Four volumes. Ed. Kenneth Ketner and James Cook. Lubbock: Texas Tech University Press.

-----. 1977. (SS) *Semiotic and Significs: The Correspondence Between Charles S. Peirce and Victoria Lady Welby*. Ed. Charles S. Hardwick & J. Cook, Bloomington: Indiana University Press.

-----. 1998. (EP) *The Essential Peirce* 2. Peirce Edition Project, Bloomington: Indiana University Press.

Pietarinen, Ahti-Veikko. 2006. *Signs of Logic: Peircean Themes on the Philosophy of Language, Games, and Communication*. Dordrecht: Springer.

------. 2008. The Place of Logic in Pragmatism. *Cognitio* 9(1): 247-260.

------. 2011. Graphs, Games, and Pragmaticism's Proof. *Semiotica*, in press.

Pietarinen, Ahti-Veikko and Lauri Snellman. 2006. On Peirce's Late Proof of Pragmaticism. In *Truth and Games*, ed. Tuomo Aho and Ahti-Veikko, 275-288. Helsinki: Acta Philosophica Fennica.

Pihlström, Sami. 2004. Peirce's Place in the Pragmatist Tradition. In *The Cambridge Companion to Peirce*, ed. Cheryl Misak, 27-57. Cambridge: Cambridge University Press.

Russell, Bertrand. 1910. Pragmatism. In *Philosophical Essays*. London: George Allen & Unwin.

Schiller, F. C. S. 1902. Axioms as Postulates. In *Personal Idealism*, ed. Henry Sturt, 47-133. London and New York: Macmillan.

------. 1907. *Studies in Humanism*. London: Macmillan.

------. 1912. *Formal Logic: A Scientific and Social Problem*. London: Macmillan.

------. 1929. *Logic for Use: An Introduction to the Voluntarist Theory of Knowledge*. London: G. Bell and Sons.

------. 1966. *Humanistic Pragmatism: The Philosophy of F. C. S. Schiller*. New York: Free Press.

70 Ahti-Veikko Pietarinen

Scott, Frederick J. Down. 1973. Peirce and Schiller and their Correspondence. *Journal of the History of Philosophy* 11: 363-386.
Sturt, Henry, ed. 1902. *Personal Idealism*. London and New York: Macmillan.

Part II – Media

Alexander Brand
University of Dresden, Germany
Stefan Robel
University of Dresden, Germany
Hegemonic governance? Global media, US hegemony and the transatlantic divide

1. Introduction

In this paper we explore the relationship between the world political role of the United States and current trends in the global media realm. Truly global media – in the form of globally operating media enterprises – have emerged only to underscore the 'pole position' of US- and Western-based media conglomerates in global communication. More often than not, this pole position is seen as a building bloc of global political hegemony or 'empire'. This argument rests on an ostensibly plausible hypothesis: that it is necessary for hegemonic governance and/or an empire to be constantly (re-)produced also – and sometimes it is even asserted *above all* – in the cultural/media realm.

Our argument, which will challenge this rather intuitive claim, is developed as follows: First, we decide on the analytical framework proper to analyze the global position of the United States with regard to the transnational media realm. In doing so, we opt for a spatially differentiated, society-oriented model of contemporary US hegemony. Under the analytical lens of US hegemony as defined here, we argue that to assume a simple correlation between the global political role of the United States and the formative influence of US-based media corporations does not allow for sufficient understanding. Although forms of hegemonic governance and the leveling of 'soft power' may to some degree indeed rest upon media (and other cultural) strategies, we identify three current trends that counter the assumption of a simple 'media-political-complex': the ambivalence of the 'Americanization' of global media; regionalization strategies in the media realm and their consequences for hegemonic governance; and, a deep rift in the transatlantic realm, which we refer to here as to the so called 'transatlantic media divide'. Thus, hegemonic governance is far more precarious even within the inner circle of US hegemony, let alone with regard to global media dynamics. Media in fact do play a crucial role in *undermining* the acceptance of US political leadership around the world, despite the preponderance of US actors in the global media and communications sector. Consequently, it is wrong to assert an automatism of hegemony/consensus through the ascendancy of communication means or an ideological strengthening of the imperial grip the United States is supposed to have on global public opinion.

2. The analytical framework: empire, or hegemony?

The foreign policy of the United States since 9/11, namely various strategic orientations as well as concrete policies of the two Bush administrations, arguably have fuelled debates on the role of the United States in world politics (Bacevich 2002; Brzezinski 2004; Czempiel 2002; Johnson 2004; Müller 2003; Nye 2002). There are discernible strands in these debates: Whether American preponderance is better described as 'hegemony' or pure 'dominance', for instance, or whether we are experiencing a new form of 'empire'. The phenomenon itself, although being debated on and off since the end of the Second World War, has been interpreted quite differently over time. From an academic point of view, however, International Relations (IR) theories to date have not yet delivered a generally accepted term, a workable definition let alone a dominant theoretical concept for analysis of the singular international role of the United States of America in the contemporary international system.

The current fad is, without doubt, the ubiquitous use of the term 'empire'. A rapidly and still growing stock of literature on the subject notwithstanding, there is no consensus even within the most prominent schools of IR if and if so, how to apply the term to the United States. We argue that the rise of the term 'empire' is mainly due to the particular characteristics of the foreign policy of the Bush administrations and the specific circumstances under which they were able to fully apply what has been dubbed 'imperialistic' characteristics to US foreign policy strategy of late: the focus on military security and interventionism accompanied by a broad neglect of multilateralism, international institutions and the virtues of diplomacy. Even before the election of Barack Obama as the 44th President of the United States – undoubtedly bringing a personal and stylistic change to the White House – it was not hard to predict that at least the very open unilateral style of US foreign policy strategy would change, regardless of the outcome of the 2008 elections.

Although it seems fair to describe some of the foreign policies pursued by the Bush administration as *imperialistic*, this does not automatically render the term 'empire' a legitimate or useful choice for the description of the global power relationship that the US has established. To be sure, imperialism, a foreign policy strategy that *aims at* the establishment of an empire is quite a different thing as an empire *in existence*. Even if we call the policies of the respective US administrations 'imperialistic', the status quo would only be ill-described by the term 'empire'.[1] Yet, the empire discourse returned to town (Cox 2003; Ikenberry 2004a, b; Mann 2004). It has been mostly applied to the analysis of US

---

[1] We are much more convinced by the argument that the Bush Administration pursued a strategy of (selective) world domination (*'selektive Weltherrschaft'*, see Czempiel 2002, 108) or a 'strategy for empire' (Loveman 2004) than we are by the semantic base line of a vast amount of literature on the United States as an empire in existence.

dominance in world politics with either harsh or rather sympathetic assessments of the strategic and normative implications of current trends in US foreign policy. Compared to the early days of the empire discourse in IR, when its main protagonists could easily get away with popularizing the term without even trying to define it (Cox 2003; Ferguson 2004) it has matured of late (Ferguson 2008; Lake 2008; Lipschutz 2009; Nexon and Wright 2007; Saull 2008; Spruyt 2008; Sterling-Folker 2008). However, the debate still offers far more 'don't's than 'do's with regard to the application of the term in IR theory on and analysis of the contemporary international system.[2]

Beyond that, as Jennifer Sterling-Folker (2008) has put it ironically and admirably to the point in the title of her essay: *The Emperor* (without wearing much else) *Wore Cowboy Boots*. With George W. Bush having left the White House, the question has been: will the US still be viewed and discussed as being an empire even by its own social science scholars? This, it is fair to say well into the second year of the Obama term, is not at all so. The theoretical debate has moved from empire straight to the newest version of a recurring theme: hegemonic decline (Lieber 2008).[3]

This leads us back to the term 'hegemony.' As long as we are not willing to give up the analytical system of formally sovereign states as a relevant organizational principle of (post)modern politics, we have to settle for a term that sticks to *power* as the basic modus of international relations. The term 'hegemony' certainly exhibits tensions with regard to imperialistic strategies, but does not preclude them fully.[4]

International hegemony[5] – as distinct from 'empire', pure dominance or simple preponderance – is to describe here "… a specific form of leadership in which the existence and continuity of the relation depends on the one hand on the power resources of the hegemon, its will and strategic competence and, on the other hand, on the basically voluntary allegiance of a group of states which are homogeneous in terms of government" (Robel 2001, 21). The establishment and persistence of such a hegemonic leadership is conditioned by the "self-restraint of power" (Triepel 1974, 34) as well as the strategic competence of the

---

[2] For a more elaborate discussion on this see Prys and Robel, forthcoming.

[3] As Lieber (2008, 50) argues: "The new declinists usually pin the blame (or credit) on the Bush administration's grand strategy (the Bush Doctrine) – a crudely unilateralist assertion of American power that disregards both the views of other countries and international law."

[4] With regard to the experience of the two Bush administrations, the question is rather: To what degree has 'hegemony' proven sustainable in the face of openly imperialistic policies?

[5] This is a broadening of the concept of Heinrich Triepel, see Triepel 1974; for a detailed overview on Triepel's theory of hegemony, see Robel 1994, 3-23. This concept seems to be much closer to the argument of Bacevich about the long history of the United States as an 'informal' empire, see Bacevich 2002.

hegemon and the *perception of legitimacy of the leadership among the follow-ers*. The leadership can only endure, if a stable long lasting consensus is reached within and between the political systems of all states concerned. This requires that political and societal stability persist within the borders of the hegemonic state while at the same time it maintains its capacity of adaptation to changes in the international system (Robel 2001, 22). On the international level, international institutions play a decisive role in creating and maintaining this consensus constitutive of hegemonic leadership. Hegemony understood this way as the exercise of leadership met by some basic consensus of the led makes it, first of all, necessary to differentiate between sub-global spheres. The above mentioned definition is only widely and generally applicable to the hegemon's relations to a core group of states. Applying a term coined by Ernst-Otto Czempiel (1993), it is referred to here as the "OECD world."[6] Other parts of the world are certainly also – and sometimes even more so – affected by the weal and woe of US hegemony, albeit generally in quite different ways. Different sets of actors and societal constellations support or oppose US hegemony in the inner core or the periphery of the unipolar system. Together with the hegemon itself there are four different realms (or regions or spaces) of hegemony which have to be differentiated to support a truly profitable analysis of hegemony: the centre, the inner and the outer circle and the so called outcasts.[7]

The hegemonic state is located in the centre of the model. Its decisions determine, to a certain (but rarely, if ever, irrelevant) extent, the existence and chances of success/leeway of the other states in the system. What we have called the '*inner circle of hegemony*' comprises the comparatively homogenous group of 'OECD-democracies'. The states in this group have in common that hegemonic leadership is in principle accepted because of the support of the overwhelming majority of the country's elites in and outside of government, as well as by the majority of 'partially official' representatives of the population on the whole (the media and the 'general public'). The general public might at times tend to show what some observers eagerly would call straits of anti-Americanism,[8] the majority feels attracted to the American system for as long as hegemony can be said to be in effect. In contrast, the sphere of influence of the *outer circle of hegemony* comprises an extremely heterogeneous group of states, reaching from the classical developing (or underdeveloped) countries and the states succeeding the former Eastern bloc to regional superpowers such as Russia, India, the People's Republic of China and Brazil. With the marked excep-

---

[6] Czempiel's notion of the *'Gesellschaftswelt'* (societal world) describes this section of the international system quite accurately. For the grounding of this concept, see Czempiel 1993, 105-132.

[7] For a further elaboration on the necessary subglobal differentiation of spheres of influence of US-American hegemony see Lempp and Robel 2006, 11.

[8] See the nuanced and empirically rich discussion in: Ruzza and Bozzini 2006; Isernia 2006.

tion of those regional powers (a case in point here is Russia) in most of the states of the 'outer circle of hegemony' significant parts of the elite on whose support the government depends secretly, if not overtly, accept US hegemonic domin-ance while significant parts of the public are either overtly anti-American or at least fundamentally question the legitimacy of US global preponderance or poli-cies designed to achieve it. The '*outcasts*' openly oppose the hegemonic US's claim to leadership, be it out of choice or by virtue of the definitional power of the hegemon as being named a 'rogue state' or belonging to the 'axis of evil' or, in former times, the 'Evil Empire', with former examples Libya and Saddam Hussein's Iraq, and the current ones Iran, North Korea and, for half a century now, Fidel Castro's Cuba.

3. Hegemony and hegemonic governance

If hegemony is understood and applied as sketched above, hegemonic gover-nance[9] is to describe the world policy of a hegemonic state
   a) together with and in relation to a comprehensive group of states (compris-ing regional powers; the inter-state component);
   b) in accordance with the (dominant ideas of) central actors of global capital-ism (the transnational component[10]);
   c) for the sake of an (at least partially genuine) improvement of world order;
   d) from which, in turn, not only the hegemon, but at least its followers in the inner circle of hegemony benefit (at least they seem to or believe they benefit);
   e) hereby evoking or bolstering consent towards its hegemonic project.
Regardless of the sub-global differentiations introduced, an overarching me-chanism can be analytically grasped consequently which seems to be at the heart of any hegemonic endeavor: the need to establish and foster some degree of consensus toward that very leadership, or, in other words: voluntary allegiance has to be fed by legitimacy.

It is this 'necessary consensus component' (Cox 1993; Gill 1993), which particularly captures our attention here. In analyzing the effect of hegemonic ideas, their development and spreading (or in asking: How do ideas, ideologies and hegemonic projects emerge and assert themselves within one society and how do they come to set the tone in international politics?), we clearly see how

---

[9] For a sensible account of 'hegemonic governance', see Beyer 2008, 17-35.

[10] It should be mentioned that we here do not elaborate theoretically on the transnational component of (international) hegemony. It would have gone beyond the scope of this chap-ter, although we concede to the critical reader that this omission is at least surprising with regard to an analysis of the reciprocal effects of transnational media conglomerates and US hegemony. Still, our aim here is to analyse the interaction of inter-state hegemony with the effects of transnational media business strategies.

transnational operations of mass media *could* enter the picture. The argument would be – often made more implicit with regard to media in general – that they may complement the effect of international organizations as instruments of hegemonic world politics (Cox 1993, 62). In this sense, the hegemon may use international institutions to legitimize and preserve the status quo by including national and transnational elites in a consensus over ideas.[11] With regard to media, more often than not, a differentiated account is missing. They are for a large part simply assumed to play a role in fostering some consensus around which US policies converge, for instance with regard to the so called 'Washington consensus', i.e. neoliberal macroeconomic restructuring (deregulation, liberalization and privatization). As Mittelman argues in this regard: "A set of organizing institutions bundles neoliberalism and globalization, and seeks to universalize the core ideas. Among these diverse institutions are *the media*, the lecture circuit, schools, and universities ..." (Mittelman 2005, 49; emphasis added). Although this seemingly undifferentiated account constitutes an invitation to problematize the role of transnationally operating US American media, it undoubtedly hints at an important aspect. To ask for 'hegemonic governance' is to ask for mechanisms of how ideas are spread, how different meanings are constructed and disseminated and how an eventual consensus is forged. In other words, it is about the achievement and contestation of discursive supremacy.

Still, 'hegemonic governance' might be an unlikely term describing foreign and world policies recently pursued by the United States, especially under the two Bush administrations. It might be a misleading concept altogether if applied to analyze the changing patterns of US foreign policy and their ordering effects on the international system only on the basis of a presumed consensus-oriented strategy. Trends and single global as well as regional policies since 2000 have underscored the fact that 'hegemonic governance' in the sense of a steering of world politics through leadership – which is not fundamentally contested – is not a stable and permanent *leitmotif* of US policy. This is true, above all, if hegemonic governance itself – as a policy style and a policy substance – is not seen as constituting a vital interest in the eyes of central decision-makers in the administration and important societal actors. However, this does not imply that 'hegemonic governance' is of no importance with regard to the definition of policy goals in the near future, the choice of certain instruments and even domestic political processes. To scrap the idea of 'hegemonic governance' or the idea of 'hegemony' as described above would mean to adjust models to current (and already changing) political trends. Not only the outcome but the turnout of voters in the US (presidential) elections in 2008 (this could be said already with some justification regarding the results of the mid-term congressional elections

---

[11] Are media, to use Murphy's term, as well 'transmission belts' for the global spread of ideas, or, in a narrower (not Murphy's) sense, acting as transmission belts on behalf of a hegemon? (Murphy 2004, 13).

in 2006) showed that the majority of Americans do not at all want anything faintly similar to the unilateral and at times imperialistic foreign policies of the Bush administration.[12] We therefore anticipate a general revitalization of the 'hegemonic governance'-interpretation with regard to the analyses of US foreign policy after 2008. Hegemony has to provide at least some façade and at most some form of genuine governance to the world to be sustainable in the middle (or longer) run.

Hegemony understood as the exercise of leadership met by some basic consensus of the led and hegemonic governance as the world policy of a hegemonic state thus can be conceptualized with some plausibility as also resting on media strategies. Rather well documented in the domestic context, the assertion of hegemony by a class of actors through influencing mass media discourses can be conceptualized on an abstract level as follows: media are able to organize publics through agenda setting, framing, news selection and the dissemination of cultural aspects and values and, more generally, through their capacity to generate and circulate knowledge, opinions and orientations. It seems also fair to assume that it is necessary for hegemonic governance in international terms (political steering based upon some basic consensus towards the existing power configuration) to be constantly (re-)produced also and, above all, in the cultural/media realm. This is not least true with regard to the fact that the most stable hegemonic constellation is probably one, in which 'hegemony' as such is hardly at the focus of debates, at least not openly problematized and contested.[13] At a very general level, the relationship between successful hegemonic governance and media consists of a supportive (in its consequences rather than in its intentions) agency of media: the spread of world views or perspectives on political events, phenomena and constellations which in turn at least do not undermine the hegemon's claim to leadership as well as more general cultural and lifestyle orientations.

---

[12] Much could be said on the domestic side: While it is generally true that US elections are decided on domestic issues, even in this regard the Bush presidency was able to provide some kind of anomaly in the form of its foreign policy record spearheaded by the disaster in Iraq. Most analysts agree that this proved crucial in the 2008 elections. There is, however, a certain disagreement regarding the decisiveness of its impact on the election outcome, see Al Jazeera International 2008; National Public Radio 2007. It seems reasonable to assume that the (by then) unpopular Iraq War played a decisive role for many more voters before the housing/financial and economic crisis kicked in.

[13] Thus and hitherto, US hegemony has been most effective while being largely 'invisible,' (Robel 2001).

4. Global media dynamics and their impact on hegemonic governance

Media thus without any doubt play an important role in the context of establishing and maintaining hegemonic governance, since they are able, on an abstract level, to organize public acceptance of policies or – more generally – political constellations. With regard to US hegemony, most accounts, although admittedly rather implicitly, assume an intersection of the political hegemony and dominance of a state (the US) with the unequal distribution of media and communication resources (biased towards US-dominated enterprises). To scrutinize this assumption, as we will do in the following section, is not to imply that US hegemony and successful operations of American media enterprises exhibit no ties at all. It is rather to question the mutuality of these ties as well as the *endurance of any mutual reinforcement*. In fact, one can detect some tendencies which might weaken the global political position of the United States, despite the fact that they are rooted in the eventual 'Americanization' of global media communication.

The building bloc of any eventual globalization of media and communications throughout the last three decades has been the process of media concentration through mergers and acquisitions of media enterprises abroad. And indeed, with regard to the global media and communications sectors, one can detect sharp asymmetries and imbalances, which seem to tilt towards 'the' United States. Undeniably, US media and communications companies have been at the forefront in globalizing media in this way, rendering the loose talk on the 'Americanization' of international media seemingly relevant again (Brand 2008). From a media economy standpoint thus no one would seriously disagree that some sort of 'Americanization' of global media communication is a fact with regard to ownership and shareholder structures. 'Americanization' therefore seems to be a valid concept to describe the exceptional position of US-based enterprises in the international media and communications sector (Chalaby 2006; Compaine 2002; McChesney 2004). Five out of seven globally operating media and communications conglomerates have their headquarters in the United States: Time Warner, Disney, Viacom, NBC Universal and News Corp. If one is to rank global media outlets according to their stock capitalization, American-based internet giants Yahoo and Google enter the scene. More difficult is the inclusion of the US American film industry in an account of global media dominance, since its ownership structure is diversified and includes a host of foreign investors. What is more, it employs a rather internationally composed group of actors and directors, and there seem to be some rival outlets on the international level (think of Bolly- or Nollywood). It is thus mainly its global distribution network which makes the US film industry a class of its own among its competitors.

Consequently, truly global media – not in the sense of a media technology, but in the form of globally operating commercial media enterprises – have emerged only to underscore the 'pole position' of US- and Western-based media conglomerates in global communication. More often than not, this pole position is seen as a building bloc of global political hegemony. That is, to proponents of this view it seems fair to intuitively draw a causal connection between the ascendancy of US media and the hegemonic position of the United States within the current world system. A characteristic feature of most of these accounts is a simple conflation of the global political position of the United States and the pioneering role of American enterprises in the media and communications realm. Xia, for instance, is particularly clear in describing CNN from that perspective as 'a media agency by order of the world's only superpower' (Xia 2003). As Biltereyst has summed up the debate on the recent wave of the 'Americanization' of international media:

> At the background of this we see the persistent hegemonic position of the United States in the construction of ... a new unipolar world order – not only in terms of geopolitics, economic, diplomatic or military power, but also in terms of its leadership in cultural, media or communication domains. (Biltereyst 2003)

As we will argue next, the relationship between the global political role of the United States and the formative influence of US-based media corporations is far more complex and, at times, ambivalent. Furthermore, the assumption of a mutually stabilizing and reinforcing relationship of American global political preponderance and the strong performance of American media outlets in domestic, and especially in foreign markets, is wrong. Although forms of hegemonic governance and the leveling of 'soft power' may to some degree indeed rest upon media (and other) cultural strategies, we are able to identify trends that counter the assumption of a simple 'media-political-complex'. Two of the following three dynamics are directly related to the global preponderance of US media and communications companies; the third dynamic is detectable even within the so called 'inner circle of hegemony', i.e. the transatlantic arena. Taken together, all three dynamics rather undermine the prospects for successful hegemonic governance as defined above, or at least they are not necessarily conducive towards upholding it.

It has been argued above, US media and communications companies hold what could be called the 'pole position' within the global media markets. But how can this extraordinary position be referred back to the political preponderance of the United States? Did the United States use its leverage to enact policies which helped business interests? For sure. Does the private media sector, in the reverse case, bolster American political primacy in world politics? Not necessarily so, especially with regard to the very workings of US-based media and communications enterprises in foreign markets.

As for the first aspect of an alleged 'media-political complex': It seems plausible to assume that US business interests have benefited from policies pursued by various American governments. Liberalization and deregulation in the domestic US American media and communications context since the 1980s – already starting with rather liberalized structures given specific American traditions – might have formed the base for global expansion strategies in this context (McChesney 2004). One can certainly push the argument further than McChesney does in simply stating that consequently the US model of media has been exported across the planet through the workings of the US government (McChesney 2004, 7). The twin argument presented here is that US administrations have either taken a very permissive and pro-liberalization/deregulation stance in bi-, pluri- and multilateral negotiations regarding questions of global media governance or exhibited a fairly clear position in so called 'global media debates' (Siochrú 2004; Siochrú et al. 2002; Zhao 2004); namely, that they regard(ed) the private sector and business actors as the legitimate class of actors in media matters. This mixture of active pursuit of liberalization of the media sectors in other regions of the world and a permissive stance with regard to deregulation combined with the safeguarding of intellectual property rights – the standard package of liberalization through international organizations – can be explained by massive lobbying efforts of US-based transnational media companies (Siochrú 2004; Siochrú et al. 2002; Zhao 2004; Freedman 2005; Wunsch-Vincent 2003).

Not to be separated from these considerations is the specific and at times vociferously articulated standpoint of the United States within the global media debates of the last three decades, namely the debate on a New World Information and Communication Order (NWICO) in the 1970s and the discussions around the World Summit on the Information Society (WSIS) 2003-2005. To sum up this position, the United States, especially the administrations involved in both debates have repeatedly and staunchly rejected the idea that global imbalances in the media and communications sector should be tackled through new domestic regulations or redistributional mechanisms to be enacted via multilateral institutions. This confirms the assessment that various US administrations have supported private-sector friendly policies as well as blocked countermeasures or policies that might have inhibited the business interests of American firms in the international realm of media and communication. American media enterprises have clearly benefited from this, but what about the reverse assumption? Indeed – from a political science standpoint – it might all boil down to the question: What to make of the largely unchecked "pole position of specific, often US ... corporations in the global cultural economy" (Bitereyst 2003, 57) and the international news business? This pole position is, as has been shown, undoubtedly also the result of official American policies and attempts on behalf of various US governments to open-up media and communications markets abroad. But it does not necessarily translate into full-scale support of US hegemony through the activities of US media enterprises.

This is most obvious with regard to various regionalization strategies of globally operating media enterprises employed by the so-called global players: by US-based media conglomerates. These companies generally strive for orienting their products towards regional and local tastes and habits for the sake of gaining market shares vis-à-vis their competitors. It is our contention that a combination of localization strategies and adaptation towards regionally specific laws, however, may exhibit interesting political implications, not least because it contradicts to some degree the globalization-as-Americanization assumption. In other words, where US-dominated global media and communications enterprises mainly cater to local tastes and agree to specific rules and laws for the sake of making profit, their actions may not be backing official US policies; to the contrary, their actions may as well have some negative feedback effects with regard to the global political role of the United States. In what follows we will try to elucidate this assumption with regard to an outstanding case: the operations of News Corp., especially in China, while the so-called Google-/Yahoo-Affair[14] could also stand as an example for the mechanism described.

Rupert Murdoch's News Corp. is certainly the 'usual suspect' if political implications of media concentration are discussed. Politically conservative, close to the Republican Party in the domestic US American context, Murdoch undoubtedly represents a class of entrepreneurs with a 'political agenda'. Although it is debatable whether this agenda resembles a 'populist conservatism', certainly most of News Corp.'s news outlets have openly advanced a broadly conservative agenda, at least in the domestic American market (Kirkland 2007). It is thus not hard to demonstrate that the news of the Fox News channel which belongs to News Corp. takes a rather unambiguous ideological stance in the domestic setting. A representative study of media coverage in the run-up to the Iraq War in 2003 thus explained: "The extent of American's misperceptions vary significantly depending on their source of news. Those who receive most of their news from Fox News are more likely than the average to have misperceptions" (PIPA/KN Poll 2003). People who got most of their information through Fox News were far more convinced than others that, for instance, there had been close ties between Al Qaeda and Saddam Hussein, that there had been a huge stockpile of WMD in Iraq before the invasion of US-led troops and that public opinion around the world was in favor of a military invasion in Iraq in Spring 2003. In that sense, Fox News operated in line with the ideological position of

---

[14] This refers to the open compliance of both companies in establishing censorship and surveillance infrastructure on behalf of the Chinese government. This in turn may cater to the interests of the Chinese Communist party and their grip on power while largely contradicting the interests of the United States in containing a potential hegemonic rival as well as in supporting domestic change within China.

its owner and helped to gain support for the (domestically not uncontroversial) strategy of the Bush administration.

The main question for our purposes, however, is: What does this tell us about *transnational activities*[15] of News Corp.? Thussu assumes in his study which explicitly targets the activities of News Corp. in foreign, especially Asian markets,[16] that it also exhibits certain political biases there (Thussu 2004). Interestingly, he *does not demonstrate* that the media products offered through Murdoch's outlets in foreign markets are as partisan as could be concluded from the products (especially news) in the US context. To the contrary, Thussu himself gives a hint that New Corp.'s activities abroad are to some degree far more 'localized' (Thussu 2004, 94). This confirms the general assessment that the success of foreign businesses in domestic media markets is increasingly dependent upon localization strategies (Banerjee 2002, 533), i.e. to employ local personal, to report on local topics, to report from a 'local perspective', in sum: to cater to local tastes. In a similar vein, Curtin in his analysis of Murdoch's international activities has asked: "To what extent can Murdoch impose uniform cultural standards on global audiences?" (Curtin 2005, 155) He makes clear that instead of using the pan-Asian satellite service STAR TV for beaming Western programming in from the outside, Murdoch was forced to localize its contents and to cater to local demands (Curtin 2005, 162). There are other indicators that seem to contradict the simple conclusion that News Corp. acts as an ideological weapon in foreign markets. First, a key feature of most joint venture arrangements in Asian markets, especially in China, is that the Murdoch part of the business mostly offers entertainment and sports (Atkins 2003; Curtin 2005, 164). That is, domestic and international political news is not the main part of News Corp.'s activities in Asian markets. On the other hand, its programming is not free of politics, but interestingly, some key decisions and positions taken by Murdoch show over time an increasing orientation towards local rules and laws and in the case of China, towards the positions of the Chinese Communist Party. That may be a reminder as to what drives US-based global media in foreign markets: unsurprisingly, its profits and the need to eventually compromise other intentions.[17]

---

[15] As Kirkland (2007) points out, News Corp. is truly internationally oriented, not least according to its revenue scheme.

[16] STAR (Satellite Television Asian Region) as part of the Murdoch media enterprise reaches an estimated 300 million people (Thussu 2004). It has about 100 million viewers, mostly in India, each day (Kirkland 2007).

[17] After all, Murdoch is frequently quoted as having spoken of Star TV as an unambiguous threat to totalitarian regimes in 1993 (Barraclough 2000, 264), a remark that did not amuse Chinese officials. For various instances of Murdoch's abiding by the rules set forth by the Chinese Communist Party, see Kahn 2007.

By now, the dropping of BBC World News from Star TV's north Asian platforms following expressions of dissatisfaction by the Chinese government as well as the concurrence – shortly after News Corp. was allowed to enter a joint venture with Phoenix TV in China – of Rupert Murdoch's son James with the official Chinese opinion that Falun Gong was indeed a dangerous cult, are almost icons of Murdoch's specific 'localization strategy' (Flew and McElhinney 2006, 292). It has become rather obvious that News Corp. is thus very much open to political pressure and influence on behalf of Chinese officials. Thus, one can clearly detect a potential de-coupling of the interests of US governments and US-dominated media. A rather neglected, but for our purposes very instructive episode in this context is told by Curtin with regard to News Corp.'s activities in the context of the Phoenix TV joint venture (Curtin 2005, 164). Phoenix TV can be said to rely on a specific version of 'Chineseness' in its news as well as entertainment programming. This very embraces the conservative cultural and political philosophies preferred by the Party leadership. On the other hand, this does not mean that the various programs cannot tackle hot topics, such as political events, elections etc. But in any case, Phoenix has to orient its reporting not only towards audience sympathies, but also to government favor. As Curtin shows, it employed a specific mixture of popular outrage and fervent nationalism in news reporting (thus testing the boundaries of what was acceptable in China itself) when the embassy of the PRC in Belgrade was destroyed by NATO. In this instance, it certainly did not – via any eventual influence of News Corp. – serve as an outpost for US public diplomacy. The whole business of the various Murdoch enterprises in kowtowing to Chinese leaders and pandering to nationalist sentiments in China may point to the fissures and cracks between the often assumed overlap of interests between US politics and US-dominated media. Obviously, ownership structures and behavior in the US domestic market do not determine the behavior of media outlets around the globe. Political biases in the United States and self-censorship as well as different biases abroad may seem contradictory at first glance, but find their explanation in the primarily economic, not political orientation of media enterprises.

A recent study on the eventual 'Murdochization' of news in India (Thussu 2007) again pointed towards the ambivalence in the reading of the political consequences of US media giants' actions abroad.[18] Thus, unlike in other countries

---

[18] This idea must be seen in the context of a burgeoning literature on the spread of a 'global corporate hegemony' through US media, i.e. the neoliberal restructuring of international media which then in turn allegedly leads to the spread of certain values like consumerism (Artz 2003; McChesney 2004; Murphy 2003). It is, however, highly questionable, whether such a dynamic would necessarily bolster US *political* dominance on a global scale. In other words, we claim that specific forms of cultural and media production, as well as specific values, might indeed have been spread by the operations of US media enterprises abroad, leading to a partial convergence around American forms of media organization and pro-

with commercially lucrative and huge markets, India does allow for foreign ownership of news channels; in this regard, Murdoch could be an actor in the politically sensitive branch of news reporting in this foreign market, and indeed has a stake in the Indian news market. What Thussu found in his analysis of the news programming which belongs to the Murdoch-owned company, was therefore a considerable degree of popularization and 'politainment' (as discussed in political programming in the US throughout recent times as well). Far more reserved is his assessment of the political implications of these forms of programming with regard to the evaluation of US policies or the world political role of the United States for that matter. Although he states that the Murdoch-owned news programs largely spread the Pentagon line on the Iraq War (Thussu 2007, 605), it seems overblown to generally accept Murdoch's activities in foreign markets as being similar in tone and effect to the US domestic market. A meaningful degree of differentiation can be introduced via the idea that there are country-specific acceptance frames which determine what can be said (or should be adapted to local/regional tastes and fitted into a regulatory framework). In economic terms, these acceptance frames effectively work as confines for the profitability (in most cases, even the very operability) of media outlets in foreign markets. More focused empirical studies (with a comparative design) might help elucidate this relationship; for the case of India, it seems safe to assume that a more overtly 'official US' storyline with regard to the Iraq War (and the fight against Islamist terrorism in general) has been acceptable and discursively accessible for political elites as well as large segments of the society.

Somewhat paradoxically, given the obviously varying strategies of US-dominated media in international settings, there has been a detectable and growing sentiment around the world which we would describe as a 'perceived Americanization'. For all its problems, the notion of 'Americanization' as dominance of US enterprises in the media realm (which does not easily translate into the spreading of only American perspectives, as has been shown) thus has some validity with regard to the *perceptions* of public opinion and governments across the world. Epitomized in a specific use of the term 'CNN-effect'[19] as the idea that CNN is a global news medium and resembles the informational dominance of the US (El-Din Aysha 2005, 196), the preponderance of American media in the global realm has become sort of an unquestioned 'fact'. As such, it has in-

---

gramming etc. This, however, need not necessarily translate into unilinear support for US preponderance, let alone hegemony as defined at the beginning. Neoliberalism might also, on the one hand, empower other actors, or, by creating societal fissures and political unrest, also have a destabilizing effect on political relationships of all sorts.

[19] This notion is to be distinguished from the usual meaning of the term in the field of *Media Studies* as the ability of media in general to exert political pressure in situations of crises and policy vacuum (Robinson 2002).

creasingly triggered counter reactions in recent years, i.e. attempts at establishing *non*-American media and, above all, sources of information around the globe. This creates a distinguishable mode of localization/regionalization, since it is pushed by the (perceptions and actions) of a different class of actors – not US media enterprises, but political as well as media elites throughout the world. As far as US hegemonic governance is concerned, this is both an indicator of a growing sentiment of, put mildly, skepticism towards US world policy as well as a destabilizing factor for further attempts at 'renewing' US hegemony, since the pluralization of media outlets, news programs and sources – most of them directly targeted at countering prevailing US perspectives! – at least potentially undermines any effort to de-problematize US preponderance (whatever form it may take politically).

These counter tendencies towards a perceived informational dominance[20] may have a profound and lasting impact on US hegemony, since their more or less explicit goal is to offer alternative world views. This is obvious with regard to the emergence of the (largely private) Arab news network Al Jazeera, the state-sponsored French international news channel France 24 (these days part of FranceMonde) as well as the Latin American network TeleSUR which is based on cooperative agreements of several Latin American governments such as Venezuela, Argentine, Cuba, Brazil among others. These developments roughly confirm the assumption that in the global media realm a 'Clash of World Views' might have begun (Meckel 2006). There is a host of most explicit references to a vaguely defined need of counterbalancing American information dominance that can be found while researching the founding of France 24, or TeleSUR for that matter. France 24's aim is to offer a decidedly *French* perspective on world politics (France 24 2007), a project developed during the transatlantic rift regarding the Iraq War; as such, it had become one of then-president Chirac's most fervently pushed political projects and finally went on air in 2006. At first glance the programmatic statement of TeleSUR's Uruguayan general director Aram Aharonian allows for a more general reading; Aharonian is quoted with the statement that the goal of the multi-state public-service television channel was to develop a tool in the battle of ideas against the hegemonic project of globalization (Burch 2007). Given the fact that the wide-spread Latin American anti-globalization sentiment can be interpreted as an extension of the (increasingly even elite-based) rejection of the projection of US power in the Western hemisphere, it is not difficult to decipher the message.

In some ways, France 24 and TeleSUR resemble a rather old-fashioned public diplomacy reaction on behalf of a government or various governments in concert. Another counter project, established through private actors with some

---

[20] For a discussion of this alleged contra-flow, as predominantly a geographical shift of production sites and capacities or rather an increase in contra-flow content, see Wessler and Adolphsen 2008.

initial government funding, which has undoubtedly evolved into a role model given its success in establishing an alternative to American news reporting, is Al Jazeera. While the Arab network itself and the interpretation of its political implications for the openness of Arab societies have already drawn a lot of attention (El-Nawawy and Iskandar 2003; Pintak and Ginges 2008; Tatham 2006), it is necessary to point out that Al Jazeera always had another 'intention' or 'effect,' namely to "break the news monopoly of the Western media" (Armbrust, no date) by establishing an *Arab* perspective. Recent developments such as the expansion of Al Jazeera Arabic to Al Jazeera International, to go global in other words, only confirm such intentions. In a very restrained manner, the network itself posts on its website that they aim at "balancing the current typical information flow by reporting from the developing world *back to the West* and from the southern to the northern hemisphere. The channel gives voice to *untold stories*, promotes debate, and *challenges established perceptions*" (Al Jazeera 2007; emphases added). That challenging 'Western perspectives' above all means challenging American perspectives has been made clear by the cooperation agreement of Al Jazeera and TeleSUR, the Latin American news network with heavy leanings towards the Venezuelan government, which was signed in 2006. This cooperation did not go unnoticed and achieved one of its purported symbolic objectives when US Representative Connie Mack declared it an arising global TV station for terrorists. As Wessler and Adolphsen make clear, however, with regard to the very (measurable) effects of establishing such an alternative perspective through Al Jazeera: "the impact of Arab news channels on the Iraq War coverage by Western channels mainly lies in showing that a different (Arab) perspective *exists – rather than in actually infusing* Western coverage with this different perspective" (Wessler and Adolphsen 2008, 458; emphasis added). From our point of view, this can be regarded a subtler form of contestation, nevertheless a challenge towards any attempted monopolization of reporting.

Although this specific form of regionalization is to be distinguished from the activities of US-dominated media, both developments occur in the same global media and political environment. Claims of American informational dominance justify the establishment of 'alternative' (not grassroots- or independent-, but non-American) international media, while the dominance of American media and communications enterprises might not fully translate into informational and/or cultural dominance of the United States. It is this peculiar relationship which forms the core of our argument about the potential for a further weakening of US hegemony not only despite the pole position of US-led media enterprises, but in a subtle way tied to it. Of course, the timing of the onset of this 'Clash of World Views', precisely in the form of resistance towards US (information) dominance, can be explained at least partially with reference to the confrontational policies of the Bush administration. However, it remains to be seen, to what degree an 'Obama effect' might weaken the resistance embodied in the media projects cited. It is our contention that since a competing media infrastructure has been established US hegemony will be constantly (at least implicitly) scrutinized. In this regard, growing criticism of the United States in publics around the world is not just, or perhaps not primarily, a 'communication problem' or the result of a failed public diplomacy strategy, but fundamentally rooted in the development of an infrastructure to articulate such sentiments.

There is, in addition to the two dynamics described, a third phenomenon which captured our attention. Here, the strength of US-dominated global media rather forms the context, while the discernable patterns of media behavior – the so called 'transatlantic media divide' – is confined to the inner circle of US hegemony, i.e. the complex pattern of relationships between political elites and societies of the United States and Western Europe. From our perspective of hegemony, this resembles the political space, in which the preponderance of the United States in world political terms is at least tacitly welcomed, at least and usually not openly contested.[21] Media in this regard, might play a crucial role either in actively fostering this consensus or rather indirectly contributing to the acceptance of US hegemony through the spread of common values and America-friendly frames. They may also be important in *not* problematizing US hegemony as such or simply not paying too much attention to questions of political asymmetries on a global scale. The case of a 'media divide' (i.e., with regard to the dynamics of the past eight years, where largely diverging patterns of reporting and commentary on US foreign and world policies have developed) then creates a problem for the upholding of hegemonic governance. Of course, one has to bear in mind that the specific policies of the Bush administrations in the aftermath of 9/11, the contours of the War on Terrorism as well as the Iraq War, may constitute a singular, special case. It is, however, our contention that the transatlantic media divide has to some degree only hinted at and amplified already existing and increasingly diverging patterns of values within the transatlantic arena.

The term 'transatlantic media divide' was coined by Paul Krugman referring to the discernable cracks in understanding, empathy and acceptance across the Atlantic, which could be felt at least since mid-2002. As Krugman wrote:

> There has been much speculation about why Europe and the United States are suddenly at such odds. … I haven't seen much discussion of an obvious point: We have different views partly because we see different news. (Krugman 2003).

---

[21] Again, the George W. Bush-episode has been identified as the exception to the rule quite early (Medick-Krakau et al. 2004). A German chancellor who wins a domestic election by explicitly distancing himself from the foreign policy direction of an American president has been a novelty in German politics since World War II.

In a similar vein, albeit with a markedly different emphasis, Richard Lambert remarked a few weeks later: "Anti-Americanism has been a feature of the European news media for years ... The past couple of years have seen a marked change of tone in the reporting and commentary on Western Europe in the US print media" (Lambert 2003). Building on these remarks, we thus define the 'transatlantic media divide' as the drifting apart in the reporting of US and Western European media on issues concerning 'the other' (side of the Atlantic), especially the respective foreign and world policies pursued, their normative evaluation and the assessment of their effectiveness. The focal point in this has been, quite understandably, the US foreign policy of the two Bush administrations, while at least tacitly, the central role of the United States in world political terms (i.e. US hegemony) has been under scrutiny as well.

The central issues in the respective reporting have been on both sides: the open unilateralism, especially of the first Bush administration (Kyoto protocol, ICC, its mostly adversarial approach to the United Nations; with a short break on behalf of European media taking the shape of '*Nous sommes tous Américains!*'-sympathy in the immediate aftermath of 9/11); the personality and character traits of exposed political actors on both sides (George W. Bush and his lack of knowledge on certain issues as well as the mocking of Chirac and Schroeder in US media); certain features of 'Bush politics' (on the European side, especially the reporting of the influence of neoconservatives); the Iraq War, its necessity as well as legitimacy questions (especially divergent assessments of military solutions on both sides), epitomized by the largely different perspectives on the efficiency of weapons inspections and the persuasiveness of Powell's speech at the United Nations; the general legitimacy of (military) power politics, with the increasingly felt (and uttered) European sentiment of a need for the EU to countercheck the United States; and the assessment of the Israeli-Palestinian conflict (where charges of anti-Semitism and willful ignorance of Israel's wrongdoings have been unevenly distributed across the Atlantic). To some degree, differences in reporting as well as especially European reservations with regard to the strong performance of US media in international markets are hardly a new phenomenon (the French demand for quotas concerning US, or generally foreign, music and films as well as a more general fear of 'Americanization' date back to the early days of the twentieth century transatlantic bargain). And, of course, there have also been and continue to be different ways of covering events within the respective political systems; in this regard, the *Wall Street Journal* is not the *New York Times*, *Fox News* is hardly the same as *CNN*, and the *Guardian* does not very much resemble *The Times*, while *Die Welt* almost certainly regards the *Süddeutsche Zeitung* as reporting from a decidedly different political angle. Thus, the contention of a 'transatlantic media divide' in no way implies a flattening of differences or heterogeneity within the respective strands of media. Empirical studies, however, have shown, that there are interesting differences between both bodies of reporting, which on the one hand, can be referred back to journalistic decisions – European and German television, for instance, based its coverage on a far broader set of sources, thus evoking a more balanced account (Lehmann 2005a, b) – or more general political-economic dynamics within the media sector: from a certain point onwards, it proved quite profitable for some media outlets to cater to the prejudices of at least some parts of the respective audiences (Lehmann 2005a, 85). Thus, in some audiences, (tacit) anti-Americanism sold, in some parts of the public, the re-naming of French fries got a favorable treatment, thus catering to anti-French attitudes almost became a pop-cultural event.

What seems to be a rather new development – and guides our understanding of the 'transatlantic media divide' precisely as both indicative of as well as amplifying fissures in the transatlantic context – then is that the differences *between* US and (Western) European coverage are markedly bigger than the degree of difference *within* both bodies of reporting. A study of the Greek coverage of the US reactions towards the terrorist attacks of 9/11 (Kaitatzi-Whitlock and Kehagia 2004) nicely illustrates this point. While the Communist newspapers in Greece largely accused the US administration of using 9/11 to create an atmosphere of war all over the world, their conservative counterparts articulated hope that the Americans would become more sensitive to the suffering of other people. Albeit focused on different aspects, both perspectives imply a profound criticism of an alleged ignorance of US policies, which hardly resembled the mainstream in US media at the end of 2001. By way of such anecdotic evidence (for lack of detailed comparative empirical studies, especially transcending the 2001-2003 years), it seems plausible to identify diverging patterns of coverage and reporting on each other on both sides of the Atlantic. Unquestionably, this tendency has to do with the policy style as well as the policy substance of US foreign policy of the Bush administrations. But there are also indicators which hint at a lasting quality of this media divide. Jaeger and Viehrig have shown that, given the obvious nationally bounded quality of worlds of perceptions, it is only to a lesser extent the diverging patterns of coverage and perspectives taken among European countries and their presses which captures the attention; far more striking is the difference between US and European reporting, respectively (Jaeger and Viehrig 2005). With regard to the Darfur crisis, European news outlets tend to focus on the roots of the conflict, while US counterparts cover its consequences; while the European media tend to address the United Nations on Darfur, the UN does not even regularly show up in US coverage. It is, thus, such subtle differences in attention and focus which may in turn be grounded in stable and diverging normative orientations and values within the respective societies (Lehmann 2005c; Medick-Krakau 2007) that are indicative of a lasting media divide despite any eventually changing style and policy substance of successive US administrations.

5. Conclusion

We conclude that the relationship between hegemonic governance and media/communication (and by that we mean cultural) issues is far more complex and, at times, ambivalent than often assumed. There is, on the one hand, no automatism concerning US hegemony in world political terms and the pole position of US-based global media. That is, although American enterprises are undeniably in the pole position vis-à-vis their competitors – US hegemony is far from being unquestioned, even within countries where US media and communications companies already have a strong position. This position has been brought about at least partially by the policies of successive US governments, but the behavior of US media in foreign markets does not necessarily bolster US hegemonic policies. If proven profitable, or the only way to have stakes in certain lucrative markets, US media employ a host of localization strategies, which might in turn even undermine US political hegemony. There seemingly is a profound ambiguity if not a paradox inherent in contemporary US hegemony with regard to the globalization of the media sector: through fostering the neoliberal restructuring of foreign and global media markets it might have helped US-based media and, at the same time, weakened a necessary precondition for its own existence, i.e. to sustain a sufficient level of support and acceptance among the subjects of hegemonic governance. This seems to be especially true with regard to the operations of media in world regions, where US hegemony does not go uncontested (think of the various China examples). The behavior of globalized US media is primary economically and profit-driven, which may well contradict political interests of the United States. We subsume this relationship under the metaphor of 'asymmetrical allegiances'.

On the other hand, American preponderance in the global media realm paralleled by US political hegemony has also provoked growing discontent and has thus arguably unleashed counter tendencies in different regions of the world, i.e. it has led to a growing diversification of media outlets around the world. The perception of an undue 'Americanization' of international media or US communications dominance has triggered what could be termed a 'Clash of World Views', increasingly weakening US attempts at discursive supremacy and, consequently, bearing the potential for challenging US hegemony. Expanding the argument to a slightly different dynamic within international media contexts, we were also able to detect a bundle of tendencies that threaten to undermine the opportunities for US leadership even in the inner circle of hegemony. The so called 'transatlantic media divide', as a divide that is indicative of as well as amplifying the drifting apart of the United States and Western Europe, bears witness to this. Thus, hegemonic governance is far more precarious even within the inner circle of US hegemony; and media in fact do play a crucial role in undermining the acceptance of US political leadership, despite the patterns of the dominance of US-based companies, enterprises and media outlets within the global media and communications sector. Consequently, it is plainly wrong to assert an automatism of hegemony/consensus through the ascendancy of communication means.

References

Al Jazeera. 2007. Corporate Profile, http://english.aljazeera.net/NR/exeres/DE 03467F-C15A-4FF9-BAB0-1B0E6B59EC8F.htm (accessed April 1, 2007).

Al Jazeera International. 2008. Can Iraq Impact on the U.S. Election? (November 19), english.aljazeera.net/programmes/insideiraq/2008/10/2008103064 711991366.html (accessed February 8, 2009).

Armbrust, Walter. n.d. Al Jazeera is not a Medium!, www.tbsjournal.com/LetterPF.html (accessed March 07, 2006).

Artz, Lee. 2003. Globalization, Media Hegemony and Social Class. In *The Globalization of Corporate Media Hegemony*, ed. Lee Artz and Yahya Kamalipour, 3-31. Albany: SUNY Press.

Atkins, William. 2003. Brand Power and State Power: The Rise of New Media Networks in East Asia. *Pacific Review* 16: 465-487.

Bacevich, Andrew J. 2002. *American Empire – The Realities and Consequences of U.S. Diplomacy*. Cambridge: Harvard University Press.

Banerjee, Indrajit. 2002. The Locals Strike Back? Media Globalization and Localization in the New Asian Television Landscape. *Gazette* 64: 517-535.

Barraclough, Steven. 2000. Satellite Television in Asia: Winners and Losers. *Asian Affairs* 31: 263-272.

Beyer, Cornelia. 2008. *Violent Globalisms. Conflict in Response to Empire*. Aldershot: Ashgate.

Biltereyst, Daniel. 2003. Globalisation, Americanisation and Politicisation of Media Research. In *Media in a Globalized Society*, ed. Stig Hjarvard, 55-89. Copenhagen: Museum Tusculanum Press.

Boot, Max. 2003. American Imperialism?, No Need to Run Away from Label, http://www.cfr.org/publication.html?id=5934 (accessed March 20, 2009).

Brand, Alexander. 2008. Amerikanisierung der internationalen Kommunikation? Implikationen für den Diskurs und die Deutungsmacht globaler Politik. In *Mediendemokratie in den USA*, ed. Matthias Fifka and Daniel Gossel, 157-180. Trier: WVT.

Brzeziński, Zbigniew. 2004. *The Choice – Global Domination or Global Leadership?* New York: Basic Books.

Burch, Sally. 2007. Telesur and the New Agenda for Latin American Integration. *Global Media and Communication* 3: 227-232.

Chalaby, Jean K. 2006. American Cultural Primacy in a New Media Order. A European Perspective. *Gazette* 68: 33-51.

Compaine, Benjamin. 2002. Global Media. *Foreign Policy*, 133, 20-28.

Cox, Michael. 2003. The Empire's Back in Town: Or America's Imperial Temptation – Again. *Millennium* 23: 1-27.

Cox, Robert W. 1993. Gramsci, Hegemony, and International Relations. In *Gramsci, Historical Materialism and International Relations*, ed. Stephen Gill, 49-66. Cambridge, New York: Cambridge University Press.

Curtin, Michael. 2005. Murdoch's Dilemma, Or: 'What's the Price of TV in China?' *Media, Culture & Society* 27: 155-175.

Czempiel, Ernst-Otto. 1993. *Weltpolitik im Umbruch. Das internationale System nach dem Ende des Ost-West-Konflikts*. München: C.H.Beck.

------. 2002. *Weltpolitik im Umbruch – Die Pax Americana, der Terrorismus und die Zukunft der internationalen Beziehungen*. München: C.H.Beck.

El-Din Aysha, Emad. 2005. September 11 and the Middle East Failure of US Soft Power: Globalisation Contra Americanisation in the New US Century. *International Relations* 19: 193-210.

El Nawawy, Mohammed, and Adel Iskandar. 2003. *Al-Jazeera*. Boulder: Lynne Rienner.

Ferguson, Niall. 2004. *Colossus. The Price of America's Empire*. New York: Penguin Press.

Ferguson, Yale H. 2008. Approaches to Defining 'Empire' and Characterizing United States Influence in the Contemporary World. *International Studies Perspectives* 9: 272-280.

Flew, Terry, and Stephen McElhinney. 2006. Globalization and the Structure of New Media Industries. In *Handbook of New Media*, ed. Leah A. Lievrouw and Sonia Livingstone, 287-306. London etc.: Sage.

France 24. 2007. About France 24, http://www.france24.com/france24Public/en/page-footer/about-france-24.html (accessed March 10, 2007).

Freedman, Des. 2005. GATS and the Audiovisual Sector. *Global Media and Communication* 1: 124-128.

Gill, Stephen, ed. 1993. *Gramsci, Historical Materialism and International Relations*. Cambridge, New York: Cambridge University Press.

Ikenberry, John. 2004a. Liberalism and Empire. *Review of International Studies* 30: 609-630.

------. 2004b. Illusions of Empire: Defining the New American Order, http://www.foreignaffairs.org/20040301fareviewessay83212a/g-john-ikenberry/illusions-of-empire-defining-the-new-american-order.html (accessed March 10, 2007).

Isernia, Pierangelo. 2006. Anti-Americanism and European Public Opinion During the Iraq War. In *The United States Contested. American Unilateralism and European Discontent*, ed. Sergio Fabbrini, 130-158. New York: Routledge.

Jaeger, Thomas, and Henrike Viehrig. 2005. Internationale Ordnung und transatlantische Wahrnehmungen: Die medial vermittelte Interpretation der Darfur-Krise in den USA, Deutschland, Frankreich und Großbritannien. Kölner Arbeitspapiere zur Internationalen Politik und Außenpolitik, AIPA 3.

Johnson, Chalmers. 2004. *The Sorrows of Empire – Militarism, Secrecy, and the End of the Republic*. New York: Henry Holt.

Kahn, Joseph. 2007. Murdoch's Dealings in China: It's Business and it's Personal. *New York Times*, June 26.

Kaitatzi-Whitlock, Sophia, and Dimitra Kehagia. 2004. "All that is Solid Melts into Air". How the September 11 Tragedy Was Presented in the Greek Press. In *U.S. and the Others. Global Media Images on "The War on Terror"*, ed. Stig A. Nohrstedt and Rune Ottosen, 131-154. Goteborg: NORDICOM.

Kirkland, Rik. 2007. Think Again: Rupert Murdoch, www.foreignpolicy.com/story/cms.php?story_id=3655 (accessed January 9, 2007).

Krugman, Paul. 2003. The Great Trans-Atlantic Media Divide. *The International Herald Tribune*, February 19.

Lake, David A. 2008. The New American Empire? *International Studies Perspectives* 9: 281-289.

Lambert, Richard. 2003. Misunderstanding Each Other. *Foreign Affairs* 82: 62-74.

Lehmann, Ingrid A. 2005a. Exploring the Transatlantic Media Divide over Iraq. *The Harvard International Journal of Press/Politics* 10: 63-89.

------. 2005b. The Transatlantic Media and Opinion Divide Over Iraq. *Peace Review: A Journal of Social Justice* 17: 357-363.

------. 2005c. Taking the Bull by the Horns (Interview), www2.diasonline.org/interview/lehmann (accessed July 2, 2007).

Lempp, Jakob, and Stefan Robel. 2006. A Tale of Two Worlds? U.S. Hegemony and Regional Development: The Case of Latin America. Dresdner Arbeitspapiere Internationale Beziehungen, DAP-15.

Lieber, Robert J. 2008. Falling Upwards. Declinists: The Box Set. *World Affairs* 171: 48-56.

Lipschutz, Ronnie D. 2009. *The Constitution of Imperium*. Boulder: Paradigm.

Loveman, Brian, ed. 2004. *Strategy for Empire – U.S. Regional Security Policy in the Post-Cold War Era*. Lanham: SR Books.

Mann, Michael. 2004. Failed Empire. *Review of International Studies* 30: 631-653.

McChesney, Robert. 2004. The Political Economy of International Communications. In *Who Owns the Media? Global Trends and Local Resistances*, ed. Pradip N. Thomas and Zaharom Naim, 3-22. London: Zed Books.

Meckel, Miriam. 2006. Kampf ums Weltbild. *Neue Zürcher Zeitung*, November 17.

Medick-Krakau, Monika. 2007. Bröckeln die Fundamente? Deutsch-amerikanische Beziehungen, öffentliche Meinung und gesellschaftliche Identitäten. In *Res publica semper reformanda: Wissenschaft und politische Bildung im Dienste des Gemeinwohls*, ed. Werner J. Patzelt, Martin Sebaldt and Uwe Kranenpohl, 539-550, Wiesbaden: VS-Verlag.

Medick-Krakau, Monika, Stefan Robel and Alexander Brand, 2004: Die Außen- und Weltpolitik der USA. In *Einführung in die Internationale Politik*, ed. Manfred Knapp and Gert Krell, 92-134. München: Oldenbourg.

Mittelman, James. 2005. *Whither Globalization? The Vortex of Knowledge and Ideology*. London: Routledge.

Müller, Harald. 2003. Supermacht in der Sackgasse? *Die Weltordnung nach dem 11.September*. Bonn: BpB.

Murphy, Patrick D. 2003. Without Ideology? Rethinking Hegemony in the Age of Transnational Media. *In The Globalization of Corporate Media Hegemony*, ed. Lee Artz and Yahya Kamalipour, 55-75. Albany: SUNY Press.

Murphy, Craig N. 2004. Global *Institutions, Marginalization, and Development*. London: Routledge.

National Public Radio. 2007. Iraq War Fades as Issue in Election (December 6), www.npr.org/templates/story/story.php?storyId=16970093 (accessed February 8, 2009).

Nexon, Daniel, and Thomas Wright. 2007. What's at Stake in the American Empire Debate. *American Political Science Review* 101: 253-271.

Nye, Joseph S., Jr. 2002. *The Paradox of American Power – Why the World's Only Superpower Can't Go It Alone*. New York: Oxford University Press.

Pintak, Lawrence, and Jeremy Ginges. 2008. The Mission of Arab Journalism: Creating Change in a Time of Turmoil. *The Harvard International Journal of Press/Politics* 13: 193-227.

PIPA/KN Poll. 2003. *Misperceptions, the Media and the Iraq War*. Report, October 2.

Prys, Miriam, and Stefan Robel. forthcoming. Hegemony, Not Empire. *Journal of International Relations and Development*, Special issue on Hierarchy in International Relations.

Robel, Stefan. 1994. Die Theorie der Hegemonialen Stabilität und amerikanische Außenpolitik nach dem Ende des Ost-West-Konflikts. Unter besonderer Berücksichtigung der Neorealismus/ Neoliberalismus-Debatte. Diploma thesis, University Frankfurt/M.

------. 2001. Hegemonie in den Internationalen Beziehungen: Lehren aus dem Scheitern der „Theorie Hegemonialer Stabilität". Dresdner Arbeitspapiere Internationale Beziehungen, DAP-2.

Robel, Stefan, and Daniel Ristau. 2008. US-amerikanische Hegemonie und das „Neue Europa". Der Irak-Krieg, die transatlantischen Beziehungen und der Fall Polen. In *Internationale Beziehungen - Aktuelle Forschungsfelder, Wissensorganisation und Berufsorientierung, Festschrift für Monika Medick-Krakau*, ed. Alexander Brand and Stefan Robel, 175-211. Dresden: TUDpress.

Robinson, Piers. 2002. *The CNN Effect. The Myth of News, Foreign Policy and Intervention*. New York: Routledge.

Ruzza, Carlo, and Emanuela Bozzini. 2006. Anti-Americanism and the European Peace Movement: The Iraq War. In *The United States Contested. American Unilateralism and European Discontent*, ed. Sergio Fabbrini, 112-129. New York: Routledge.

Saull, Richard. 2008. Empire, Imperialism and Contemporary American Global Power. *International Studies Perspectives* 9: 309-318.

Siochrú, Sean. 2004. Global Institutions and the Democratization of Media. In *Who Owns the Media? Global Trends and Local Resistances*, ed. Pradip N. Thomas and Zaharom Naim, 23-42. London: Zed Books.

Siochrú, Sean, et al., eds. 2002. *Global Media Governance. A Beginner's Guide*. Lanham: Rowman & Littlefield.

Spruyt, Hendrik. 2008. "American Empire" as an Analytic Question or a Rhetorical Move? *International Studies Perspectives* 9: 290-299.

Sterling-Folker, Jennifer. 2008. The Emperor Wore Cowboy Boots. *International Studies Perspectives* 9: 319-330.

Tatham, Steve. 2006. *Losing Arab Hearts and Minds. The Coalition, Al-Jazeera and Muslim Public Opinion*. London: Hurst.

Thussu, Daya Kishan. 2004. Murdoch's War – A Transnational Perspective. In *War, Media, and Propaganda. A Global Perspective*, ed. Yahya Kamalipour and Nancy Snow, 93-105. Lanham: Rowman & Littlefield.

------. 2007. ‚Murdochization' of News? The Case of Star TV in India. *Media, Culture & Society* 29: 593-611.

Triepel, Heinrich. 1974. *Die Hegemonie – Ein Buch von führenden Staaten*. Aalen: Scientia. (Originally published in Stuttgart 1943).

Wessler, Hartmut, and Manuel Adolphsen. 2008. Contra-flow From the Arab World? How Arab Television Coverage of the 2003 Iraq War Was Used and Framed on Western International News Channels. *Media, Culture & Society* 30: 439-461.

Wunsch-Vincent, Sacha. 2003: The Digital Trade Agenda of the U.S.: Parallel Tracks of Bilateral, Regional and Multilateral Liberalization. *Aussenwirtschaft* 58: 7-46.

Xia, Guang. 2003. Globalization at Odds with Americanization. *Current Sociology* 51: 709-718.

Zhao, Yuezhi. 2004. The State, the Market, and Media Control in China. In *Who Owns the Media? Global Trends and Local Resistances*, ed. Pradip N. Thomas and Zaharom Naim, 179-212. London: Zed Books.

Subarno Chattarji
University of Delhi, India
Mass-mediated terror: some transnational media representations of the 2005 London bombings

The series of bomb blasts in London on July 7, 2005 reinforced the terrible cyclicity of acts of terrorism aimed at civilian targets. This paper focuses on selected print media analysis originating from India, Pakistan, the UK, and the US in the immediate aftermath of the attack. The London bombings lacked the spectacle that planes crashing into the twin towers had, but they marked a significant milestone in the 'war on terror' given that the terrorists were homegrown.

Most media commentators noted the care with which the Secret Organization of al-Qaeda in Europe, the organization that claimed responsibility for the attacks, chose the setting. The G-8 summit in Gleneagles formed a stunning backdrop and drove home the point, if at all it needed to be reinforced, that even the most powerful states are impotent in the face of terrorism. As Alex Standish, editor of *Jane's Intelligence Digest*, said:

> 'It is absolutely impossible to prevent a determined terrorist – particularly a suicide bomber.' Professor Michael Clarke, director of the Centre for Defence Studies at King's College London, reiterated the fact that 'the scale of the attack on Europe's premier financial centre and the venue of the 2012 Olympics was carefully calibrated. The bombs that knocked London off-balance must have had at least 24 people involved in planting them, he said. (Lall 2005, 13)

Mass transit systems being targeted at rush hour drew immediate parallels with the Madrid train bombings of March 2004. In this context the then London Mayor Ken Livingstone's comment that such attacks target the working people rather than prime ministers or presidents was very apposite. Livingstone overlooked the fact that in his city even wealthy financial advisers take the tube, but that apart he inadvertently highlighted a basic disjunction in the functioning of some democracies.

As some media analysts in the US and UK noted, there was an air of inevitability about the London bombings, not in a fatalistic sense, but in terms of the politics of Tony Blair's support for the US-led war in Iraq. It is common knowledge that Blair stood by President Bush in the face of the largest civil society protests in Britain since the Vietnam War.[1] Some of those very people who opposed Blair's policies seemed to suffer for them. This is an example of the dysfunction of democracy mentioned earlier. The irony was further strengthened by

---

[1] In a video broadcast on al-Jazeera on 4 August 2005, in the wake of the 7 July London bombings, al-Zawahiri addressed the British people: "Blair has brought you destruction to the heart of London, and he will bring more destruction, God willing" (Atwan 2006, 78).

Blair speaking about the resilience of the British people and comparing their situation to the tribulations of the Blitz. Undoubtedly London's citizens displayed stoicism and courage of a rare order, but to be commended by their leader whose policies might be perceived by the citizenry as partially responsible for their targeting could be galling. While media reports and analyses noted a cause-and-effect syndrome they did not perceive the deeper structural problems that affect modern democracies, where leaders in effect do not seem to need the consent of their people to go to war. Blair's grandstanding, of course, totally ignored this although, to be fair, Blair was not the only one of his kind. Prime Minister Berlusconi of Italy and the former Prime Minister of Spain, were just two examples of European leaders who joined the war effort despite the demonstrable reluctance of segments of their populations. The gap between the leaders and the populace and its implications for democratic functioning are analyzed by Suman Gupta:

> The view that what people express in a democracy has nothing to do with what a leader does unquestionably offends the deep sense of democracy, the minimum linguistic definition of democracy that now, ... underlines all modern conceptualizations of democracy at some level. Bush's view that 'The role of the leader is to decide policy based upon the security' makes precisely that point. It smacks precisely of the kind of totalitarianism that is often instinctively posited against the minimum understanding of democracy. (Gupta 2006, 179)

Unlike the unfortunate Aznar who faced and lost an election a couple of days after the Madrid bombings, Blair won a third term, albeit with a reduced majority. Aznar's electoral loss was seen by some media analysts as a type of collective appeasement of terrorism and failure of democracy while others argued that the Spanish election results were a sign of democratic maturity.[2]

Much of the media commentary in the immediate aftermath of July 7 revolved around the past, present, and future of al Qaeda. For instance, the *Washington Post* carried a piece which analyzed the ways in which al Qaeda's operations have altered since 9/11. The authors highlighted the fact that the classic terrorist cells are no longer the mode of organization, that al Qaeda has gained a lot of mileage and recruits from the ongoing conflict in Iraq, and that the corporate hierarchical structure originally attributed to the organization by some commentators in the immediate aftermath of 9/11 no longer holds true.

> Indeed, Zarqawi's pledge to bin Laden has offered a model of the new kind of al Qaeda outsourcing. 'From al Qaeda's point of view, it makes it look like they're in on the biggest action going right now in Iraq,' said the former US intelligence official, speaking on condition of anonymity. 'From Zarqawi's point of view, it's brand

---

[2] See Subarno Chattarji, 'What is the Spanish word for appeasement?' in Nalini Rajan, 2007, 101 -115.

recognition – you're a franchisee, whether Burger King or al Qaeda.' (Coll and Glasser 2005, A01)

The corporate lingo is indicative of a certain analytical superficiality, as if dealing death or burgers were of equal moral value. Behind the comparison, however, is the contrast between a corporate West that peddles positive life styles and products ('Our way of life' as Blair and Bush put it) and a corrupt, immoral Islamic civilization that deals in indiscriminate death. The latter is made clear a little later in the same piece.

> 'I do not really believe there is such a thing as al Qaeda, the organization; there is al Qaeda, the mindset,' said Yosri Fouda, senior investigative reporter in London for the al-Jazeera satellite television network, the only journalist known to have interviewed Sept. 11 planners Khalid Sheikh Mohammed and Ramzi Binalshibh. 'This is what I find much scarier. Your ability to predict is reduced to a minimal level.' (Coll and Glasser 2005, A01)

Fouda's authority is bolstered by his Arab/Islamic pedigree and by the fact that he interviewed 9/11 planners, but what he said is as essentialist as the comments of most non-Arab analysts. The realms of analysis on al Qaeda almost always end up in this cul-de-sac and in a crucial manner heighten the 'us-versus-them syndrome' that the terrorists wish to foster.

It did not help, of course, that sections of civil society reacted in atavistic ways and attacked either Muslims or Sikhs. One lamentable fallout of the July 7 outrage was the rupturing of tenuous community links: "Even as anguished leaders of Britain's 1.5 million strong Muslim community told TOI [*Times of India*] of the hate mails that had started to flood their websites and pour into email inboxes, the Muslim Association of Britain (MAB) significantly advised the faithful on how to avoid vigilante attacks" (Lall 2005, 12). More bizarrely Sikhs were the target of attacks, with a gurdwara in Kent being firebombed (reported in the *Sunday Times of India*, July 10, 2005). The latter was a replay of the post-9/11 scenario where ignorance and hate coalesced to create fear and loathing within a country. Britain takes justifiable pride in its multiculturalism and the fact that London is one of the most cosmopolitan cities in the world. Even so, hate mail and a firebombing could be construed as stray incidents they exposed vulnerabilities within that multicultural fabric.

One possible explanation for the disruption of carefully constructed societal bonds is the cause and effect proposition I pointed to earlier. An aspect of this argument is that Tony Blair's Britain had this attack coming as a result of his stalwart defense of US policies in Iraq. In fact Tariq Ali believes that "it did not matter whether or not London's attackers were linked to the al Qaeda. What was certain, he said, was they were a by-product of deep despair, Muslim impotence and rage at Western acts of occupation" (Lall 2005, 13). Ali's formulation moves the rage beyond Iraq to other geographies, specifically Palestine, and perhaps a wider historical anger and discomfort at the processes of modernity and their consequences as felt in the Middle East since World War II.[3] As Jason Burke writes: "For many Arabs and many Muslims across the world, I knew, the image of tanks rolling into a refugee camp in Gaza represented every humiliation ever visited on the ummah or the Arab nation or both by the West. The course of the conflict in Israel-Palestine was a powerful symbol of their own powerlessness" (Burke 2006, 105). The causal framework kicks into motion every time there is such an attack and the 'Muslim world' (as if it were a homogenous entity) is asked to respond to it. It is interesting, of course, that the responses from the 'Muslim world' are often absent or inadequate in the aftermath of atrocities such as the London bombings. Thus while citizens in Britain and elsewhere protested against the war in Iraq there were no corresponding mass protests against the Madrid or London bombings in the 'Muslim world.'

An article on MSNBC.com syndicated by the Associated Press dealt specifically with this aspect of Muslim response. Datelined Cairo the piece began with condemnation and cause: "Islamic leaders condemned the London bombings, though many on Friday insisted the United States and Britain, with their wars in Iraq and Afghanistan, are ultimately to blame for fueling militant violence. Increasing voices, however, say the Arab world has to stop adding 'but' to its denunciations of terrorism" (July 8, 2005). The fact that American and British policies and actions can have any contributory influence towards creating a sense of disaffection or hatred is considered heretical because the former act only for the good of the benighted Arab communities. The same sense of ingenuous innocence was expressed after 9/11 when President Bush, among others, mused why the US was hated and came to the conclusion that it was because of the freedoms and the way of life that the West represents. The post-9/11 debate allowed minimal space, if at all, for distinguishing between analysis and justification. This distinction is made and then blurred in the AP article:

> The chain of blasts in central London, claimed by an al-Qaeda-linked group, once again had Arabs walking a fine line: denouncing bloodshed and terrorism while trying to explain the growth of Islamic militancy.
> 'We are not trying to justify, only to analyze,' wrote Abdel-Bari Atwan, who lives in London and is editor-in-chief of the *Al-Quds Al-Arabi* newspaper. 'We or any of our family members or friends could have been among the victims in London.'

---

[3] While decrying the evils of 'modernity' al-Qaeda and their cohorts are not averse to using technologies such as the internet emerging from the apostate West. "Hamid Mir, the Pakistani journalist and bin-Laden biographer, described how he watched al-Qa'ida men fleeing US bombardments of their training camps in November 2001: 'Every second al-Qa'ida member [was] carrying a laptop computer along with his Kalashnikov,' he reported" (Atwan 2006, 117). Chapter 4 of Atwan's study of al-Qaeda, 'Cyber-Jihad', discusses in detail the interface between technology and terrorism.

'But we must emphasize that the wars being waged now against Muslims in Iraq and Afghanistan and Palestine are the best way to recruit more terrorists and to expand the circle of armed attacks in the entire world,' he said.

That stance was exactly what Khaled al-Huroub, a Palestinian writer living in Cambridge, England, said Arabs must avoid.

'It's wrong even to say this is a crime we condemn but we must understand the reasons behind it — this could be seen as a justification,' he wrote in the London-based Arab daily *Al-Hayat*.

He called for 'a clear-cut position, with no "buts," calling a crime as it deserves to be called.'

The article couldn't be more accurate when it describes the "fine line" that Arabs have to take in such a situation. Khaled al-Huroub's refutation of Atwan's argument points precisely to the cleft in which Muslims find themselves. There can be little doubt that certain policies accentuate "the circle of armed attacks in the entire world" or they serve, as King Abdullah II of Jordan pointed out in an interview with CNN International on July 9, 2005 to provide an excuse to extremist elements within the Islamic community. Whatever the case and however reprehensible, such attacks are not ahistorical actions neither are they acts of God. To say that analysis can be seen as justification and therefore it is best to avoid such analysis is to fall into a political and moral abyss. It is this kind of abyss that created the 'You're either with us or you're with the terrorists' syndrome in the aftermath of 9/11. One kind of absolutism feeds another and leads to mind numbing horrors. An obvious paradox of the G-8 summit was that it aimed to reduce African debt and to 'make poverty history', while world leaders thus far have not addressed issues of poverty, illiteracy, and dispossession in the Arab world. The latter might help to reduce the new recruits for extremism. Of course, a crime must be called a crime, but the "clear-cut position" advocated by al-Huroub may not provide solutions for either the West or the Arab world because of entangled networks of distrust, hate, fear, and prejudice. For a Palestinian writer to posit such dangerous clarity was a poignant pointer to the difficulty of expressing complex issues in a nuanced fashion in the public sphere.

Thomas L. Friedman in "If it's a Muslim problem, it needs a Muslim solution" offered a clear analysis and even a solution to the problem of Islamic terror. He began by expressing solidarity with the victims: "Thursday's bombings in central London are profoundly disturbing. In part, that is because a bombing in our mother country and closest ally, England, is almost like a bombing in our own country" (Friedman July 9, 2005). He then went on state that jihadi attacks are an assault on "open societies" which "depend on trust," and that trust is diminished by such assaults. Friedman is entirely right about the demolition of trust as was evident from the hate mail and attacks on minorities within Britain, and he articulates this without ambiguity:

When jihadist-style bombings happen in Riyadh, that is a Muslim-Muslim problem. That is a police problem for Saudi Arabia. But when al-Qaeda-like bombings come to the London Underground, that becomes a civilizational problem. Every Muslim living in a Western society suddenly becomes a suspect, becomes a potential walking bomb. When that happens, it means that the West is going to be tempted to crack down even harder on their own Muslim populations. (Friedman July 9, 2005)

Friedman gets to the nub of what Abdel-Bari Atwan calls the perpetuation of circles of suspicion, hatred, and violence. Friedman also admits that since the West has no obvious target to retaliate against it will do so in a crude and blanket manner "by simply shutting them out, denying them visas and making every Muslim in its midst guilty until proven innocent." Friedman's solution to this downward spiral in Muslim-Western relations is to advocate that Muslims do their own policing: "The greatest restraint on human behavior is what a culture and a religion deem shameful" (Friedman July 9, 2005). He gives two examples of such change: the Palestinian ceasefire with Israel and King Abdullah's conference in Amman calling on moderate Muslims to retrieve their faith from the hands of extremists. Without a doubt there are Arab societies where moderate voices have been sidelined. There is a sense, however, in which Friedman places sole responsibility on Muslim societies to reform themselves or face the wrath of an intolerant and paranoid West. The truism of cultural and religious shaming hides an essentialist bias: that Islamic culture does not deem acts of terror as shameful. One wonders if the same argument would apply to Abu Ghraib or Guantanamo Bay in terms of what the dominant culture or religion values. In conclusion Friedman avers that "The double-decker buses of London and the subways of Paris, or the markets of Riyadh, Bali and Cairo, will never be secure as long as the Muslim village and elders do not take on, delegitimize, condemn and isolate the extremists in their midst" (Friedman July 9, 2005). While I do not disagree with this argument, I am also concerned that Friedman absolves the West of any responsibility and agency in this terrible cycle of violence and counter violence. His arguments are reasonable up to a point but they seem underpinned by a white Anglo-Saxon bias, evident in the phrase "our mother country." Considering that the US is not exclusively the land of white immigrants anymore many citizens of the US would disagree with that appellation, even if they were entirely sympathetic to the victims in London.

Pakistan media anxieties

At the same time as media debates were being played out in Britain and the US in the aftermath of the London bombings, there was intense media scrutiny and anxiety in Pakistan. Pakistan was most sensitive to the reactions in the West as two of the London bombers, Shahzad Tanveer and Haseeb Hussain, had received training in Pakistan. A few examples from Pakistani media highlight not only the interconnected and global nature of terrorism but also the local and regional reverberations of such an event.

Najmuddin A. Shaikh, wrote in *The Dawn*:

> If it is established, as one fears it will be, that Shahzad Tanveer and Haseeb Hussain did attend training camps in Pakistan, then the consequences will be as grim as President Musharraf fears. It should perhaps be the catalyst which will help him convince the naysayers among his advisers and associates that the game of running with the hares and hunting with the hounds is no longer an option. (Shaikh 2005)

The Dawn editorialized on July 10, 2005:

> Pakistan has reason to be particularly on guard [against Muslim stereotyping and bashing] because of the way its territory has been used by all kinds of terrorist and militant organizations. Irrespective of what the present military-led government may say or do, we have not been able to quite shake ourselves free of our past association with the Taliban and our encouragement of militant tendencies. We may have come out of our previous state of denial, in which we refused to differentiate between sectarian parties and 'jihadi' groups, but recognition of the link between the two has not led to forceful enough action on either front. The fact that wanted persons are regularly unearthed within Pakistan shows that the country remains a beehive of terrorists. (Editorial July 10, 2005)

Shaikh and *The Dawn* editorial highlighted fundamental contradictions and connections in Pakistan domestic as well as foreign policy in that domestic compulsions – particularly the need to establish an 'Islamic' identity and credibility – led to support for the Taliban in Afghanistan and the insurgency in Indian occupied Kashmir. A subtext "of running with the hares and hunting with the hounds" was precisely the interminable struggle over Kashmir and the ways in which successive Pakistani governments had kept that conflict at the forefront to bolster its own sense of national self.

An editorial in *The Nation*, "A Common Struggle," noted certain historical connections, sometimes ignored in Western media:

> It is not without reason that Pakistan should appear in the press again and again as a source of recruits or infrastructural facilities in terror operations. It was here that the US-led West, with the help of General Zia at the helm, created the Frankenstein that stalks it now. Pakistan was used as a training ground by the CIA and European agencies for radical elements collected from all over the world, including Britain. Their role in the Afghan struggle against the USSR was glamourised by the western media. It was at this time that the seminaries in Pakistan were radicalised by one superpower to overthrow the other, making full use of what Mr. Blair now calls an 'evil ideology.' This said, what is needed now is to launch a common struggle against terrorism instead of indulging in mutual recrimination. (Editorial July 23, 2005)

While retrieving often elided histories and connections it is interesting that this editorial projected Pakistan as a site that was "used" by the West albeit "with the help of General Zia at the helm." This representation obscures the active role played by General Zia-ul-Haq in the Islamicization of Pakistan as well as the ways in which subsequent Pakistani governments and its intelligence agencies actively supported the Taliban in Afghanistan. *The Dawn* was much more forthright and accurate in characterizing Pakistan as a "beehive of terrorists." The disjunction between these media analyses is indicative of larger fissures within the Pakistani polity in their attitude toward Islam, modernity, the West, and the US. These contradictions came to the fore post-9/11 with the former ruler of Pakistan General Parvez Musharraf's decision to become a 'frontline ally' in the war on terror and side with the United States.[4] The intense media focus in the immediate aftermath of the London bombings highlighted a schism within the nation and "running with the hares and hunting with the hounds" is an accurate summation of the contraries within a complex Muslim country. The media debates were also indicative of the transnational nature of Islamic jihad and although Tanveer and Hussain were British born their training in Pakistan, indeed their parents' links to Pakistan as immigrants, were enough to arouse in the UK a broader suspicion of the enemy within. While Friedman reached out to the "mother country" in sympathetic solidarity Pakistani media were embarrassed by the atrocities propagated by their prodigal sons.

I have looked at some media analysis within the first week of the carnage in London and the brief focus is instructive in that the contours of the media debate were set within that week. Indian newspapers and television largely used syndicated material or depended on a lone correspondent. Some of them such as Chidanand Rajghatta, the US correspondent for the *Times of India*, bravely and repeatedly highlighted recent and past terror attacks in India, from the Mumbai blasts to Ayodhya. This was to indicate that India too belongs to the comity of nations blighted by terrorism. From the Indian point of view there was a certain satisfaction in seeing Pakistan being pilloried for its support of terrorism and the condemnation from the West fed into a sense of national grievance given India's experiences with terrorism, particularly in Kashmir. As in the West, Indian media too highlights acts of Islamic terrorism to the exclusion of all other kinds.[5]

---

[4] Post-9/11 fault lines in Pakistan's response to terrorism were evident in the siege of the Lal Masjid (Red Mosque) and, more recently, in the direct ways in which Pakistan was implicated in the Mumbai attacks of November 2008. See William Dalrymple, July 23, 2007, http://www.newyorker.com/reporting/2007/07/23/070723fa_fact_dalrymple. The unreliable nature of Pakistan's support in the war on terror was repeated in the US media. See, for example, Carol Grisanti, July 25, 2007, http://www.msnbc.msn.com/id/19955166

[5] For an analysis of the elisions in Indian media on terror agents see Subarno Chattarji *Tracking the Media: interpretations of mass media discourses in India and Pakistan*, 2008, Chapters 2 and 4.

The fact that the London bombings were covered in detail in the Indian subcontinent is indicative of the ways in which acts of terror impact on local and regional politics, either through some direct connection (as in Pakistan) or through competitive demonizations. The fact that Tanveer and Hussain were of Pakistani heritage and had trained in Pakistan was, from India's point of view, a reiteration of the perfidious 'other' across the border. The contours of the discussion in the West were disappointing largely because they were so tied to defending the moral and political primacy of the West, and the Indian media latched on to that strain. The Pakistani media almost universally condemned the attacks but they were more reluctant to absolve the West of all responsibility. This interface is perhaps one space where we perceive alternatives, where analysis is not seen as justification or questionable patriotism, and where the terror unleashed on London would not become another excuse for greater surveillance of domestic constituencies (the I-Card project in the UK) or racial profiling of visitors and immigrants.

References

AP. 2005. After Bombings, Arabs Debate whom to Blame: Islamic Leaders Condemn London Attack; Some Say U.S., Britain Fuel Violence. July 8, http://www.msnbc.msn.com/id/8514909/

Atwan, Abdel Bari. 2006. *The Secret History of al-Qa'ida*. London: Abacus.

Burke, Jason. 2006. *On the Road to Kandahar: Travels through Conflict in the Islamic World*. London: Penguin.

Chattarji, Subarno. 2007. What is the Spanish Word for Appeasement? In *21st Century Journalism in India*, ed. Nalini Rajan, 101-115. New Delhi, Thousand Oaks, London: Sage Publications.

------. 2008. *Tracking the Media: Interpretations of Mass Media Discourses in India and Pakistan*. New Delhi, London: Routledge.

Coll, Steve and Susan B. Glasser. 2005. Attacks Bear Earmarks of Evolving Al Qaeda. *Washington Post*, July 8, A01.

Dalrymple, William. 2007. Letter from Pakistan: Days of Rage: Challenges for the Nation's Future. *The New Yorker*, July 23, http://www.newyorker.com /reporting/2007/07/23/070723fa_fact_dalrymple

Editorial. 2005. *The Dawn*, July 10, http://www.dawn.com/2005/07/10/ed.htm

Editorial. 2005. *The Nation*, July 23, http://nation.com.pk/daily/july-2005/23/editorials1.php

Friedman, Thomas L. 2005. If it's a Muslim Problem, it Needs a Muslim Solution. *New York Times*, July 9, http://www.nytimes.com/2005/07/08/ opinion/08friedman.html

108   Subarno Chattarji

Grisanti, Carol. 2007. What's Next for Musharraf? Pro-democracy Leaders to Islamic Leaders Add to Political Pressures. 25 July, http://www.msnbc.msn.com/id/19955166

Gupta, Suman. 2006. *The Theory and Reality of Democracy: A Case Study in Iraq*. London, New York: Continuum.

Lall, Rashmee Roshan. 2005. Britain Copes with Life after Mayhem. *Times of India*, July 9, 12.

------. 2005. Attacks a By-product of Muslim Rage. *Times of India*, July 9, 13.

Rajan, Nalini ed. 2007. *21st Century Journalism in India*. New Delhi, Thousand Oaks, London: Sage Publications.

Shaikh, Najmuddin A. 2005. London Blasts' Impact on Pakistan. *The Dawn*, July 15, http://www.dawn.com/2005/07/15/op.htm

William R. Glass
University of Warsaw, Poland
James R. Keller
Eastern Kentucky University, USA

Movies and foreign policy: from *The Third Man* to *Zentropa*

The premise of this essay is that popular fictional films might be used to under-stand the era in which they were originally made and viewed. In other words, popular films, and even those with more limited circulation, can be used as cul-tural documents to analyze issues and attitudes at a particular moment in Ameri-can history. Additionally, they can be used to chart change over time by compar-ing two movies that deal with similar issues but were made in different eras. The two films under consideration here allow us to look at how European film mak-ers have evaluated the intentions and motives of American foreign policy toward the reconstruction of Europe after WWII.

Made over 40 years apart, *The Third Man* (1949) and *Zentropa* (1991) re-flect a change in the evaluation of America's contribution to European recovery. Both films question the motives for American involvement, but while *The Third Man* acknowledges the potential for good in American efforts, *Zentropa* paints a darker picture. In part the different perspectives result from the historical cir-cumstances of the years in which they were released. Appearing at the beginning of the Cold War, *The Third Man* presents a basically positive assessment of America's role, but appearing after America's misuse of power in Vietnam, the debate over nuclear weapons in Germany, and most important, after the fall of the Berlin Wall and the end of the Cold War, *Zentropa* is a more pessimistic im-age of America's economic and political interests abroad.

The criticism of these two films generally does not read these films as ex-tended commentaries on American foreign policy but at the same time neither is the politics of the films ignored. Generally, film critics' initial reviews of both films emphasized the entertainment value of the movie and the technical aspects of the film makers' craft. For example, Bosley Crowther, *New York Times* film critic, described *The Third Man* as "essentially a first-rate contrivance in the way of melodrama-and that's all. It isn't a penetrating study of any European problem of the day … It doesn't present any 'message.' It hasn't a point of view. It is just a bang-up melodrama, designed to excite and entertain" (Crowther 1950). The stature of the film has grown over the decades and so has the recog-nition of its politics (Ebert 1996, Dirks, and Miller 1997). For example, Gary Giddins of the *New York Sun* sees its main character as screenwriter Graham "Greene's first evisceration of the 'quiet American,' the well-meaning innocent abroad" (Giddins 2007) The first reviewers of *Zentropa* were overwhelmed by director Lars von Trier's technical tricks to tell his story, which, according to *New York Times* critic Stephen Holden, was "the only conventional aspect of a film that is an almost impudently flashy and knowing exercise in post-modern cinematic expressionism" (Holden 1992; see also, Ebert 1992 and Savlov 1992). Over a decade later on the occasion of the DVD release of the film, Bill Weber catalogued those elements that so caught the attention of the reviewers, noting that the film "has a singular look dominated by the actors' placement in a multi-planed mise-en-scène employing front and rear projection, restless tracking shots, and a few lurid intrusions of color (the reds of blood and emergency brakes) in its silver-and-gray, eternal-night monochrome" (Weber 2008). While cinematic techniques can be used by skilled film makers to reinforce the intended meaning of the their movies, this essay will focus on narrative and character as the factors that most directly convey these films' discussion of American aid to post war Europe.

American foreign policy in the years after World War II, the origins of the Cold War, and the place of the reconstruction of Europe in the policy of containment are as contentious of topics as any in American historiography. This essay is not the place to rehash these debates, but general lines of interpretation range from those historians, like William Appleman Williams, who emphasize the pre-eminent need of the American capitalist system for expanding markets as the driving force behind American policies to others, like John Lewis Gaddis, who, while acknowledging the economic undercurrents in American actions, point to the necessity of stopping the expansion of a Stalinist version of communism in order to maintain freedom and democracy in western Europe and the rest of the world. Whether seen as the means of enabling Europeans to buy American products (Williams 1972, 272) or as a humanitarian relief effort to stabilize economically and politically war devastated Europe and so contain communism by undercutting its ideological appeal (Gaddis 2005, 32), the Marshall Plan was the most concrete expression of the effort to rebuild Europe by injecting billions of dollars into the economies of various nations. Neither *The Third Man* nor *Zentropa* directly reference the Marshall Plan nor are the actions taken by their characters connected to this policy. The exact time of the events in *The Third Man* are not specified while those in *Zentropa* occur before the development of the Marshall Plan. Moreover, *The Third Man* focuses on the actions of individual Americans while *Zentropa* more squarely addresses the machinations of officials of the American occupation by including them as secondary characters. With these caveats, it is important to note that these films generally do not comment on promoting democracy and human rights but rather focus on American economic interests, and in this way analyze dramatically rather than historically the motives of post war aid policies toward Europe.

Based on an original screenplay by Graham Greene (who later turned it into a novel), directed by Carol Reed, and released in America in 1950, *The Third Man* focuses on Holly Martins who comes to Vienna at the invitation of his old college friend Harry Lime. Martins comes to Europe for the economic opportunity provided by Lime's offer of a job. Holly believes that Harry directs a medical charity and wants Holly to write about the work perhaps as a means of drumming up donations. Thus the initial impression is that Martins is an opportunist and Lime a humanitarian. Holly learns that Lime has been killed in a traffic accident and that Major Calloway, a British member of the occupation police, believes that Lime was involved in a black market scam selling diluted penicillin. Martins becomes determined to disprove Calloway's charges. Because he cannot speak German, he enlists the aid of Lime's girlfriend, Anna, a Czech refugee whom Lime supplied with forged papers to enable her to avoid being returned to her communist dominated homeland. Calloway's evidence of Lime's guilt shatters Martins' illusions and awakens Holly to the way Harry intended to use him. To Anna after Calloway's revelations, he explained that Lime sold his penicillin for "Seventy pounds a tube. And he asked me to write about his great medical charity. I suppose he wanted a Press Agent. Maybe I could have raised the price to eighty pounds." For Harry, profits and a market not charity were his paramount concern even if that meant sacrificing his best friend and his lover.

While the film condemns economic gain as a justification for American involvement in European reconstruction, it also suggests that political concerns are inadequate motives for American interest. In the tense, early years of the Cold War, American politicians used the specter of communist expansion to convince the American people of the necessity of economic aid to Europe. American assistance in the form of programs like the Marshall Plan was useful for achieving political ends. For a movie released in these years, the absence of both sinister, communist Russians or direct exposition of communist aggression in *The Third Man* is somewhat surprising. The villains are not Russians bent on dominating central Europe but rather an American and his European associates intent on personal economic gain. Russians appear in only a few scenes, more as bureaucrats doing their jobs in a mindless, orderly fashion. Yet the few scenes are coded in such a way to remind audiences of the evil intent of the Russians. Apparently these scenes were too subtle for producer David Selznik as he wrote Greene and Reed that "We frankly made the Russians the heavies, in pursuit of the girl. All of this has been eliminated, even what was in the original script. We must insist upon its return, for patriotic reasons, for purposes of the picture's importance and size" (quoted in "Making"). As evidenced by what appears in the film, Greene and Reed ignored this demand. In any case, in 1950, *The Third Man* did not need much exposition to remind audiences of the broader political circumstances of the film's setting. Churchill's Iron Curtain speech, the announcement of the Truman Doctrine, the effort to force Russian troops out of Iran, the success of communists in China, the development of the Marshall Plan, Russian testing of atomic weapons, the formation of NATO, and the Berlin airlift were but a few of the events that the press and politicians used to remind

people of the communist threat. Anna, then, serves to represent the plight of refugees and displaced persons who became pawns in the power struggle between
East and West in the early years of the Cold War. On the one hand, Greene and
Reed clearly portray Anna as threatened by the Russian bureaucrats who wish to
return her to Czechoslovakia, but they also suggest she is a victim of American
exploitation. The origins and nature of Lime's interest in her are never made
clear. Perhaps he had genuine romantic feelings for her; perhaps she was nothing more than a convenient sexual partner. In any case, Lime provided her with
the documents she needed to stay in Vienna, and she came to have a deep romantic attachment that even evidence of Lime's black market crimes and self
interest could not break. But when Calloway's investigation of the black market
threatened Lime's livelihood and life, Lime sacrificed Anna, trading the truth
about her nationality for protection from the Russians. On the other hand, Holly's concern for Anna seems to come from a combination of romantic infatuation and anxiety for her status as a refugee. Holly eventually recognizes that Anna will not be able to love him and makes a deal with Calloway to trade Anna's
safety in return for setting a trap for Lime. This action would seem to suggest
that Martins was acting out of humanitarian motives to rescue displaced persons.
His sacrifice of Harry for Anna would seem to suggest that Holly learned the
lesson that America must forego its economic interests to achieve its political
goals of stopping communist aggression. However, Anna sees the true nature of
this transaction, that her needs and those of other displaced persons are secondary to the political ends of the two superpowers. When she forces Holly to admit
that he and Calloway are not insuring Anna's safety out of the goodness of their
hearts, she pointedly tells Holly, "If you want to sell yourself, I'm willing not to
be the price."

Holly and America must learn to act not for economic profit nor for political
advantage but for the pure motive that a common humanity requires assisting
those in need without regard to personal or national gain. This lesson Martins
learns when Calloway brings him face to face with the effects of Lime's black
market scam. After seeing his plans to save Anna fail, Holly decides to leave
Vienna, remarking that Anna's "right. It's none of my business." Holly's decision to leave implies the possibility of America giving into the temptation to
withdraw from world affairs, to return to its pre-WWII isolationism. On the other hand, Calloway's efforts to secure Holly's help signify European desire to
have American assistance in economic recovery and the maintenance of their
political freedom. But the film suggests that American help should be delivered
in ways that take into account European needs not American interests. Calloway
has one last card to play. He arranges for Martins to leave but on the way to the
airport stops at a children's hospital where the staff has used some of Lime's
diluted penicillin to treat meningitis. As Holly tours the hospital, no dialogue is
spoken neither are the faces of the children shown; all we see is the growing

horror on Holly's face as he views the results of Lime's greedy quest to exploit for profits the needs of people in war devastated Vienna. After the tour Martins agrees to bait the trap for Lime. American exploitation must be eliminated for the benefit of the children.

That point is reinforced by the climatic chase in the sewers of Vienna. As Harry tries to escape, he kills Sergeant Paine, Calloway's assistant. Just as Europe had borne the brunt of Nazi aggression leaving America virtually untouched so Paine takes Lime's bullet to protect Holly. Accepting his responsibility as well as his complicity, Martins picks up Paine's gun and kills Lime. America itself must put aside its inclination to take advantage of the post war chaos and act out of compassion for the needs of the war's victims. Thus while Holly seems to have learned the lesson of acting for humanitarian reasons and suggests an optimistic assessment of America's role in post war Europe, the ending is more ambivalent than this simple reading. Anna and Holly meet at Harry's funeral but she ignores him, disdaining even to look in his direction. Anna's indifference to Holly's presence and her refusal to acknowledge him on the cemetery road suggests that America's actions to this point may have alienated some Europeans.

Premiering at the 1991 Cannes Film Festival as *Europa*, released in the US the following year with the title *Zentropa*, and written and directed by Danish film maker Lars von Trier, *Zentropa* shows its central character moving from humanitarian ideals to a realization of the exploitive nature of American policies, just the opposite arc from Holly Martins. An idealistic American youth, Leopold Kessler, who was AWOL during the war because he could not bring himself to betray his German heritage, has returned to the country of his ancestral origins in order to "show this country a little kindness." However, the young man's good intentions are undermined by the corrupt and self-interested political factions that are jockeying for power within the chaotic German state. Von Trier uses Kessler's personal odyssey through post-WWII Germany to cast doubt on the popular image of America rescuing Western Europe from economic devastation and political tyranny.

The film revolves around a single pervasive metaphor. The reconstruction of Germany is represented by the redevelopment of the Zentropa railway. Thus German society is, literally and figuratively, attempting to get back on track. Kessler attempts to facilitate the country's recovery by taking a job as conductor of the train's sleeping car. The railway signifies both the country's fascist past and its economic future. Kessler is taken on a tour of the train in which he discovers cars he "never knew existed." The imagery of the film then reveals the train's deployment in the transportation of Jews to concentration camps during the war. Later in the film, Kate Hartman, daughter of the railway's owner, admits that Zentropa carried "Jews to concentration camps" during the war and "American Officers, first class, afterwards." Kessler's uncle expresses concern over the train's direction and the country's future, thus revealing his fear of the past and uncertainty of the future: "There's the feeling that I don't know in which direction the train is moving. I don't know if we are going forwards or backwards. Or what I thought was forwards has suddenly become backwards." Kessler's uncle captures the essence of Germany's predicament: the inability to construct a new state without employing the remnants of the former power structure.

Moreover, the administration of the train is shown to be in the hands of former Nazis. The uniforms of the train conductors are reminiscent of SS regalia, and the rigid discipline imposed upon the employees invokes the stereotype of Nazi efficiency. When Kessler is reviewed for promotion, his inspectors are caricatures of SS officers, rigorously imposing rules and regulations that have no reasonable foundation. The caricature alludes to the irrelevancies of military discipline that demands unquestioning obedience. Kessler is plainly incapable of living up to the expectation of his inspectors. In this aspect of the film, the notorious German efficiency that proved so effective in the enterprises of the war is redirected toward economic recovery, toward capitalist enterprises. Indeed, Max Hartman, the owner of Zentropa, had former Nazi affiliations which he is forced to deny in order to maintain control of the railway.

Additionally, the American occupation force is shown to be less altruistic than self-interested, exploiting its military advantage and sacrificing humanitarian interests for economic gain. Because the American military believes Max Hartman vital to the reconstruction of Germany's transportation system and because all German industrialists must prove that they had no Nazi affiliations in order to maintain their position of authority, Colonel Harris, of the occupation force, coerces a Jewish man, caught stealing food from an American commissary, into confirming Hartman's innocence. The Jewish man is compelled to maintain that Max fed and hid him during the war. The incident reveals the American commitment to Germany's economic future exceeds the desire to ferret out and punish former Nazis. The American interest in the demilitarization of Germany is also shown to be hypocritical. Leopold Kessler learns that many Americans owned German industries during the war, and as he and the Hartman family witness the Allies' destruction of cranes, owned by the IG-Farben industry, an action ostensibly intended to "prevent the rise of another German military power," the Hartman son reveals that the American's have first seized the company's chemical patents and then destroyed its production capacity in order to eliminate industrial competition, thus guaranteeing America's economic supremacy.

Perhaps the most startling condemnation within the film is that of Kessler himself who on the surface appears to be the only innocent. He was AWOL from his military duties because he felt that his German heritage and his American citizenship created a divided loyalty. In conversation with a priest at the

Hartman residence, Kessler is told that God finds it easier to forgive those who "fight fervently for a cause" even if that cause is ultimately wrong. The only group whom "God won't forgive" are "unbelievers, who take no sides." Paradoxically, Kessler's refusal to take a side in the fight is both his guilt and his innocence. His innocence is a temptation to all factions within the social conflict, who attempt to exploit him for their own gain. The Werewolves, a terrorist organization trying to undermine German reconstruction and restore the old order, blackmail him, threatening to kill his wife, Kate, if he does not place a bomb on Zentropa; Colonel Harris manipulates Kessler into spying on Kate who is believed to have Werewolf loyalties; and Kate herself misuses her relationship with Leopold in order to advance her terrorist organization's agenda. After her exposure, she reminders her husband that he "is the only criminal;" because he was not "working for either side," he was easily manipulated by both.

The release of *Zentropa* in the early 1990s invites its comparison to the important social changes in Germany and Europe beginning in 1989. In this context, the film can be read as an enactment of the desire of some Europeans to see a lessening of American influence, be it political, cultural, or economic, and of their hopes for a reinvigorated European presence in the world occasioned by the reunification of Germany and the development of the European Union. This conflation of Germany with Europe is reinforced by von Trier's own words: "I'm obsessed with Germany. For Denmark, it's a very big neighbour. Germany is a symbol. It is Europe" (quoted in Galt 2005, 3). Less than a year after the film's release, European leaders signed the Maastrich Treaty laying the foundation for new levels of cooperation and integration on the continent. In the film, the relationship between Leopold (America) and Kate (Germany) turns out to be a calculated scheme for the advancement of an insidious plot by a nationalistic German organization, and Kessler's naïveté is one of the principal facilitators of this plot because he fails to discern her true loyalties. The narrative voice of the film is a hypnotist who is manipulating the experiences of Kessler. The entire narrative is a subjective experience revealing Kessler's nightmarish anxieties, and in the film's final monologue, the hypnotist reminds his subject: "you want to wake up to free yourself of the image of Europa, but it is not possible." Curiously, missing from the film are references to the ostensible reason for American aid: a rebuilt, capitalist, and democratic Germany (and Western Europe) would serve American foreign policy goals of containing communism. If Russians were only in the background in *The Third Man*, they are not seen in *Zentropa*. Their absence in a film after the end of the Cold War, when coupled with the mesmerizing images of Kessler's body drifting down a river and out to sea when Zentropa goes off the track at the end of the film, is a rather unambiguous statement from von Trier that the time has come for Europe to be rid of American control and influence.

In conclusion, these films portray America's intervention in the internal affairs of other nations as a humanitarian venture. In *The Third Man*, Lime is, outwardly, a part of a positive program to help Europe recover from the devastation of the war while his work is actually destructive of human life. Moreover, when Martins kills Lime, he destroys the exploitative dimension of American interests and affirms America's potential to act out of altruistic motives. On the other hand, in *Zentropa*, when Kessler blows up the bridge and sends the train careening off the tracks, he not only destroys the Germans and American military personnel, he destroys himself. He recognizes the corruption of all involved in the reconstruction of Germany after the war, and his own death constitutes the destruction of American naïveté, the destruction of America's belief in its own good intentions. Moreover, the very same process that gets Zentropa back on track also guarantees the financial success of American business interests at the German's expense.

References

Crowther, Bosley. 1950. Movie Review: The Third Man. *New York Times*, 3 February. http://movies.nytimes.com/movie/review?_r=1&res=9A02E4D B1E39E43BBC4B53DFB466838B649EDE (accessed 14 July 2009).

Dirks, Tim. n.d. Review of *The Third Man (1949)*. Filmsite, http://www.filmsite.org/thir.html (accessed 15 July 2009).

Ebert, Roger. 1992. Zentropa. *Chicago Sun-Times*, July 3. http://rogerebert.suntimes.com/apps/pbcs.dll/article?AID=/19920703/REV IEWS/207030301/1023 (accessed 14 July 2009).

------. 1996. *The Third Man* (1949). *Chicago Sun-Times*, December 8. http://rogerebert.suntimes.com/apps/pbcs.dll/article?AID=/19961208/REV IEWS08/401010366/1023 (accessed 14 July 2009).

Gaddis, John Lewis. 2005. *The Cold War*. London: Penguin Books.

Galt, Rosiland. 2005. Back Projection: Visualizing Past and Present Europe in *Zentropa*. *Cinema Journal* 45: 3-21. http://www.jstor.org/stable/3661077 (accessed 15 July 2009).

Giddins, Gary. 2007. Who is Harry Lime. *New York Sun*, May 22. http://www.nysun.com/arts/who-is-harry-lime/54980/ (accessed 15 July 2009).

Holden, Stephen. 1992. Technique! Allusion! Leitmotif! *New York Times*, May 22. http://movies.nytimes.com/movie/review?res=9E0CE0D61E3FF9 31A15756C0A964958260 (accessed 14 July 2009).

The Making of The Third Man. Film Forum. http://www.filmforum.org/ archivedfilms/making3rdman.html (accessed 14 July 2009).

Miller, Laura. 1997. Personal Best: The Third Man. *Salon*, March 21. http://www.salon.com/march97/miller970321.html (accessed 15 July 2009).

Savlov, Marc. 1992. Review of *Zentropa*. *The Austin Chronicle*, September 18. http://www.austinchronicle.com/gyrobase/Calendar/Film?Film=oid%3a13 8691 (accessed 15 July 2009).

The Third Man. 1949. Directed by Carol Reed.

Weber, Bill. 2008. Europa. *Slant Magazine*, December 12. http://www.slantmagazine.com/film/film_review.asp?ID=4026 (accessed 15 July 2009).

Williams, William Appleman. 1972. *The Tragedy of American Diplomacy*. New York: W. W. Norton.

Zentropa. 1991. Directed by Lars von Trier.

Lars Lierow
George Washington University, USA
"I urge that you transmit that message to the nations of the Earth": *The Day The Earth Stood Still* and postwar international communication

Audiences in 1951 would have recognized *The Day the Earth Stood Still* as a variation of science fiction narratives they already knew from radio serials, comic books, magazines, and, of course, the movies of the 1940s. Yet *The Day the Earth Stood Still* also contained elements now considered trademarks of cold war science fiction films, while at the same time its overtly political message against nuclear militarization remains unique. The movie is loosely based on the science fiction short story "Farewell to the Master" story by Harry Bates and has many elements in common with other science fiction movies from the 1950s which likewise revolved around a confrontation between Americans and aliens from outer space or strange mutant creatures. Through the fantastic format, these movies alluded to and exaggerated the threat of Soviet communism. Associating communism with their imagery of eerily unknowable or grotesque others, movies like *The Invasion of the Body Snatchers*, *The Blob*, *Them!*, *Red Planet Mars*, and many others also incorporated themes of mind control and conformity.[1] *The Day the Earth Stood Still*, however, does not quite fit that template because it represents the alien as a friendly visitor who must be protected from a hysterical and narrow-minded mob, and therefore, according to Peter Biskind (1985, 58, 71), could be labeled "radical" or "left-wing" science fiction. Contemporary commentators also noted that the movie does not easily fit the science-fiction/alien invasion formula of that time.[2]

What distinguishes *The Day the Earth Stood Still* is its explicit critique of US cold war politics and militarism, in particular with regard to a possible nuclear confrontation with the Soviet Union. Set in Washington, D.C., the movie advocates mutual international understanding and international peace. After a flying saucer, which brings the alien Klaatu (Michael Rennie) and Gort, a tall intergalactic peace-enforcing robot, lands on the national mall, it is immediately surrounded by armed soldiers and tanks as well as a crowd of curious, but frightened, onlookers. When Klaatu pulls a futuristic device from underneath his suit, he is wounded by a shot and taken into military detention – from which he escapes and moves into a boarding house, disguised as an American. In order to

---

[1] Jeffrey Sconce analyzes a series of similar movies from that era which capitalize on a fascination with the human brain and the possibilities of psychological/neurological manipulation.

[2] Compare the contemporary reviews by R.L.C and Bosley Crowther. Also compare the more recent analysis by Tony Shaw (2007, 140-144).

demonstrate the seriousness of his mission and to convince Professor Barnhardt (Sam Jaffe) to convene a meeting of the world's most intelligent scientists and philosophers, Klaatu brings the world to a standstill for half an hour. He is chased and almost killed, but is able to deliver his message – that the inhabitants of the earth should cease their cold war arms race, which threatens other planets, lest they want to risk the destruction of planet earth by Gorts – a kind of robot superpolice that ensures harmonious relations between the planets by the threat of their destructive powers.

The movie opens with scenes that establish the encounter with the alien visitor unmistakably as a matter of global importance. Close-ups of radar stations, hurried phone calls, and news broadcasts detect and announce the flying saucer's arrival. A long sequence strings together scenes of different countries as they receive the news, interspersed with a soundtrack of radio broadcasts announcing the arrival of the alien visitor. This theme continues, as the movie repeatedly draws attention to how news media shape the public reception of the alien Klaatu. The media excitement and public service announcements stand in contrast to the ordinariness of Klaatu. Klaatu's mission is to deliver a message to the entire world regarding the cold war nuclear arms race. The opening scenes of *The Day the Earth Stood Still* are instrumental in combining the two themes of communication and global politics.

When *The Day the Earth Stood Still* came out, the United States had been involved in the Korean War for about a year. Moreover, two years before the movie's release, the Soviet Union had tested its first atomic bomb. An ambiguous mix of fear and confidence characterized the public response, as a nuclear war seemed a distinct possibility.[3] The idea of a world government was being actively promoted during the late 1940s by scientists who warned of the uncontrollable destructive capacities but had by the early 1950s increasingly come under criticism (Boyer 1985, 29-98). The world-government movement "was something of a hybrid, briefly bringing together people of vastly different orientations to whom the atomic crisis gave, at least superficially, a common outlook" (Boyer 1985, 44). In this political climate, the movie takes an explicit political stance. Klaatu's insistence on a meeting of representatives from all nations comes close to endorsing a world government as a means to prevent nuclear warfare. *The Day the Earth Stood Still* participated directly in these cold

---

[3] Paul Boyer (1985, 22-25) has compared the results of consecutive polls taken after the 1945 attacks on Hiroshima and Nagasaki which, taken together, indicate a shift in public attitudes toward the atomic bomb. He finds that toward the end of the 1940s, opinion surveys found Americans increasingly willing to admit anxieties about a possible nuclear war. Elaine Tyler May (2008, 25) reports Gallup Poll results from 1950 which show that 61 percent of the respondents supported the use of the nuclear bomb by the United States in the event of another war, but that at the same time almost half of the respondents (53%) were certain American communities would be the target of nuclear attacks.

war debates, and nuclear warfare becomes one of its dominant themes. Its understanding of politics and the solution it offers, however, is shaped by the intersection of the political discourse with the postwar discourse about mass communication.

This essay argues that the movie *The Day the Earth Stood Still* adopts a view of US cold war politics in which mass communication and propaganda ranked as strategic tools which could supplement, or even provide an alternative to the nuclear arsenal. This view was fostered through the government's active collaboration with the nascent field of communication research. The field itself was characterized by its ambivalent reinterpretation of *propaganda* as a pernicious foreign threat but also as a useful and legitimate method to achieve the United States' own military and political ambitions. Communication research thus took on a cold war liberal frame of reference (Gary 1996, 135-136, 144 -145). The movie illustrates how broadly these ideas concerning mass communication circulated into popular culture; and the communication subtext renders the movie's anti-war message itself more ambivalent.

Mass media like radio, television, and newspapers are, in fact, an integral element of *The Day the Earth Stood Still*. Throughout the movie, recurrent scenes of radio announcers as well as characters reading newspapers, listening to the radio, and watching television[4] are used to characterize the postwar United States as a media-saturated society. The filmmakers also employ media technology as a narrative device. Toward the end of one telling scene of a news broadcast, for example, a close-up of a television set in the studio showing the flying saucer that has just landed fills the movie screen. The close-up then dissolves to reveal the events on the national mall. This transition by way of a TV screen on the movie screen addresses the audience as a media audience and acknowledges the media's role in shaping the perception of real events.[5] That *The Day the Earth Stood Still* articulates its critique of US postwar society and global politics through this understanding of a media society is not at all incidental. The discourses about mass communication and global politics became closely joined in early stages of the cold war. In fact, they often co-constituted each other so much that even a film like *The Day the Earth Stood Still*, which seeks to critique the cold war common sense, incorporated the vision of a mass communication domain very much like the one mass communication research developed.

---

[4] The radio and television announcers in *The Day the Earth Stood Still* were the real-life announcers Drew Pearson, H.V. Kaltenborn, and Elmer Davis whose voices and faces were familiar to postwar audiences.

[5] This play with realism and mediation also alludes to the 1938 broadcast of Orson Wells' *War of the Worlds* radio drama which was thought to have caused widespread panic because of its believability. In the drama, the threat posed by alien invaders is revealed through successive radio bulletins.

This connection is particularly apparent in the solution to global nuclear annihilation which the film envisions. It displays a preference for interpersonal communication which acts as supplement or counterpoint to mediated communication, focusing on Klaatu's quest to deliver the message and his direct personal interactions with Helen Benson (Patricia Neal) and Professor Barnhardt. Mass communication research similarly developed theories stressing the role of prominent individuals and group interaction as a safeguard against the possibly undemocratic propaganda power of mass media. Being able to understand mass communication – and utilize it – was thought of as a distinct strategic advantage as the United States fought in World War II and entered the early cold war. Communication theory constructed images of political and social relations, democratic processes like elections, regional and class differences; and they put forward ideas about how a basic political stability, a consensus is to be achieved.

In close collaboration with government agencies and cold war propaganda and psychological warfare institutions, communication research developed a theoretical outlook that was anchored, on the one hand, in the vision of an international political domain being tethered together via channels of mass communication and, on the other hand, the positive reframing of propaganda as *education*, or simply *international communication*. The institutional alliances and the prestige of communication research as a reliable and usable science shaped an interpretation of global politics through the lens of communication. This interpenetration of the political and social science discourse that gave cold war politics a sense of manageability filtered into *The Day the Earth Stood Still*. The movie adopts the faith of postwar liberals in communication and psychology as political strategies. Its political leaning is thus ambiguous and cannot easily be characterized as "left-wing," despite its outright critique of US nuclear militarism.

1. Mass communication research emerges as a cold war social science

Mass communication research in the United States emerged as an autonomous field and a politically expedient social science during the 1940s and 1950s. It merged approaches from sociology, psychology, political science, propaganda studies, and public opinion research into one *single* paradigm (Delia 1987; Gitlin 1978; Glander 2000). This paradigm defined the new field and understood communication as the flow of bits of information and stimuli from medium to audience. In addition, the researchers focused primarily on *effects*, e.g. changes in opinion or behavior mass communication could possibly trigger, and preferred quantitative methods like survey interviews and content analysis. Statistical aggregate data and charts about the likelihood of certain effects and the distribution of public opinion were characteristic of the field (Czitrom 1982, 122-146).

As a champion of detailed, methodologically intricate quantitative investigations that communications research became known for, Paul Felix Lazarsfeld added to the reputation of the communication research. He became one of the publicly recognized experts on communication during the postwar era.[6] One of the most influential communication researchers of that era, he became the director of the Bureau of Applied Social Research at Columbia University, where he conducted studies on marketing, voting behavior, and propaganda that significantly shaped the terminology and outlook of the field.

The government took an urgent interest in the nascent field. In fact, the transformation of communication research since its beginnings in radio research and public opinion studies and the increase of dedicated research institutions and degree-granting programs was bolstered by the field's alliance with politics. Like other social sciences at that time, communication research was expected to deliver rational answers and to assist in the engineering of a stable national and global order.[7] Research projects were sponsored – overtly and covertly – by US government agencies which had an interest in understanding the workings of propaganda as well as in rendering transparent the attitudes, political leanings, voting tendencies, susceptibility to media campaigns of different population segments – at home and abroad (Glander 2000; Simpson 1994; Gary 1996; Czitrom 1982).[8] Communication research was a central component in the national security efforts of World War II and the nascent cold war and became part of the quest to develop an invisible psychological, non-deadly superweapon that could match the powers of nuclear weapons as envisioned by the Joint Chiefs of Staff in 1951 (Robin 2001, 41-56).[9] As Christopher Simpson underlines "it is unlikely

---

[6] His earlier studies on radio soaps, for example, were cited by the popular press as trustworthy evidence against their supposedly mind-numbing effects on housewives (Gould 1942; Hutchens 1943, 1944). In the 1950s he also spoke before the Kefauver Senate Committee on Juvenile Delinquency regarding the effects of television on adolescents, where he made the case for a more rational, better-funded research agenda in order to debunk speculations about television's harmful effects on the minds of children and adolescents (Lazarsfeld, 1955).

[7] Terence Ball characterizes postwar social sciences and their intimate relationship with the government as one of increasing interdependence, in which the scientists received funding but also increased legitimacy in exchange for knowledge that supported, for example, military and propaganda campaigns.

[8] On the development of social sciences in the cold war climate also compare Ball and Robin.

[9] Historical studies from inside Communication and Media Research that look back at their history barely mention this relationship. Two studies that on the other hand foreground the ties with the propaganda and intelligence apparatus are: Simpson and Glander. Instead of a single unified program on psychological warfare that matched the scale of the Manhattan Project of atomic weapon research many individual projects and think tanks assumed this task. One noteworthy example in the context of the Korean War was the Project Revere, conducted by Stuart A. Dodd at the University of Washington, which investigated the pos-

that communication research could have emerged in anything like its present form without regular transfusions of money for the leading lights in the field from US military, intelligence, and propaganda agencies" (1994, 4). In the process, communication research emerged as a typical social science of the early cold war period.

2. Mass communication and politics in a shrunken world

This desire for trustworthy insights into communication was undergirded by an assumption, as this section shows, that mass media had achieved the potential to reshuffle and reorganize international political and social relations, because like an electronic nervous network they would now connect nations and peoples across the world. According to this logic, the United States were now confronted with an unprecedented situation in which political concerns at home were inseparable from global affairs because of the media. Media executives and researchers alike commented on the ability of mass communication to shrink the world. The president of NBC, Sylvester Weaver, for example, thought that television could turn the "entire world into a small town, instantly available, with the leading actors on the world stage known on sight or by voice to all within it" (Spigel 2001, 16). Weaver's televisual fantasy was preceded by the encounter of the world through radio. In the late 1930s through the 1940s, the events leading up to World War II were brought to American audiences through radio either first or in particularly dramatic ways (Ackerman 1948; Horten 2002, 21-39). Anthropologist Margaret Mead similarly attributed the concern with communication to "the enormous advance in technology and the resulting shrinking of the world into one potential communication system" (1948, 17).

David Sarnoff, the head of the Radio Corporation of American and a planner behind *The Voice of America* propaganda radio project, propounded the possibilities of "transoceanic TV" to integrate distant nations into a shared mediated world experience. He envisioned, for example, that television will make available "the violent reality of distant battlefields ... on the home front" as well as "international meetings, sports events and human everyday living [as] almost a firsthand experience." Sarnoff saw television as a potential tool of global "human brotherhood" and proposed a "Vision of America" program to "sell democracy abroad." To circumvent these programs from being jammed, he proposes to use microwave signals that bounce between airplanes functioning as relays – a method he dubs "radio air-lift," referencing the recent Berlin air lift in which the US supported West Berlin during a Soviet embargo (Sarnoff 1950, 108). Sarnoff was obviously not interested in a global problem-solving conversation.

---

sibility to drop leaflets to trigger the spread of messages from person to person (Robin 2001, 100-101).

He was convinced of the effectiveness of media campaigns that project a favorable image of American life abroad.

Two roles for the US – steward in world affairs or participant in a political ecumene – were being negotiated in the postwar thought on mass communication. The shrunken world could be a global sphere of conversation but also the terrain for precisely targeted persuasion campaigns via the channels of communication. In many cases it was imagined as a hybrid, with US propaganda reframed as education campaigns and benevolence. Lyman Bryson, in his foreword to the 1948 collection of conference papers dealing with communication as a scientific concept and a unique characteristic of world culture and politics, *The Communication of Ideas*, surmised that a "statesmanship of communication" should be developed under the guidance of communication research (Bryson 1948, 7-8). Bryson suggested that the US develop a global leadership role, using "the machines for conveying thought to wide mass audiences from a single diffusion point" not so much to indoctrinate the "world community," but instead as instruments of education (1948, 4). By recasting propaganda as a form of gentle paternalism, without questioning the necessity for US political dominance, Bryson tried to differentiate between two scenarios of the postwar future with its powerful mass communication technologies and institutions. The optimistic faith in global education campaigns offered a rhetorical counterpoint possibility of global propaganda, which was deemed undemocratic and did not match the national self-image of the United States.

This kind of thinking paralleled the rationales behind UNESCO's mass communication project. The preparatory report on mass communication for the December 1946 General Conference also characterized mass media as a modernizing force which dissolves barriers between the world's nations, pushes them closer together into a relationship characterized by mutual understanding but also vulnerability. The creation of this political and cultural co-habitat per mass communication is, however, also represented as potential threat as well as a unique opportunity. Imagining national audiences tethered together, the report stated, that

> [b]efore the advent of radio, film and publications with mass circulation, most people in all parts of the world lived in cultural isolation, unaware of the diversity of ways and standards of living elsewhere ... The media of mass communication have helped to destroy this conservation and sense of stability, and have projected through the world in its place a stimulating but alarming picture of change and diversity. (UNESCO's Program of Mass Communication, 519-520)

The UNESCO report called upon the craft of communication researchers to facilitate and organize this conversation in order to reestablish a sense of global stability.

Underlined by the movie's opening sequences, this image of the shrunken world is fundamental to *The Day the Earth Stood Still*. Klaatu at one point admits that he has learned English by listening to radio broadcasts. The movie dramatizes the potential of communication technology to reduce distances and encourage global stability and peace by extending this fantasy to outer space. *The Day the Earth Stood Still* underlines the importance of mass media in establishing social and political ties with its recurrent scenes of television and radio broadcasts.

The idea of global communication as an alternative political strategy in the cold war conflict is driven home by Klaatu's actions. He refuses to deliver his message to one single government and instead insists on speaking to representatives from all nations. Klaatu's power depends on his ability to command the attention of global and domestic audiences. While he encourages peaceful exchange among the nations of the earth, he is in control of his message and its distribution. Klaatu reveals his intentions and the reason for his visit in one-on-one conversations first to Professor Barnhardt and later, during the half hour of world paralysis, to Helen Benson before he addresses a larger crowd gathered around his space ship. *The Day the Earth Stood Still* contrasts Klaatu's earnest conversations with the exaggerated news reports. Klaatu's position parallels the ambivalent political stance of US communication research. In other words, he is the kind of statesman of communication that Lyman Bryson might have had in mind, because his well-intentioned propaganda sets off the unreliable and undemocratic mess media messages.

3. Klaatu's personal influence: The ambiguities of interpersonal and international communication

One scene in particular encapsulates how the movie adopts the ambivalent discourse on mass communication and cold war politics. On the first morning after Klaatu's arrival, the residents of the boarding house are gathered around the breakfast table. As they eat, the boarders listen quietly to radio broadcast about the "menace from another world" and read the daily news. The camera pans across the faces of the people at the table, before they begin discussing whether the "spaceman" is indeed a threat or a friendly visitor. Their different responses highlight the public's possible susceptibility to media-generated hysteria. When Helen Benson suggests that the alien could be afraid himself, another boarder chuckles and later suspects that he is in fact a Soviet invader: "If you want my opinion, he comes from right here on earth, and you know where I mean," raising her eyebrows and emphasizing the last words. Only Helen, who later assists Klaatu in fulfilling his mission remains calm and dares to voice a different opinion. This scene mirrors the hypotheses of personal influence, highlighting the distribution of mass communicated information within the social group and underlining through the character of Helen the possibility for resistance to mass media influences.

The idea that interpersonal communication has the potential to offset the influence of mass mediated messages and propaganda was codified into theory by Lazarsfeld and his colleagues, particularly in their influential studies *The People's Choice* (1948) and *Personal Influence* (1955). Their approach came to be called the *limited-effects paradigm* (Chaffee and Hochheimer 1985). The general thrust of their argument, in a nutshell, was that creating desired effects – like voting decisions, product purchase – was so immensely complicated, because the voters and consumers were pressured by a vast range of alternative and competing influences. Therefore worries about wholesale manipulation of opinion through media – and thus the possible corruption of democracy – were supposed to be entirely unfounded. This proposition was articulated in the concepts of the *opinion leader* and the *two-step flow* which both mean that information and influences do not reach individuals directly but via detours – often interpersonal talk in the community; and they can be deferred or set off by other influences.

Yet the limited-effects paradigm contained an important ambiguity. The studies were also answering how public opinion can be directed, how campaigns can achieve their effects despite the complicated reception process the researchers mapped out. Toward the end of their study on voting behavior *The People's Choice*, the researchers suggest to utilize personal contacts – "amateur machines" – for effective campaigning. "The most successful form of propaganda ... is to 'surround' people whose vote decision is still dubious so that the only path left to them is the way to the polling booth" (Lazarsfeld et al. 1948, 158).

What is at stake within the narrative of *The Day the Earth Stood Still* is both the penetration of Klaatu's message of global/intergalactic peace and the audience's resistance to exaggerated descriptions of the threatening spaceman which are relayed via newspapers and broadcasts. Even while the movie reverses the premises, criticizing domestic civil defense propaganda and valorizing the *alien*'s messages, its conception of how a preferred message influences target audiences follows the theories outlined by the politicized communication research. That is, Klaatu's success to deliver his message to a larger crowd by the end of the movie is predicated on his ability to convince influential and cooperative individuals, Helen Benson and Professor Barnhardt.

Mass communication research thought of itself in pursuit of basic laws of social relations and of mass media in society that would apply universally – at home and abroad. The domestic focus is apparent in the investigations of the election process and studies on marketing. The international scope embraced the subfields political communication and international communication which carried on the legacy of propaganda research. The domestic and the international domain of mass communication research were not clearly separated. Because they were looking for basic laws, the insights they gained and the theories they developed were thought of as applicable in both realms.

A case in point that illustrates the overlap between domestic and international concerns is the two-step flow. It was developed explicitly in *Personal Influence* (1955) after it had been "discovered" in *The People's Choice* (1944) and initially stated as a hypothesis. However, the theory was developed first and tried out in a project of the United States Information Agency (USIA) (Simpson 1994, 73). Communication relations at home were a subset of the larger global system of communications. This perspective considered each national audience, including the one at home in the US, susceptible to forms of media/communication influence, from inside (the own government or media companies) and from outside (foreign influence). The challenge then appeared twofold: on the one hand to manage those relations to protect the US population and exert influence over others; on the other hand to utilize the international communication system for diplomacy – to create mutual understanding and peaceful, harmonious relationships.

Under the banner of *political communication* and *international communication*, social scientists openly thought about the uses of their craft and investigation methods in order to shape political developments. Wilbur Schramm, who headed the communications department at Urbana, Illinois, acknowledged the relations between communication research and political strategies in the text books that he edited for the teaching of communication research. Schramm's working assumptions was that basic understanding of communication principles yielded knowledge directly applicable to foreign societies and their audiences as well as to psychological warfare. In the *Public Opinion Quarterly*, then the key publication of the field, articles were published frequently that dealt with such questions as what image of the United States should be projected abroad, how does foreign propaganda work, what images of foreign countries are dominant in the US, what are the attitudes toward communism, etc.

While *The Day the Earth Stood Still* critiques official US ideologies and political strategies, it imagines the international matrix in ways similar to theories produced by government-supported communication and propaganda research. In presenting its possible solution, the movie contrasts rational and irrational responses to mass-mediated messages; and it contrasts direct person-to-person relations with broadcasts and newspapers that incite the mob. Inter(galactic)national peace and nuclear weaponry do not constitute the only pairing of options contrasted. The film also ponders the proper and democratic behavior in an international mass communication environment. Part of its critique, in fact, is aimed at improper ways – which lead to the near-fatal shooting of Klaatu. Down to the idea that interpersonal relations can offset media messages and that a strong personality (an opinion leader) can save the day – and bring earth closer to peace, the movie's representation of communicative relations in an international domain coincides with ideas established in communication research.

This analysis does not mean that either Hollywood or social scientists borrowed ideas directly from each other. Rather it suggests that both participated in a liberal discourse on democracy that negotiated the threats and possibilities of mass communication and ended up resting their hopes on individuals who would take over specific communication roles in their local group environments. In other words, Klaatu's message is *good* information not just because of its content but also because of the way in which it is received and "processed" by the people. That is what legitimizes it, associates it with idealistic, honest characters – adding up to a plausible alternative to contemporary politics despite the fact that the alternative articulated by Klaatu is backed by the threat of violence. *The Day the Earth Stood Still* shares a vision of proper, sober, democratic conduct under the conditions of cold war in a mass mediated global society.

References

Ackerman, William C. 1948. U.S. Radio: Record of a Decade. *The Public Opinion Quarterly* 12.3: 440-454.

Ball, Terence. 1989. The Politics of Social Science in Postwar America. In *Recasting America: Culture and Politics in the Age of Cold War*, ed. Lary May, 76-92. Chicago: University of Chicago Press.

Biskind, Peter. 1985. Pods, Blobs, and Ideology in American Films of the Fifties. In *Shadows of the Magic Lamp: Fantasy and Science Fiction in Film*, ed. George Slusser and Eric S. Rabkin, 58-72. Carbondale: Southern Illinois University Press.

Boyer, Paul. 1985. *By the Bombs Early Light: American Thought and Culture at the Dawn of the Atomic Age*. New York: Pantheon.

Bryson, Lyman, ed. 1948. Problems of Communication. In *The Communication of Ideas: A Series of Addresses*. New York: Institute for Religious and Social Studies, distr. Harper.

Chaffee, Steven H., and John L. Hochheimer. 1985. The Beginnings of Political Communications Research in the United States: Origins of the 'Limited Effects' Model. In *Mass Communication Review Yearbook*, ed. Michael Gurevitch and Mark R. Levy, 74-104. Beverly Hills: SAGE.

Coe, Richard L. 1951. Planetary Visitor Lands In District. *The Washington Post*, October 11.

Crowther, Bosley. 1951. The Screen in Review. *New York Times*, September 19.

Czitrom, Daniel J. 1982. The Rise of Empirical Media Study. In *Media and the American Mind: From Morse to McLuhan*, 122-146. Chapel Hill: University of North Carolina Press.

Delia, Jesse G. 1987. Communication Research: A History. In *Handbook of Communication Science*, ed. Charles R. Berger and Steven H. Chaffee, 20-98. Beverly Hills: SAGE.

Gary, Brett. 1996. Communication Research, the Rockefeller Foundation, and Mobilization for the War on Words, 1938-1944. *Journal of Communication* 46.3: 124-147.

Gitlin, Todd. 1978. Media Sociology: The Dominant Paradigm. *Theory and Society* 6.2: 205-253.

Glander, Timothy Richard. 2000. *Origins of Mass Communications Research During the American Cold War: Educational Effects and Contemporary Implications*. Mahwah, NJ/London: Lawrence Erlbaum Associates.

Gould, Jack. 1942. One Thing and Another. *New York Times*, October 25.

Horten, Gerd. 2002. *Radio Goes to War: The Cultural Politics of Propaganda During World War II*. Berkeley: University of California Press.

Hutchens, John K. 1943. Are Soap Operas Only Suds? *New York Times*, March 28.

------. 1944. Soap Opera Addicts. *New York Times*, May 28.

Lazarsfeld, Paul F. 1955. Why Is So Little Known About the Effects of Television on Children and What Can Be Done? *The Public Opinion Quarterly* 19.3: 243-251.

Lazarsfeld, Paul F., Bernard Berelson, and Hazel Gaudet. 1948. *The People's Choice: How the Voter Makes up His Mind in a Presidential Campaign*. 2nd ed. New York: Columbia University Press.

Lazarsfeld, Paul F., and Elihu Katz. 1955. *Personal Influence: the Part Played by People in the Flow of Mass Communications*. Glencoe, IL: Free Press.

May, Elaine Tyler. 2008. *Homeward Bound: American Families in the Cold War Era*. Updated 20th Anniversary Edition. New York: Basic Books.

Mead, Margaret. 1948. Some Cultural Approaches to Communication Problems. In *The Communication of Ideas,* ed. Lyman Bryson, 9-26. New York: Harper.

Robin, Ron. 2001. *The Making of the Cold War Enemy: Culture and Politics in the Military Industrial Complex*. Princeton: Princeton University Press.

Sarnoff, David. 1950. Our Next Frontier ... Transoceanic TV. *Look,* September 12: 108.

Schramm, Wilbur Lang, ed. 1948. *Communications in Modern Society: Fifteen Studies of the Mass Media*. Urbana: University of Illinois Press.

------. 1954. *The Process and Effects of Mass Communication*. Urbana: University of Illinois Press.

Sconce, Jeffrey. 1996. Brains from Space: Mapping the Mind in 1950s Science and Cinema. *Science as Culture* 5.23: 277-302.

Shaw, Tony. 2007. *Hollywood's Cold War: Culture, politics, and the Cold War*. Amherst: University of Massachusetts Press.

Simpson, Christopher. 1994. *Science of Coercion: Communication Research and Psychological Warfare, 1945-1960*. New York: Oxford University Press.

Spigel, Lynn. 2001. *Welcome to the Dreamhouse: Popular Media and Postwar Suburbs*. London: Duke University Press.

UNESCO's Program of Mass Communication: I. 1946. *The Public Opinion Quarterly* 10.4: 518-539.

Wise, Robert, dir. 1951. *The Day the Earth Stood Still*. Perf. Michael Rennie, Patricia Neal. Twentieth-Century Fox.

Francesca de Lucia
University of Oxford, UK
Representations of ethnicity in a postmodern gangster film: the Coen Brothers' *Miller's Crossing*

1. Introduction

The aim of this paper is to analyze the way in which the film *Miller's Crossing* (1991) by the Coen brothers gives a post-modern treatment of the ethnic motif that marks in different fashions the gangster genre, as well as merging together different cinematic elements. In her book *The Politics of Postmodernism*, Linda Hutcheon defines postmodernism thus:

> Postmodernism takes the form of a self-conscious, self-contradictory, self-undermining statement. It is rather like saying something whilst at the same time putting inverted commas around what is being said. The effect is to highlight or "highlight" and to subvert or "subvert" and its mode is therefore a knowing and ironic, or even "ironic" one. Postmodernism's distinctive character lies in this kind of wholesale "nudging" commitment to doubleness or duplicity. (Hutcheon 1990, 1)

She adds that elements of parody are an intrinsic part of the postmodern narrative: "parody – often called ironic quotation, pastiche, appropriation – is usually considered central to postmodernism" (Hutcheon 1990, 89). All these traits are visible in *Miller's Crossing*'s representation of the ethnic mobster. The film performs an ironic subversion of this motif, combining disparate influences and themes to produce an innovative variation of the classical gangster film. I will now proceed to describe the different influences which appear in *Miller's Crossing*, especially those deriving from the gangster films of the 1930s and from Francis Ford Coppola's film *The Godfather* (1970), before going on to show how these intermingle in the Coen brothers' film and, in particular, in its treatment of ethnicity.

2. The early gangster film

As a genre, the gangster movie first started to develop in the context of the aftermath of Prohibition and in the early Depression era. Novels and films evoked the rise and fall of characters more or less directly inspired by real-life gangsters of Italian descent such as Al Capone, embodying both the desire of transgression and the consumerist urge of the Prohibition period and the bleaker, disillusioned mood of the Depression years. The most significant examples of the genre of the pre-war gangster film are represented by Mervin Leroy's *Little Caesar* (1931) and Howard Hawks' *Scarface* (1932), based respectively on novels by W. R.

Burnett and Armitage Trail. Hence these early works, which focus on figures loosely based on Al Capone, were produced by non-ethnically identified authors. While the mobsters at the centre of the narratives are of southern Italian descent, explicit references to their immigrant background remain vague and circumscribed. The sense of a hazy and symbolic ethnic identity is reinforced in the film adaptations by the fact that the characters of Rico Bandello in *Little Caesar* and Tony Camonte in *Scarface* are played by Jewish actors (respectively Edward G. Robinson and Paul Muni). This element suggests a generic blurring of ethnic identity and also possibly hints indirectly at the presence of Jewish gangsters, whom the predominantly Jewish Hollywood establishment might have been less willing to represent directly. It is also significant in the light of the common condition of racial ambivalence in which Jewish and southern Italian immigrants found themselves when they first settled in the United States in the early twentieth century, being considered subaltern to groups of Northern European descent according to the social Darwinist trends popular at the time. Moreover, this ambiguous interplay between Italian and Jewish figures has a significant part in the representation of characters belonging to these two ethnic groups visible in *Miller's Crossing*. In the 1930s, figures such as Al Capone and his fictional projections were perceived as embodiments of a general desire for transgressive behavior and their Italian background became an emblem of the immigrant heritage of most Americans. George De Stefano underlines the appeal of the protagonists of *Little Caesar* and *Scarface* in the context of this difficult historical period: "Like the Depression-era audiences in the 1930s, the gangsters wanted to escape poverty; Italians and Jews could also relate to the struggle of a Rico Bandello and Tony Camonte to break out of the immigrant ghetto" (De Stefano 2006, 75). Even though these characters are members of criminal organizations, they were often represented as isolated individualists dominated by a personal quest for success and power.

3. The impact of *The Godfather*

While the gangster genre dwindled in the 1940s and 1950s, it would be revived in the 1970s through the huge success of *The Godfather*, first in Mario Puzo's book and then especially in Coppola's films. *The Godfather* reinterprets the material of the pre-war gangster movie, however endowing its vague ethnic/immigrant component with a specific southern Italian dimension. Thus, in discussing the novelty constituted by *The Godfather*, Vera Dika writes:

> *The Godfather* then, must be seen as an important moment in the evolution of the gangster genre. This film accomplishes an elaborate *return* [italics in the original], also to the old-style gangster film, one complete with the criminal as a central character and with the convention of the Italian American criminal ... *The Godfather*

expands the gangster story and the representation of ethnicity beyond all previous renditions. (Dika 2000, 82)

In presenting a more realistic representation of Italian American immigrant life, *The Godfather* places an emphasis on various immigrant customs, as well as placing the focus on the myth of the immigrant family as an anti-assimilationist instrument of power, as well as introducing the idea of the family as criminal enterprise. Because of its enormous success, *The Godfather* has been the object of several pastiches and parodies, including for instance John Houston's *Prizzi's Honor*, closely based on Richard Condon's novel of the same title, which subverts several of *The Godfather*'s themes, especially in connection to gender roles and the part they play in the process of assimilation, or Harold Ramis' *Analyze This* (1999), which at times enacts a direct parody of Coppola's work. Hence to a certain extent, *Miller's Crossing* inscribes itself in the tradition of the reworkings of *The Godfather*, as well as undergoing the influence of the gangster films of the 1930s.

4. Ethnic images in *Miller's Crossing*

Miller's Crossing, the work of Jewish American directors, draws elements from the early gangster films and from *The Godfather*, and also combines representations of Jewish, Italian and Irish American syndicates. *Miller's Crossing* by the Coen Brothers obviously borrows and pastiches several of the stylistic conventions of the gangster films of the 1930s. Much of the movie takes place in dingy nightclubs or small offices; all the male characters are well-dressed and wear fedora hats, which assume an emblematic connotation; the main female character combines the stock images of the flapper, the gun moll, and the destructive *femme fatale*. As James J. Mottram points out:

This is the Coens dismantling the genre, an exploration of what lies beneath the long coats and the fedoras ... And it's here that we return to the central motif of the hat – which, as the titles suggest, must be stripped and blown away from the gangster. To put it bluntly, the incongruity of an urban gangster in the woods, minus an important part of his armour, suggests that the Coens are about to debunk the myth of the 1930s gangster embodied by the likes of Paul Muni's Tony Camonte and James Cagney's Tom Powers. (Mottram 2000, 61)

The Coens put a far stronger emphasis on ethnic elements, distancing themselves from the vague and generic use of ethnicity of the original 1930s gangster. *Miller's Crossing* also bears the influence of Coppola's *Godfather*, reworking some of its themes. Yet unlike Puzo and Coppola, the Coen Brothers do not seek to achieve an effect of authenticity. The film includes representatives of three groups traditionally associated with Prohibition-era gangsterism, including not only Italian characters but also Jewish and Irish ones. *Miller's Crossing* plays with ethnic stereotype and each character behaves according to the clichés of his group: the Italian Johnny Caspar (Jon Polito) talks incessantly, gesticulates exuberantly and has an obese wife and son, while the Irish Tom Reagan (Gabriel Byrnes) displays a detached and melancholy attitude as well as a tendency to drink heavily, and the Jewish Bernie Bernbaum (John Turturro) is inclined to constant whining and devious behavior, according to the Shylock/Fagin stereotype. The deliberate use of cliché is intensified by the abundance of demeaning ethnic labeling such as "eytie," "potato-eater" or "sheeny." The use of figures who appear as little more than caricatures, and the simulation of the atmospheres and stylistic devices of early gangster films conveys a strong sense of unreality. As suggested by Fran Mason:

> There is no ideology of freedom or oppression, no moral judgement on gangster corruption or criminality, no engagement with characters' emotions which are presented as cold postmodern desire … In this depthlessness, *Miller's Crossing* offers a postmodern spectacle of generic imagery and attaches this to the foregrounding of its iconography. (Mason 2002, 152)

5. Cinematographic influences

While the Coen Brothers do not seek to give a convincing representation of the Prohibition-era underworld nor a mythical evocation of ethnic organized crime, their film can also be read as a pastiche of *The Godfather*'s depiction of the family as a criminal enterprise. The influence of Coppola's work is visible in the first scene, which is almost a parody of the opening of *The Godfather, Part I*; in both films, an unseen voice is speaking in emotional tones. When Johnny Caspar is revealed, he is almost a caricature of Salvatore Corsitto playing Amerigo Bonasera: both men are balding, dark-skinned and wear moustaches, yet Caspar's rotundity and frenetic speech obviously signify that he is a comic character. As in *The Godfather*, the character is presenting a request to an invisible listener, whose gaze presumably corresponds to the frame of the camera. Leo (Albert Finney) is eventually shown sitting impassively in front of Caspar, but, unlike Don Vito, he minimizes Caspar's complaint. Instead of a charismatic, almost almighty leader, Leo is an arrogant and unsympathetic syndicate boss, and Bonasera's dramatic tale of disillusionment and injustice is replaced by a rant against a petty criminal with the ludicrously alliterative name of Bernie Bernbaum. At this stage, Caspar's ethnicity is still unclear, since his repetitive use of Yiddish terms and his nervous talkativeness may associate him also with a Jewish cliché. The confusion between Italian and Jewish ethnicity is highly significant in light of the influence of the 1930s gangster film on *Miller's Crossing*. In the film versions of *Little Caesar* and *Scarface*, Italian American mobsters were played by Jewish actors, suggesting a sense of continuity between two groups who found themselves in the same ambivalent racial position at the early stage of their settlement in the United States, as well as hinting at the existence of Jewish syndicates. This notion is reinforced by the fact that *Miller's Crossing* upturns the situation of *Little Caesar* and *Scarface* in the character of Bernie, who is played by the Italian American actor John Turturro. Eventually, Leo will reveal that Caspar's real name is Giovanni Gasparro; he is thus the only one of the film's ethnic gangsters to have Anglicized his name, yet any wish Caspar might have for assimilation is contradicted by his being constantly referred to by a variety of anti-Italian slurs.

6. Ethnic aesthetics

Other elements related to Italian culture indirectly derived from *The Godfather* will emerge in relation to the theme of the family. From this point of view, the Coens operate a deconstruction of the myth of the criminal syndicate as a family in various ways, distorting the mythical ethnic family as it appears in *The Godfather* saga. Indeed, this element is introduced early on with the reference to the connection between Verna and her brother Bernie, which turns out to have incestuous implications. The family motif is also presented in a more conventional key in the character of Caspar. The latter's status as a *paterfamilias* contrasts the manipulative and unstable dalliances the other characters engage in. Instead of a moll or a homosexual lover, Caspar has the comic caricature of the traditional Italian family: his wife and small son are obese, as he is, and the former behaves according to the cliché of the overanxious southern mother, explaining in Italian that she is worried that her overweight child is not eating enough. Later, Caspar displays a contradictory combination of impatience and indulgence towards his little boy. The southern Italian family functions as a farcical element in a film with an otherwise bleak atmosphere, suggesting a rejection of the glorification of the traditional family unit present in Puzo and Coppola's work. This notion surfaces again in the scene where Caspar tries to force the corrupt mayor to give jobs to his two cousins, who are presumably newly arrived immigrants, as they do not speak English; their quality of quaint caricatures is underlined by their comic resemblance, since they have identical egg-shaped bald heads and handlebar moustaches. The Italian theme appears in a slightly more serious form only on one occasion: when Caspar's acolytes bring Tom to Miller's Crossing to look for Bernie's corpse. Throughout the scene, an Italian gangster can be heard singing a dialect song in the background; nevertheless, this does not serve to make a comment on the character's ethnicity, but rather to create an effect of alienation and incongruity, since the melancholy ballad accompanies a violent and macabre scene involving the recovery of the decomposing body of a murdered man. Ethnic music is used in a similar way also in connection with the Irish American characters: the traditional Irish song "Danny Boy" accompanies with a sense of contrast the scene of a prolonged shooting. Like other symbolic elements in the film, such as Tom's fedora, these music-related ethnic signifiers are ultimately devoid of deeper meaning. *Miller's Crossing* is a postmodern combination of different genres and motifs, where ethnicity is used in an ironic and playful way. As Jewish American film makers, the Coen Brothers do not only appropriate clichés connected to their own background (visible in the character of Bernie) but also of other ethnic groups, suggesting a more fluid and broad conception of contemporary ethnic identity.

References

Burnett, W. R. 1984. *Little Caesar. Four Novels*. London: Zomba.

Condon, Richard. 1982. *Prizzi's Honour*. London: Michael Joseph.

Coen, Ethan, dir. 1990. *Miller's Crossing*. Perf. Gabriel Byrnes, Marcia Gay Harden, John Turturro. Circle Films.

Coppola, Francis Ford, dir. 1972. *The Godfather, Part I*. Perf. Al Pacino, Marlon Brando. Paramount Pictures.

De Stefano, George. 2006. *An Offer We Can't Refuse: The Mafia in the Mind of America*. New York: Faber and Faber.

Dika, Vera. 2000. The Representation of Ethnicity in *The Godfather*. In *Francis Ford Coppola's "The Godfather" Trilogy*, ed. Nick Browne, 76-107. Cambridge: Cambridge University Press.

Houston, John, dir. 1985. *Prizzi's Honour*. Perf. Jack Nicholson, Kathleen Turner, Anjelica Houston. ABC.

Mason, Fran. 2002. *American Gangster Cinema: From "Little Caesar" to "Pulp Fiction"*. Houndsmills: Palgrave.

Mottram, James J. 2000. *The Coen Brothers: The Life of the Mind*. London: Butler and Tanner.

Puzo, Mario. 1969. *The Godfather*. London: Heinemann.

Ramis, Harold, dir. 1999. *Analyze This*. Perf. Robert DeNiro, Billy Crystal. Warner Bros.

Trail, Armitage. 1997. *Scarface*. London: Bloomsbury.

Anna Mazurkiewicz
University of Gdańsk, Poland
Coverage of Polish presidential elections (1989-2005) in the *New York Times* and *Chicago Tribune*

Until 1980s majority of Americans considered communist-dominated Poland as one of many captive nations in East Central Europe. The birth of "Solidarity" and its subsequent crackdown by the imposition of martial law changed the popular perception of Poland and Poles in the US to more friendly and sympathetic (Mazurkiewicz, 2009, 97-121). As the compromise reached during the Round Table Talks of 1989 paved a way for a peaceful transition to democracy and set a precedent for other nations of the area, the American media observed developments in Poland with growing interest. While inquiring how long this "sentimental" interest lasted, this paper attempts to present the evolution and differences in opinions expressed in the US on Poland's maturing democracy. Based on the evaluation of Poland's leaders from an American perspective, the central question that I want to address is: How did the American image of Poland change from the fall of communism to current times.

I am aware that the examination of the American interest in the process of building democracy in Poland should be conducted on different levels including at least: diplomacy, international politics, economic relations and migration history, public opinion polls and content analysis of both public and private American media. However, with the purpose of revealing the main, altering trends in American attitude towards post-Communist Poland I have decided to select and compare corresponding sets of sources i.e. American press reports on Polish presidential elections over the sixteen year span.

The decision to pick the coverage of popular elections comes from a well rooted conviction that they embody democracy's essence: people's choice. If democratic government rests on the axiom that "the supreme power is retained by the people" (CIA 2007, xviii), then the foreign media observations on the periodically renewed electoral process leading to exercising this power indirectly (through a system of representation, and delegated authority) are well worth analysis.

Furthermore, the evolution of the American attitude to any given presidential candidate or incumbent office holder was more feasible to study than the ever changing Polish party formations. In addition, the regularity of direct presidential elections between 1990 and 2005 (with the exception of the 1989 election of Wojciech Jaruzelski) offered a chance for a snapshot look at changes that took place in Poland. In the period that I will consider, voter turnout in presidential elections has always been higher compared to parliamentary elections. The record (68.2%) was set in the second round of balloting in 1995, when Lech Walesa faced Aleksander Kwasniewski in the race for the Polish presidency (Lisiak

2005). Only recently, in 2007, the voter turnout in parliamentary elections (53.88%) was higher than in the preceding presidential elections in 2005 (50.99%), which means that there was an increased number of voters in parliamentary elections and a decreased number in the presidential vote. However, this most recent turn, promptly observed by the Americans (Ek 2008, 2) lies outside of the scope of this analysis.

Reporting to the American people, the US journalists not only chronicled but also evaluated the progress of developing democracy in Poland. Thus its readers were able to learn if people were free to voice their opinions, if the election's results were not manipulated, and whether civil society was emerging. The latter feature of a young democratic country could be observed both on the basis of voter turnout, as well as on people's connection to their leaders, thus answering questions concerning the Polish leaders' legitimacy. I find it especially interesting to look into the matter of maturing democracy in Poland from the vantage point of the longest modern, uninterrupted and effective democratic tradition in the world. Especially that such analysis allows us to look into both the evolution of Poland's image in America and the changes observed in the US press.

On the basis of the research conducted to date (Mazurkiewicz 2002), I have decided to limit my analysis to two major US dailies: The *New York Times* and *Chicago Tribune*. This particular choice is justifiable for a number of reasons i.e.: they represent entirely different editorial policy, their political preferences can be contrasted as liberal vs. conservative respectively, their readership is as different as the cosmopolitan Big Apple is to the American Midwest. Moreover, they use different news services and syndicates. Although the *New York Time*'s circulation vastly surpasses that of the *Chicago Tribune* both are regarded as opinion leaders and hence offer an opportunity of comparing diverse points of view.

1. The papers: Big Apple vs. Windy City

The *New York Times*, established in 1851 is currently the third largest American daily. Four years older than its New York counterpart, with roughly half the circulation, the *Chicago Tribune*, is currently the eighth most read daily in the US (BurrellesLuce 2008). However, long-term comparison of their circulation shows that despite significant domination by the *New York Times*, both papers suffered a significant decrease in their circulation from 1995 to 2008. While twenty years earlier (from 1974 to 1995) the New York's paper saw a significant increase in its circulation, *Chicago Tribune* already faced stagnation and a sharp drop in sold copies of its Sunday Edition. By 1998 the *New York Times'* average daily circulation was over million copies (1 066 658), while *Chicago Tribune* lagged behind with 673 508 issues. (*Time* 1974; Almanac 1996; Facts About Newspapers 1999, 18).

The New York paper's supremacy over the *Chicago Tribune* comes from the fact that nearly half of its circulation lies outside the New York metropolitan area, whereas the *Chicago Tribune* focuses on the Windy City and its vicinity. According to the anniversary publication, the transformation of The *New York Times* into a truly national newspaper begun in 1980, when the paper first began publishing a national edition (McFadden 2001; Golka 2004, 144-156; 169-172).

The *New York Times'* traditional editorial policy "All the News That's Fit to Print" was introduced by Adolph S. Ochs, when he purchased the paper in 1896 thus saving it from bankruptcy (Friel and Falk 2004, 89-90). The line is still printed by the paper in the top, left corner on its front page. In terms of political views, this New York's paper is commonly regarded as representing liberal bias (Okrent 2004b, 4:2).

As early as 1940 the *New York Times* pages indicated a global outlook. Later, at the times of rising competition with television, the paper's owners decided to invest into foreign correspondence, focusing mainly on providing information rather than commentary. With the escalation of the cold war, and the growth of US foreign entanglements, the *New York Times* soon became a paper of the record in the area of American foreign policy (Shepard 1996, 166-186).

In the beginning of 1990s the *New York Times* managed to uphold its leader's position in the arena of foreign relations coverage. However, with the 2003 revelations of misinformation and plain lies published by the paper (Jayson Blair and Judith Miller affairs) serious doubts regarding *New York Times'* credibility surfaced (Herbert 2003, A21; Steinberg 2003, A31; Friel and Falk 2004, 104-114; Okrent 2004a). Nevertheless, the paper won the highest number of Pulitzer Prizes (100, plus 59 finalists) thus exceeding all competing newspapers (Pulitzer Prizes, 2009).

Although the *Chicago Tribune*'s staff won far less Pulitzer Prizes compared to the *New York Times*, the journalists who occupy editorial desks at the Tribune are not self-deprecating. The editors of the paper gladly oversaw the Tribune print additional line underneath the title: "The world's greatest newspaper." Although this slogan is no longer printed on the front page, the Tribune Company had it registered as a trademark already in 1910, and renewed five times since then – most recently in 2001 (USPTO-TARR, 2011). Isolationist turned anti-Communist, leaning towards the Republican Party, the *Chicago Tribune* was commonly recognized as a conservative publication in an American Midwest state with a visible Polish ethnic minority. Especially on the electoral map of American politics, the importance of the city's concentration of ethnic Poles cannot be underestimated.

Therefore, not surprisingly, Chicago's biggest newspaper provided its readers with interesting coverage on developments in Poland in 1980s and from

1989 to 1995 it continued to dispatch several of its correspondents to cover the presidential elections in Poland. However, during the 2000 and 2005 elections it chose to rely on its European correspondent Tom Hundley to cover the events.

Whereas editorial commentaries constituted a significant 9% of all articles on Polish elections that appeared in the Tribune, in all, a third of its coverage on Poland came from "the wire" (Associated Press, Reuters and other news services) including 5% from The *New York Times*' News Service. The key reporters who sent information on Poland combined authored little over 40% of the total election coverage. J. A. Reaves authored 17% of all articles on Poland's elections, which was more than any other of the correspondents in Poland: Tom Hundley (14%), Paula Batturini (7%), and Robin McNulty (2%).

In the case of the *New York Times*, the sources of information on Poland 1989-1995 were dominated not by the wires (12%), but by correspondents' coverage. The single highest contributor was Stephen Engelberg, whose reporting from Poland constituted 36% of all articles. Following his lead were Jane Perlez (17%) and John Tagliabue (9%). Occasionally Henry Kamm (2%), A. M. Rosenthal (3%) and others wrote on the Polish elections. All in all, foreign correspondents' reporting generated 67% of all articles devoted to Polish elections (1989-1995). What is interesting in the case of the *New York Times* is the relatively low percentage of editorial commentary devoted to the Polish electoral process – 4% of all articles.

The sharp contrast between the insignificant number of articles devoted to the Polish elections in more recent times, 2000-2005, and in 1989-1995 is striking. In both papers' cases the pieces written by correspondents from Poland were a minority compared to the number of wire-based articles. Moreover, the single digit number of articles devoted to the presidential elections in Poland (2000-2005) coincides with the changed character of both the commentary and nature of their coverage. Compared to the earlier years' political reshuffling, the more recent elections arose little interest, Polish economic and international relations receiving far more attention. Based on looking at those years it may be observed that although the events in Poland were no longer making the headlines, they were still considered of concern to the American interests in the region.

In the year 2000, the *Chicago Tribune*'s Tom Hundley wrote on the presidential election, but his correspondence was outnumbered by the wire-based coverage. The single name that dominated the *New York Times*' coverage on Polish politics in 2000 was that of Steven Erlanger, Central European bureau chief.

Just like in 1989, sixteen years later the presidential elections were preceded by the parliamentary ones, by just a few weeks. Since the key players: major parties' leaders and presidential candidates were the same people (Donald Tusk), or brothers (Jaroslaw and Lech Kaczynski) the press commentary focused on the Kaczynski brothers-Tusk rivalry and oftentimes it referred to both ballots in the same text.

In 2005, the *Chicago Tribune*'s Tom Hundley, who had briefly returned to Poland to cover the elections, wrote only two articles from Warsaw. All in all, four ballot-related articles appeared in the Chicago's paper. . Naturally, there were more publications on Poland regarding for example the country's economic growth, travel and alleged CIA run jails. Still, juxtaposed against the period 1989-1995, the period 2000-2005 is hardly comparable in terms of coverage. Even though the discrepancy is large, when comparing the *New York Times'* coverage of the 2005 election to its Chicago based counterpart it is possible to see double the number of pieces on Polish elections in the Big Apple's paper. That was at least partly due to the work of the *Times'* European correspondents (from Berlin, Frankfurt, or Paris offices), but also thanks to the journalists working for the International Herald Tribune, which since 2003 was owned exclusively by the *New York Times*. Therefore, undoubtedly, throughout the period analyzed the *New York Times* continued to surpass the *Chicago Tribune* both in foreign coverage abilities and space devoted to it. How different was their coverage on Poland, or was it?

The comparative analysis of both papers' coverage of elections in Poland, from Wojciech Jaruzelski (1989) to Lech Kaczynski (2005), may help to unveil not only the changing American attitude towards Poland but also differences in interpreting the political changes occurring in one of the many countries of East-Central Europe. Focusing on Polish leaders' portrayal in the American daily press the reader shall observe which of the presidents was found the most promising, and was presented as offering the biggest chances for political stabilization and economic development, enhancing Polish-American cooperation. How did the opinion on Lech Walesa change? Was Wojciech Jaruzelski's image unilateral? Was Aleksander Kwasniewski's election perceived as the return of the old guard? How did American journalists interpret the Kaczynski brothers' victories in both the presidential and the parliamentary elections in 2005? Despite the dramatic changes occurring in Poland, are there any common themes of continuity to be found in their presentation in the selected dailies? Was the picture of Poland created by the *Chicago Tribune* and the *New York Times* different? How did it evolve? What does their coverage on Poland tell us about the papers themselves?

2. The year of the great change: 1989

By the late 1980s nobody could have predicted how the communist regime would respond to democratic reforms. Right before the parliamentary elections of 1989, the American National Public Radio reported: "Polish leader general Wojciech Jaruzelski today hinted he might use a show of force to maintain the social order. Jaruzelski made the statement on state run television just two days before Poland's partially free elections in more than 40 years" (NPR, Jun. 2, 1989).

Just a little over a month later, the same general Jaruzelski was the only candidate to run for the office of president. The post was reinstated on the basis of the Round Table Agreements and its holder was to be elected by the National Assembly. According to these Agreements signed on April 5th, while the parliamentary elections to the upper chamber of the National Assembly (Senate) were to be free, balloting for the lower chamber (Sejm) was restricted. Majority of seats were guaranteed for the communists and their allies. Only 35% of the seats in the Sejm were designated for open contest, which meant that any candidate, not only Solidarity-supported one, could run (Borodziej and Garlicki 2004, 10-12).

The results of the first round of balloting which took place on June 4th, 1989 were shocking to both the regime and the Solidarity. The popular rejection of the regime was sweeping. The regime's so-called "national list" which had been designed to assure top communist party leadership's swift election to the lower chamber of the Polish parliament was entirely rejected by the voters who tended to cross out all the names listed on it. Few of the other communist recommended candidates to the Sejm were elected during the first round of voting. None of the regime's candidates got elected to the country's newly reinstated Senate, to which balloting was free and unrestricted, i.e. with no quotas for the communists. The final results of the elections, after the unavoidable, second round of balloting (June 18th) indicated that 99 out of 100 seats in the Senate were taken by the Solidarity-affiliated candidates, as were all openly contested 161 seats in the Sejm.

As there are 560 members of the National Assembly, the number of votes needed for Jaruzelski's election was 281 (50%+1). The Polish United Workers Party (PUWP) with its allies (Social Democrats, Peasants et al.) theoretically could have provided a sufficient 299 majority. However, the PUWP's formerly faithful coalition partners could no longer be trusted. On election day, July 19th, 537 valid votes were cast, which caused prolonged deliberations as to whether the ballot should be secret and what would be the number necessary for Jaruzelski's election (537:2 = 268.5). Some deputies argued that 50% was not 268 but 269, and therefore the number of votes needed to elect Jaruzelski was 270. Eventually, the members of the National Assembly voted openly and agreed that the simple majority would be 270 votes. That turned out to be exactly the number of votes that the general received. Had it not been for Solidarity's tacit support his election would have not been possible (Sprawozdanie Stenograficzne 1989).

Both of the papers noticed this "hairbreadth victory," election without a single vote to spare. Their interest in the Polish developments was significant. In the months of June and July 1989 the *New York Times* published 72 articles on Polish developments, while the *Chicago Tribune* published 48. Two days after the election the *New York Times* published the following commentary: "Gen. Wojciech Jaruzelski won election to Poland's new, more powerful presidency by the narrowest of margins Wednesday. Yet in a sense he now has a broader mandate than past Communist leaders who claimed 99.9 percent support. That's because his victory was made possible only by the freely decided action of freely elected Solidarity members of the new Parliament" (Poland's Mandate and Challenge 1989, A.28). A day earlier its Chicago counterpart published the following correspondence from Paula Batturini: "This hairbreadth victory was a reminder that the society blamed Jaruzelski for the imposition of martial law" (Batturini 1989b, C4).

A day later the *New York Times* correspondent in Warsaw John Tagliabue cited Solidarity leaders' later saying that supporting Jaruzelski was a big mistake, which cost them their credibility (Tagilabue 1989, 12). His colleague working for the *Chicago Tribune* consequently focused her attention on Jaruzelski's leadership of the violent crackdown aimed at destroying Solidarity in 1981 (Batturini 1989a).

While the New York paper focused on implications coming from the fact that the general's election was possible due to freely orchestrated, indirect support of Solidarity members who invalidated their ballots, the Chicago paper interpreted the election result as a punishment for imposing martial law. The difference in coverage was noticeable. However, if compared to the opinion piece entitled: "Jaruzelski: General to Jailor to Poland's Savior," published in the *Los Angeles Times* by a former *New York Times* correspondent (Szulc 1989, 1:5) it seems that the *New York Times*' commentaries were not as openly supportive of Jaruzelski's role in Poland. At least not in 1989.

Commentaries openly favorable to Jaruzelski – so striking in light of his image from the early 1980s – appeared in bigger numbers in 1990, when it was obvious that he was about to relinquish his powers peacefully to provide for the first free presidential election in Poland since pre-war times (Mazurkiewicz 2005, 67-96).

3. First popular presidential election: 1990

In May 1990, the then third largest American daily – *Los Angeles Times* published on its front page an article by Charles T. Powers under the headline: King Lech No Longer Royalty, calling him "Lech the Tiresome" (Powers 1990a, A1). As Walesa begun his "war on top," turning against his former allies, aides and colleagues, and increased his criticism directed at the first non-Communist prime minister, Tadeusz Mazowiecki, the general tone of the American press towards Solidarity's hero was already changing to a less favorable one. His public statements that he had the moral right to become president, and that he did not want to but had to, put the majority of American reporters off (Mazurkiewicz 2004). Given the broader context of the US press' reaction to Walesa's moves, the two dailies under analysis here, gave Walesa relatively big credit of trust. By spring of 1990 the *New York Times* observed: "Listening to Lech Walesa talk politics is like staring at an Impressionist painting from two inches away: It doesn't make sense unless you take a few steps back and view the whole canvas" (Stephen Engelberg 1990a). The *Chicago Tribune*'s evaluation of the opposition leader was simply glowing: the paper's editors called Walesa the "antidote to populism," "not a demagogue," "not an intellectual but a man of genius instinct," who was "equipped with [a] genius sense of popular mood" (Krymkowski 1990). This evaluation was printed before the first round of balloting in the first popular presidential election in Poland ever.

The results that came out after the election of November 25th were as shocking to the American observers as they were to Poles themselves. A "Man from Twin Peaks" (Powers 1990b, A 1:6) or "A candidate from Mars" (Szulecki 1990, A14:5) received more votes than the first non-Communist Prime Minister. Stanislaw Tyminski's sudden political career aroused doubts as to whether a man residing in Canada, holding three citizenships (Canadian, Peruvian and Polish) was even eligible to run in the presidential election. As explained by Andrzej Zoll, just because there were no legal provisions requiring that a candidate reside in Poland, he was eventually allowed to run (Zoll 2000, 13).

The first free election in post-Communist Poland turned out to be democracy's first tough lesson. The perils of Tyminski's unexpectedly good showing were noticed by the US press. Having obtained 23.1% of the vote he was to face Lech Walesa (39.96%) in the runoff on December 9th, his odds of winning being hard to predict by the foreign observers (PKW 1990a, 5-6).

The *New York Times* which arguably favored Mazowiecki called his result a "vote of protest" (Engelberg 1990b, 8). Although leaning more towards Walesa than Mazowiecki, the *Chicago Tribune* felt sorry for the prime minister whose "embarrassing" result was considered to be the price paid for economic reforms that brought even more hardships to people already disadvantaged under Communism (Pfaff 1990, C3).

Walesa's run for the presidency became an example of the continuing experimental path of political and economic reforms in Poland. No precedent existed for dismantling the Communist system. Therefore Poland was a test case for many observers, both in the West and in the former Eastern Bloc. With the unexpected turn of events – both papers not only openly supported Walesa in the runoff but began ridiculing Tyminski. Once the results were in and it became obvious that Walesa won a splendid victory receiving a stunning 74.25% of the popular vote (PKW 1990b, 115) – the biggest voice of support ever expressed in the history of the Third Republic – the *Chicago Tribune* called Tyminski "a spy, who aimed at orchestrating counterrevolution" (Reaves 1990). This was a sigh of relief rather than celebration of victory. Tyminski's surprise showing in Poland with his Peruvian wife, his unconventional campaign methods (suffice it to mention that he continued to publicly threaten Walesa with a material he supposedly had in a black briefcase) and the shockingly good first round result gave rise to widely circulating gossips that he was some kind of a foreign spy, or an agent of the *ancient regime*.

Interestingly enough, Walesa who before the second round of votes was represented almost as an incipient dictator – in the second round became a savior – the only man who could save Poles .... from themselves. However with the election over, the *New York Times* returned to the original question on Walesa's political abilities. Just two days after the runoff, the editors of the New York paper asked: "Is Walesa really a Democrat" (Editorial 1990, 26)?

The general tone of the post-election commentaries published in the US press focused on the new divisions that characterized Poland. It was no longer divided along the ideological and political lines that had distanced the opposition from the regime; Poles were split along economic and educational lines. Poverty, lack of prospects, and disillusionment with politics were replacing the optimism and the hopes that had been put into the process of transformation (Mazurkiewicz 2004). Low voter turnout during the 1991 parliamentary elections (43%) confirmed those opinions. However by 1993, over half of adult Poles decided to go to polls and choose their representatives in the National Assembly. This time the results indicated a rejection of the post-Solidarity rule. Both Sejm and Senate's majorities went to a newly created post-Communist Alliance of the Democratic Left (Sojusz Lewicy Demokratycznej), based on the newly established social democratic party.

4. The return of the old guard?

Although at one point there were seventeen candidates registered to run for the post of president, with Walesa's first presidential term coming to a close in 1995, from the outset of the campaign the US press focused its attention on the Walesa-Kwasniewski rivalry. However the American journalists did not consider Kwasniewski's successful campaign as a sign of a return of the old guard. Instead the 1995 presidential election was presented as a particular threshold, a meeting between the past and the future (Spolar 1995, A21).

Both papers under analysis here interpreted the rivalry in a similar style but with entirely different emphasis. While the *New York Times* wrote that young Poles view Walesa as an emblem of the past, an "ancient history" (Perlez 1995a, 1.10), the *Chicago Tribune* stated firmly: "ex-communists cannot be trusted" (Hundley 1995a, C3). Interestingly enough, while Kwasniewski's political orientation was interchangeably described as social democrat, post-Communist, ex-Communist, or former Communist, he was the one who was recognized as the much younger and media savvy embodiment of modernity, Walesa was most commonly referred to as an emblem of the past.

Generally, Kwasniewski was presented as Walesa's antithesis. More information was given on his personality than on his career within the ranks of the Communist party.

In November, debates between Walesa and Kwasniewski aired on the Polish national television station prompted comparisons to the 1960 Nixon-Kennedy debates (Perlez 1995b, 10). Surprisingly enough, it was Walesa who looked old, tired and weary, whereas Kwasniewski appeared freshly minted, and much younger than the eleven year age difference might have suggested.

While the *Chicago Tribune* presented the electoral process as an old-style confrontation, "Walesa Foe Face Off at Electoral Crossroads" (Hundley 1995a, C3), on the same day the *New York Times* emphasized the changes that occurred in Poland's politics, "Media wise Walesa's Foe Copies Style of Clinton." (Perlez 1995c, 4). Both papers analyzed Kwasniewski's campaign by looking for recent US based presidential campaign examples: Perlez by simply calling it "Clintonesque" (Perlez 1995c, 4); Hundley by writing that Clinton was Kwasniewski's role model (Hundley 1995a, C3).

In the runoff Walesa lost his bid for reelection by 3.4% (PKW 1995a, 304). In both papers the election results were covered as a Churchill-like fall of the great hero, who won the war but lost the election, but at the same time, Kwasniewski's victory was not interpreted as a holdup of political and economic reforms (The Fall of a Polish Patriot 1995, 20; Hundley 1995b, N1).

In sum, the dominant theme of the US dailies analyzed hereby was that the choice made by the Poles meant choosing the future over the past and that Walesa's failure to win a second term was predominantly considered to be his personal failure, not the country's departure from the democratic path. Soon Kwasniewski proved to be the president who would receive the most favorable coverage in the American press to date of any Polish leader.

5. One man match: 2000

Kwasniewski's first term in office concluded with Poland's membership in NATO and probable admission to the European Union. The presidential campaign of 2000 got the least coverage of all aforementioned. What seemed as a swift reelection was perceived as a sign of stabilization.

This time however the differences between the two papers showed all too clearly. One of the hot issues of the rather dull campaign was a presidential candidate screening process – employed for the first time before a Polish election. All thirteen candidates had to state openly if they ever cooperated with the Communist regime's intelligence or security services. While the *New York*

Times' Tina Rosenberg wrote: "Even if Mr. Kwasniewski had been an informer, that would be irrelevant today. He presided over Poland's accession to NATO" (Rosenberg 2000, A18:1). The *Chicago Tribune* was openly critical of the likely reelection: "Kwasniewski, little-known outside Poland, is everything that Walesa is not: smooth, tan, neat dresser and an unapologetic member of what was once Poland's Communist Party" (Hundley 2000). So, while one paper stressed the irrelevance of the past, the other implied that the social democratic coalition is nothing more than the continuation of the Communist party.

Out of Kwasniewski's many opponents, it was the leader of the Solidarity's Electoral Action (AWS), victorious in the 1997 parliamentary elections – Marian Krzaklewski that grasped most attention. Second in the race for the presidency – Andrzej Olechowski – was mentioned only briefly. However, while presenting the situation in Poland in 2000 the *New York Times* focused not only on the politics, predicting Marian Krzaklewski's humiliating defeat, but mostly on gathering ordinary people's opinions on how their lives improved during the ten years of reforms. Stephen Erlanger who travelled in Poland around the time of the election presented a picture of a country doing much better than it felt. "The signs of new prosperity are all over Poland" – asserted *New York Times'* correspondent. (Erlanger 2000, A1). The picture painted by the *Tribune's* correspondents was not that positive. A report from Lech Walesa's conference in Olsztyn was sent from a "tidy but struggling city," the workers were "the group that has been left behind by the rapid transformation of Poland's economy" and Lech Walesa himself was "like the polka - an instantly recognizable symbol of Poland for the outside world, but an object of scorn and ridicule within the country" (Hundley 2000). Still however, the Chicago paper's focus on Walesa is rather striking in the face of the (foreseeable) election results.

President Kwasniewski won his re-election with 53.9% of the vote in the first ballot, which was interpreted as a sign of consolidation of democracy in Poland. Lech Walesa, running for a third time in a row, got 1.01% of the vote (PKW 2000).

6. Eyes on Poland again 2005

Within the next five years the American interest in the political developments in Poland increased again. In the first presidential race since Poland joined the European Union, the first in the post 9/11 world, for the first time two post-Solidarity parties confronted each other with no major competitor from the post-Communist, or generally speaking, left side of the political scene. From the *Tribune's* perspective the Polish elections revolved around the "Europe-wide issue of just how far to go in sacrificing old welfare state protections for the promise of an American-style economy" (Gera 2005, 5).

The fact that twin brothers – Jaroslaw and Lech Kaczynski – were running for both of the country's top posts was also a factor in the increased coverage in the US. As mentioned before, both parliamentary and presidential elections took place only fourteen days apart. It was in 2005 that for the first time in the short history of popular election of the president of Poland the first round winner lost in the runoff. It was at this time that the differences between the *Chicago Tribune* and the *New York Times* are to be observed most clearly.

Both post-Solidarity leaders running for the presidency were presented in a manner that left no doubt to the reader whom the paper favors. The *New York Times*' description said: "Mr. Tusk has long been a committed free marketer, believing that Poland needs to reduce regulation, social spending and taxes to spur economic growth ... Mr. Kaczynski has been a kind of big-government conservative – a social democrat on economic matters but a deeply religious traditionalist on issues like divorce, abortion and homosexual rights." (Bernstein 2005).

In an article published on the same day, the *Chicago Tribune* presented Donald Tusk as "a pro-business candidate committed to stimulating entrepreneurship with low taxes and deregulation," and Lech Kaczynski as "a pro-market lawmaker and Warsaw's socially conservative mayor ... [who] wants to keep Poland's Roman Catholic values reflected in the law, for instance by preserving anti-abortion laws and preventing same-sex marriages" (Gera 2005, 5).

The differences in tones are slight, by reading both papers an American reader may get the impression that both Polish candidates could be branded Republicans; Tusk in the field of economics, Kaczynski in social matters. The meaning of presenting Tusk in the New York paper as an ardent follower of the free market ideology vs. a candidate opposed to the areas of civil rights already acknowledged by the majority of US society leaves no doubt as to which candidate is favored. Furthermore, the cosmopolitan Big Apple's paper, focusing mainly on the foreign affairs programs dismissed Kaczynski's ideas as bad, particularly in regards to future Polish policy towards Russia and Germany (Dempsey 2005, A13).

In the case of the *Chicago Tribune*, pro-business Tusk is contrasted with pro-market Kaczynski, who by the way wants the traditional values to be reflected in the county's laws. Given the fact that the daily from Chicago printed more and better photos of Lech Kaczynski, devoted more space to describe his Solidarity-related biography and went as far as to compare the Kaczynski brothers to the Kennedys and Bush brothers leaves no doubt which paper underscored which candidate (Hundley 2005, 1.1). If there only was a clear-cut distinction between liberal and conservative groups on the ever changing Polish political scene both papers would have undoubtedly underscored opposite parties.

7. Conclusion

As the presidential elections proved to be defining moments of Poland's recent history, they attained the biggest attention of the two analyzed dailies in 1990. Within the next 10 years it was reduced to almost negligible. The dynamic changes in Poland resulted in striking changes in the perception of Polish leaders. One rose from a traitor to Poland's savior, the other fell from a hero to a villain. Furthermore, of all of Poland's presidents elected after 1989, surprisingly enough it was the post-communist leader whose election received the most favorable treatment by the American media. As a matter of fact, it is in this case that the difference between the editorial policies between the two dailies was most clearly observed.

Whereas in the elections of 1989, 1990 and 1995 the stakes were much higher – with the future of Poland uncertain in both economics and politics – the perils of the reestablished and maturing Polish democracy were widely reported and commented in both of the analyzed papers. During that time, the editorial coverage of the dailies went rather along similar paths. Over those electoral years the single, common point of interest and analysis was Lech Walesa.

However, by 1995 differences between the *New York Times* and the *Chicago Tribune* started to take shape, becoming clearer by the year 2000. As Poland's political situation became more stable, the US press' biases were mirrored in their approach to the Polish leaders. Moreover, while the *New York Times* tended to evaluate the Polish political leaders on the basis of their policy plans and perspectives they bore for the future, thus showing a more pragmatic, future-oriented approach, the *Chicago Tribune* showed a more historical approach focusing its attention on their to-date records.

All in all, by 2005 Poland was no longer evaluated on the grounds of the system's stability but on the basis of the political programs, economic progress, and foreign policy plans of the candidates. Indirect adaptation of the American political philosophy was reflected in the application of editorial policy to articles published on Poland. Liberal vs. conservative was thus confirmed.

Despite the momentous changes that occurred in Poland between 1989 and 2005, I observe similarities in the American outlook on Poland's political scene. One of the common themes to be found in the political commentaries is that – despite the fast growing economy, Poland's accession to NATO and European Union – the Poles were still divided between those future-oriented and those possessed by the past.

The final conclusion of this analysis of the articles published by the Chicago's and New York's leading dailies is that between 1989 and 2005, Poland's political, strategic and economic place has definitely changed. The editors and journalists of both newspapers no longer evaluated Poland's political stability and democratic standards, but interpreted the changes outlined by the incoming leaders' in the light of Poland's foreign policy and economic progress.

References

Almanac. 1996. Information Please, Atlas & Yearbook 1996. Boston, New York.

Batturini, Paula. 1989a. Jaruzelski No Regrets for Martial Law in 1981. *Chicago Tribune*, July 18.

------. 1989b. Jaruzelski Wins Polish Presidency. *Chicago Tribune*, July 20.

Bernstein, Richard. 2005. Polish Election Appears Headed for a Runoff. *New York Times*, October 10.

Borodziej, Włodzimierz, and Andrzej Garlicki, eds. 2004. *Okrągły Stół. Dokumenty i materiały [Round Table. Documents and Papers]*. Vol. 4. Warsaw.

BurellesLuce. 2008. *Top Newspapers, Blogs & Consumer Magazines*. http://www.burrellesluce.com/top100/2008_Top_100List.pdf (accessed June 17, 2008).

Central Intelligence Agency. 2007. *The CIA World Factbook 2008*. New York: Skyhorse Publishing Company Inc.

Dempsey, Judy. 2005. Warsaw Mayor is Poised to Win Runoff in Poland. *New York Times*, October 24.

Ek, Carl. 2008. Poland's New Government: Background and Issues for the United States. *Congressional Research Service Report for Congress*, February 15, www.fas.org/sgp/crs/row/RS22811.pdf *(accessed June 15, 2008)*.

Engelberg, Stephen. 1990a. There is a Method to Walesa's Meandering. *New York Times*, April 15.

------. 1990b. Émigré From Canada Running Well in Poland. *New York Times*, November 19.

Erlanger, Stephen. 2000. Despite Soaring Prosperity, Poland Still Isn't Sure of Itself. *New York Times*, August 25.

Facts About Newspapers. 1999. *A Statistical Summary of the Newspaper Industry Published by the Newspaper Association of America*. http://www.naa.org/info/facts99/ (accessed May 25, 2008).

The Fall of a Polish Patriot. 1995. Editorial. *New York Times*, November 21.

Friel, Howard, and Richard Falk. 2004. *The Record of the Paper. How the New York Times Misreports US Foreign Policy*. New York: Verso.

Gera, Vanessa. 2005. In Poland, Close Presidential Vote Likely to End in the Runoff. *Chicago Tribune*, October 10.

Golka, Bartłomiej. 2004. *System medialny Stanów Zjednoczonych. [Media System in the United States]*. Warsaw: WSIP.

Herbert, Bob. 2003. Truth, Lies and Subtext. *New York Times*, May 19.

Hundley, Tom. 1995a. Walesa Foe Face Off at Electoral Crossroads. *Chicago Tribune*, November 19.

------. 1995b. Legendary Wałęsa Breathes Fire In Defeat. *Chicago Tribune*, November 21.

------. 2000. Lech Walesa No Longer Electrifies Fellow Poles. *Chicago Tribune*, September 17.

------. 2005. Polish Electorate Gets Double Vision. *Chicago Tribune*, August 1.

Krymkowski, Daniel H. 1990. Poles Need Walesa's Steadying Hand. Editorial. *Chicago Tribune*, November 19.

Lisiak, Marcin, ed. 2005. Komunikat z konferencji prasowej Państwowej Komisji Wyborczej w dniu 7 października 2005 r. o godz. 12:00 [Polish Electoral Commission's Press Communiqué of October 7, 2005]. Warsaw: PKW. http://www.pkw.gov.pl/pkw2/index.jsp?place=Lead07&news_cat_id=1829&news_id=6341&layout=1&page=text (accessed February 12, 2008).

Making Poland's Democracy Work. 1990. Editorial. *New York Times*, December 11.

Mazurkiewicz, Anna. 2002. Wybory prezydenckie w Polsce w latach 1989-1995 w zwierciadle opiniotwórczej prasy północnoamerykańskiej [Polish Presidential Elections (1989-1995) in the Opinion Leading Titles of the American Press]. *Zeszyty Prasoznawcze* 1-2: 107-124.

------. 2004. Polish Presidents 1947-2000 from the American Vantage Point. *East European Quarterly* 37: 4.

------. 2005. American Attitudes on Two Attempts to Establish Democracy in Poland, 1947 and 1989. *Polish American Studies* 62: 1.

-----. 2009. *Wolne i nieskrępowane? Prasa amerykańska wobec wyborów w Polsce w latach 1947 i 1989. [Free and Unfettered? American Press and Elections in Poland in 1947 and 1898]*. Gdańsk: Wydawnictwo Uniwersytetu Gdańskiego.

McFadden, Robert D. 2001. 150th Anniversary: 1851-2001: 150 and Counting: The Story So Far. *New York Times*, November 14.

NPR (National Public Radio). 1989. *All Things Considered Archival Audio Recording*. BurellesLuce CDRom.

Okrent, Daniel. 2004a. Weapons of Mass Destruction? Or Mass Distraction? *New York Times*, May 30.

------. 2004b. Is The New York Times a Liberal Newspaper? *New York Times*, July 25.

Perlez, Jane. 1995a. Young Poles view Walesa as Passé. *New York Times*, November 12.

------. 1995b. Nixon-Kennedy Move-Over! *New York Times*, November 16.

------. 1995c. Media wise Walesa's Foe Copies Style of Clinton. *New York Times*, November 19.

154   Anna Mazurkiewicz

Pfaff, William. 1990. Walesa Must Win. *Chicago Tribune*, December 9.
PKW. 1990a. Wyniki głosowania w dniu 25 listopada 1990 r. [Election Results of November 25, 1990]. Warsaw.
------. 1990b. Wyniki ponownego głosowania w dniu 9 grudnia 1990 r. [Results of the Second Round of Balloting on December 9, 1990]. Warsaw.
------. 1995. Wyniki głosowania w dniu 19 listopada 1995 r. Sprawozdanie Państwowej Komisji Wyborczej [November 19, 1995 Election Results. State Electoral Commission's Report]. Warsaw.
------. 2000. Protokół o wynikach glosowania na kandydatów na prezydenta RP przeprowadzonego w dniu 8 października 2000 r. [Polish Presidential Elections Results' Protocol of October 8, 2000]. Warsaw. www.pkw.gov.pl (accessed March 1, 2009).
------. 2005. Wybory Prezydenta Rzeczypospolitej Polskiej zarządzone na dzień 9 października 2005 r. [Polish Presidential Elections Ordered to Take Place on October 9, 2005]. Warsaw. http://www.wybory2005.pkw.gov.pl/PZT1/PL/WYN/W/index.htm (accessed February 13, 2008).
Poland's Mandate and Challenge. 1989. Editorial. *New York Times*, July 21.
Powers, Charles T. 1990a. King Lech No Longer Royalty. *Los Angeles Times*, May 20.
------. 1990b. Walesa Headed for Landslide Polish Victory. *Los Angeles Times*, December 10.
Pulitzer Prizes Web Page. http://www.pulitzer.org/ (accessed March 12, 2009).
Reaves, J. A. 1990. Walesa Gets Landslide. *Chicago Tribune*, December 16.
Rosenberg, Tina. 2000. A Polish Election Vexed by Communist Spies. *New York Times*, August 11.
Shepard, Richard F. 1996. *The Paper's Papers. A Reporter's Journey Through the Archives of the New York Times*. New York: Random House.
Spolar, Christine. 1995. Polish Voters Face Choice of Memories. *Washington Post*, November 18.
Sprawozdanie Stenograficzne z posiedzenia Zgromadzenia Narodowego Polskiej Rzeczpospolitej Ludowej. 1989. Warsaw.
Steinberg, Jacques. 2003. Editor of Times Tells Staff He Accepts Blame for Fraud. *New York Times*, May 15.
Szulc, Tad. 1989. Jaruzelski: General to Jailor to Poland's Savior. *Los Angeles Times*, August 27.
Szulecki, Witold Jarosław. 1990. The New Force in Poland Is Candidate "From Mars". *New York Times*, November 27.
Tagilabue, John. 1989. Support for Jaruzelski Splits Solidarity. *New York Times*, July 21. *Time Magazine*, 1974, January 21.
Trademark Registration for "World's Greatest Newspaper", 71053238, United States Patent and Trademark Office (USPTO), Trademark Applications

and Registrations Retrieval (TARR), http://tarr.uspto.gov/servlet/tarr?
regser+serial&entry=71053238 (accessed February 26, 2011)

Working Press of the Nation by the National Research Bureau. 1990. New York:
Farrell Pub. Corp.

Zoll, Andrzej. 2000. Moje wybory [My elections]. In: *10 lat demokratycznego prawa wyborczego Rzeczypospolitej Polskiej (1990-2000) [10 Years of the Democratic Electoral Law in the Republic of Poland (1990-2000)]*. Ed. Beata Tokaj, Marcin Lisiak and Kazimierz W. Czaplicki, 7-21. Warsaw: Krajowe Biuro Wyborcze. http://www.pkw.gov.pl/gallery/ 00/9.pdf (accessed February 2, 2009).

Grzegorz Nycz
Jagiellonian University, Poland
The role of strategic communications, public diplomacy and international broadcasting in the United States' 'War Against Terror' in the Middle East

1. Introduction: the war on terror and information warfare

This paper discusses the evolution of US government international information policy in the context of US security strategy after 9/11, with a special focus on the Middle East. The analysis refers to US public diplomacy and international broadcasting as important instruments of the "war on terror." The author attempts to present a critical perspective on President Bush's efforts to synchronize civilian and military information policies, undertaken in order to provide coherent "strategic communication"[1] framework.

Mark Leonard defined strategic communications within the area of public diplomacy as actions pursued to improve the country's image abroad (Leonard 2002, 15). According to Jarol Manheim, strategic political communication "involves not only the selective distribution of political information but, under certain circumstances, the prevention of its distribution (e.g. news management) as well" (Manheim 1991, 7).

The Bush administration's concept of strategic communication aimed at coordinating civilian and military means of information warfare, in order to increase support for American operations in the main theaters of the "war on terror" and shape the attitudes of Muslim public opinion. In late 2001, the Bush administration began to reinforce instruments of ideological pressure by linking public diplomacy, broadcasting and other PR activities of government agencies. Those policies were subdued to goals of national security strategy formed after 9/11, which included the strengthening of US political and ideological influence in Muslim countries (Pilon 2007, 218-223). However, in the first months after 9/11 it became clear that the United States lacked institutional and conceptual basis for pursuing information policies, which could effectively increase the support for American foreign policy in the Middle East. To improve US capabilities in the area of international information, the Bush administration sponsored

---

[1] According to the Pentagon, strategic communication is "the focused United States government processes and efforts to understand and engage key audiences in order to create, strengthen, or preserve conditions favorable for the advancement of US Government interests, policies, and objectives through the use of coordinated information, themes, plans, programs, and actions synchronized with other instrument of national power." See Joint Chiefs of Staff, Joint Operation Planning, Joint Publication 5-0, December 2006. http://www.dtic.mil/doctrine/jel/ new_pubs/jp5_0.pdf

media campaigns, targeted mainly at audiences in the broader Middle East. Importantly, the strategic impact of these efforts was undermined by fatal flaws of the US-led antiterrorist campaign, especially the inaccurate intelligence reports of Iraqi weapons of mass destruction, which reduced the credibility of US government.

1.1. Instruments of American public diplomacy – an overview

Historically, public diplomacy evolved from various governmental efforts to influence foreign populations through media, cultural and scientific programs, propaganda campaigns, and other "soft" dimensions of international politics. Since the Cold War era, public diplomacy was perceived as an instrument of global influence, connected with "soft," non-military means of foreign policy (Kegley and Wittkopf 1991, 112). According to the well known concept of Joseph Nye, "soft power" may be understood as the ability to shape political preferences of foreign nations, based on cultural, ideological and institutional influence of the state (Nye 2002, 8-9).

As Mark Leonard noted, though public diplomacy is often linked with propaganda, in fact it aims at defending the image and reputation of a country by correcting misconceptions and communicating national points of view with the understanding of other countries and cultures. According to Leonard, public diplomacy may be characterized in three main dimensions – news management, strategic communications and relationship building. News management supports traditional diplomacy by addressing the foreign public, strategic communications allows governments to improve the country's brand by carefully planned media campaigns, while relationship building aims at creating stable networks with key individuals in foreign countries (Leonard 2002, 11-19).

Edyta Wolfson indicated, that after World War II the scope of diplomacy was broadened to include not only foreign officials, but also citizens of other countries. The phrase "public diplomacy" was coined to describe governmental efforts to communicate with foreign people (Wolfson 2008, 201). The significance of public diplomacy in foreign policy had been recognized during the Cold War. The East-West struggle and processes of decolonization emphasized the influence of international public opinion, powerful enough to shape the policies of great powers (Pilon 2007, 124-125).

Since World War II, American public diplomacy and international broadcasting have been closely interconnected. Voice of America (VoA), launched in 1942, was a primary instrument of the US administration to counter the propaganda of the Axis. After the War, VoA became an important tool of US government in ideological warfare with the Kremlin. During the Cold War, the American public diplomacy apparatus was run by the United States Information Agency (USIA), launched in 1953. USIA administered Voice of America, while in 1950s and 1960s other important instruments of the Cold War ideological warfare – Radio Free Europe (founded in 1949) and Radio Liberty (founded in 1951) – were financed by the CIA. In 1973 Radio Free Europe and Radio Liberty were placed under the supervision of the Board of International Broadcasting, a federal body. In 1994, the latter institution was replaced by the Broadcasting Board of Governors, an autonomous agency, built to control the media supported by the US government (Wolfson 2008, 210-221).

2. To "win hearts and minds" – war of ideas or propaganda?

US national security strategy formed after 9/11 focused on the means of reducing the terrorist threat to the United States and its vital interests, by preemptive actions and increased American political and military activity in countries which housed terrorists. The focal point of this strategy was to strengthen American influence in the Middle East. The US national security strategy of 2002 indicated that in order to secure a victory in the fight against international terrorism, the United States was supposed to wage a "war of ideas," and to support "moderate and modern government in the Muslim world, to ensure that the conditions and ideologies that promote terrorism do not find fertile ground in any nation." Methods of this policy included the use of "effective public diplomacy to promote the free flow of information and ideas" (US National Security Strategy 2002, 32).

Within the framework of a new security strategy, the US government was shaping a communications strategy, presented under the well known Vietnam-era phrase to "win hearts and minds" of foreign citizens, especially in Muslim countries. In fact, after proclaiming the war on terror, the US government made huge effort to influence the audience in Muslim and Arab countries by using the dissemination of information, public diplomacy and military propaganda. As Donald Rumsfeld stated "in this war, some of the most critical battles may not be fought in the mountains of Afghanistan or the streets of Iraq, but in the newsrooms in places like New York and London and Cairo and elsewhere" (Rumsfeld 2006).

Following the incorporation of the United States Information Agency into the State Department in 1999, the main tasks referring to international information and building of US image abroad were undertaken by Under Secretary for Public Diplomacy and Public Affairs. From October 2001 until March 2003 this office was held by Charlotte Beers (a former advertising executive), appointed by Secretary of State Colin Powell, who had expected that Beers would be able to use private sector techniques to improve the US perception abroad (Tiedeman, 2004). In 2002 Charlotte Beers introduced two media campaigns – "Shared Values" and "Muslim Life in America." Television programs "Shared Values" and publications about daily life of American Muslims were trying to convince the audience that the US government was not fighting with Islam. The campaign informed viewers about religious freedoms of Muslims in the United States and emphasized similarities between American and Muslim values, such as religious zeal and respect for family. Unfortunately for the Bush administration the campaign was perceived as propaganda and several countries – Egypt, Lebanon and Morocco, among others – refused to broadcast the programs. The campaigns were criticized as too naive, but the State Department estimated that they reached around 288 million people all over the world (Marquis, 2004).

To support the ideological dimension of the war on terror, the Bush administration expanded the international information apparatus. In the first months after 9/11, new bodies devoted to information management were formed by the White House, National Security Council, Department of State and Department of Defense. In October 2001, the Department of Defense created the Office of Strategic Influence (OSI), which was providing information to foreign media in order to increase support for the US-led "war on terror" and to reduce the appeal of terrorist's propaganda (Defense Science Board, 2001 and 2004). OSI was formed because the administration noticed that the bombings of Afghanistan caused hostility towards the United States in Muslim countries. The new institution caused huge controversies – including accusations of placing disinformation and covert military propaganda in the media (Nye 2007, 155). The New York Times reported in February 2002 that the Office of Strategic Influence was pursuing military psychological operations to influence foreign audiences (Dao and Schmitt, 2002). As a result, in the end of February 2002 the Office of Strategic Influence was dissolved by Donald Rumsfeld (Defense Science Board 2004).

Other new bodies were created by the White House. On the eve of Operation Enduring Freedom in Afghanistan the White House formed a network of Coalition Information Centers, which linked Washington, London and Islamabad. Coalition Information Centers were using PR experts to respond to news events and the propaganda of the Taliban and Al Qaeda. In the following months, the Centers' tasks were undertaken by the Office of Global Communications in the White House, formed in 2002. The Office was engaged in promoting goals of the war on terror and US intervention in Iraq, by preparing appealing news stories and, among others, revealing the brutality of Saddam Hussein's regime. The Office of Global Communications was criticized by experts and journalists as a "propaganda office" and in 2005 its responsibilities were assumed by the National Security Council (Defense Science Board 2004).

2.1. US information policies in the Middle East after 9/11

After the Taliban regime was overthrown, the Middle East became the main theatre of the war on terror and primary target of US military and non-military operations. The centrality of the region in US international policy was emphasized by the Middle East Partnership Initiative (MEPI), announced in December 2002 by Colin Powell. MEPI, among its other dimensions, aimed at increasing

US ideological influence in Arab countries. Within the framework of the Middle East Partnership Initiative, about 100 million dollars was provided for public diplomacy efforts – such as programs to bring high school graduates or undergraduate students from Arab countries to American universities.

US efforts to influence Muslim societies included new government-sponsored media – Radio Sawa and television channel Al-Hurra. Radio Sawa, launched in March 2002 by the Broadcasting Board of Governors, was supposed to replace the unpopular Voice of America broadcasts in Arabic. The radio, based in Dubai, was combining modern music with the news; the goal was to reach young people between 17 and 28 years of age in the Middle East and North Africa. As the US Congressional Research Service observed, those efforts were rather unsuccessful. Radio Sawa gained the audience, but only because of the music, Arab listeners weren't interested in political programs (Sharp 2005). Television channel Al-Hurra (in Arabic "the free one"), launched in February 2004, was built in order to provide an alternative source of information for the audience of Al-Jazeera. The Al-Hurra channel, based in Virginia and funded through the Broadcasting Board of Governors, resembled typical satellite channels focused on the news. American media questioned the idea of Al-Hurra, arguing that the government-sponsored station would lack credibility. In fact, the new channel did not gain popularity; after the first year of its broadcasts, less than 4 percent of Arab audiences picked it as their second choice for news. Al-Hurra programs had mixed reviews and the channel was criticized for being patronizing (Sharp 2005).

It is important to note particularly controversial US attempts to influence the media in Iraq. In 2004 the US military authorities in Iraq helped to create the Baghdad Press Club, which was considered useful in promoting the coalition's efforts to bring stability to Iraq. In late 2005, media reports indicated that the Pentagon was paying Iraqi journalists to publish information prepared by US military officials. The Pentagon hired a Washington-based PR consultant, who paid the journalists in Iraq for publishing stories showing US policies in a favorable light, without revealing the source of information. In 2006 the Department of Defense investigation confirmed that such practices were taking place. Donald Rumsfeld insisted that those actions were justified (Rumsfeld 2006). Most of the media stories financed by the US government were considered truthful, but the methods of military information policy raised accusations that the army had pursued covert propaganda (Cloud 2006).

3. Strategic communication fiasco?

After 9/11, US public diplomacy resources were significantly increased. In 2001 the State Department spent US \$434m on public diplomacy programs, while in 2003 the funding rose to \$600m (Advisory Group on Public Diplomacy 2003).

Nevertheless, since 2003 public opinion polls showed decreasing support for the US-led war on terror and the decline of US image abroad. The credibility of the US government was shattered by inaccurate intelligence reports on Iraqi WMD to justify the operation Iraqi Freedom. According to the Pew Report (see below), respondents in Muslim countries and in Western Europe were convinced that US and British leaders lied about Iraqi weapons of mass destruction (Pew Report 2004 and 2006).

Notably, the abuse of prisoners in Abu Ghraib prison and the violation of humanitarian standards at Guantanamo Bay did more harm to US image and prestige, than any media campaign could restore. Nevertheless, some observers argued that well conducted US information projects combined with foreign aid brought significant results, reflected in raised support for US policies abroad. US humanitarian aid to Indonesia after the tsunami in December 2004 and US aid for Pakistan after the earthquake in October 2005, carefully covered by US government press services, were considered as very successful projects, which helped to improve America's image in those countries (Kessler and Wright 2005).

The polls might suggest that the efforts of the second Bush administration to repair damages caused by failed US policies in the previous had some impact on public opinion in Western Europe and in particular Muslim countries. However, those efforts could not diminish anti-American sentiment, triggered by intervention in Iraq.

Table 1. Did US and British leaders lie about Iraqi WMD or were they misinformed?

Jordan	they lied – 69%	they were misinformed – 22%
Turkey	they lied – 66%	they were misinformed – 14%
Pakistan	they lied – 61%	they were misinformed – 8%
Morocco	they lied – 48%	they were misinformed – 21%
Britain	they lied – 41%	they were misinformed – 48%
US	they lied – 31%	they were misinformed – 49%

Source: Pew Report: A Year After Iraq War, 2004

Table 2. Favorable opinions of the US (%)

	2000	2002	2003	2004	2005	2006
Great Britain	83	75	7	58	55	56
France	62	63	43	37	43	39
Indonesia	75	61	15	_	38	30
Pakistan	23	10	13	21	23	27
Jordan	-	25	1	5	21	15
Turkey	52	30	15	30	23	12

Source: Pew Global Attitudes Report, 2006

Table 3. Support for US "War on Terror" (%)

	2002	2003	2004	2005	2006
Britain	69	63	63	51	49
France	75	60	50	51	43
Jordan	13	2	12	12	16
Indonesia	31	23	-	50	39
Pakistan	20	16	16	22	30
Turkey	30	22	37	17	14

Source: Pew Global Attitudes Report, 2006

4. Conclusions

Public diplomacy, international broadcasting and the concepts of strategic communication tend to cross a thin line between information and propaganda. The controversial methods of the US-led war on terror proved that the abuse of power may refer not only to military interventions, but also to the flow of information. The misguided strategy of the Bush administration in the Middle East resulted in a dramatic fall of support for US foreign policy. Consequently, mismanaged media campaigns could not overturn anti-American tendencies, strengthened by Operation Iraqi Freedom and other unilateral instruments of US foreign policy after 9/11. The modest effects of media campaigns of the Bush administration and failed attempts to "win hearts and minds" of Muslim communities seem to indicate that even well-orchestrated efforts fail, as long as they are not followed by coherent actions.

Despite many analyses criticizing bureaucratic and institutional deficiencies within US public diplomacy, American interventionism itself might be a more significant message to foreign audiences, than all government-sponsored communication efforts and media campaigns. To conclude, the long-lasting dilemma whether national interests justify sending biased information seem to be less important than the question of long-term US strategy in the "Global Balkans," based on multilateral concepts which may gain local support without waging regular war, or the war of ideas (Brzezinski 2008, 130-132).

References

Brzeziński, Zbigniew. 2008. *Druga szansa.* Trans. M. Szubert. Warszawa: Świat Książki.

Cloud, David S. 2006. U.S. Urged to Stop Paying Iraqi Reporters. *The New York Times,* May 24.

Dao, James, and Eric Schmitt. 2002. Pentagon Readies Efforts to Sway Sentiment Abroad. *The New York Times,* February 19.

Joint Chiefs of Staff. 2006. *Joint Operation Planning.* Joint Publication 5-0. December 26.

Kegley Jr, Charles, and Eugene Wittkopf. 1991. *American Foreign Policy. Pattern and Process.* New York: St. Martins.

Kessler, Glenn, and Robin Wright. 2005. Earthquake Aid for Pakistan Might Help U.S. Image. *The Washington Post,* October 13.

Leonard, Mark, Catherine Stead, and Conrad Smewing. 2002. *Public Diplomacy.* London: Foreign Policy Centre.

Manheim, Jarol B. 1991. *All of the People, All of the Time. Strategic Communication and American Politics.* Armonk, NY: M.E. Sharpe.

Marquis, Christopher. 2004. Promoter of U.S. Image Quits for Wall St. Job. *The New York Times,* April 30.

Nye, Joseph. 2002. *The Paradox of American Power. Why the World Only Superpower Can't Go It Alone.* Oxford: Oxford University Press.

------. 2007. *Soft Power, Jak osiągnąć sukces w polityce światowej.* Trans. Jakub Zaborowski. Warszawa: Wydawnictwa Akademickie i Profesjonalne.

Pew Global Attitudes Report. 2006. http://pewglobal.org/reports/display.php?ReportID=252

Pew Report: A Year After Iraq War. 2004. http://pewglobal.org/reports/ display.php?PageID=796

Pilon, Juliana. 2007. *Why America is such a Hard Sell. Beyond Pride and Prejudice.* Plymouth: Rowman & Littlefield.

Report of the Advisory Group on Public Diplomacy for the Arab and Muslim World. 2003. *Changing Minds Winning Peace, A New Strategic Direction for U.S. Public Diplomacy in the Arab & Muslim World.* Submitted to the Committee on Appropriations, U.S. House of Representatives, October 1, 2003. Washington D.C.

Report of the Defense Science Board Task Force on Managed Information Dissemination, October 2001. Washington, D.C.: Office of the Under Secretary of Defense For Acquisition, Technology, and Logistics.

Report of the Defense Science Board Task Force on Strategic Communication, September 2004. Washington, D.C.: Office of the Under Secretary of Defense For Acquisition, Technology, and Logistics.

Rumsfeld, Donald. 2006. New Realities in the Media Age: A Conversation with Donald Rumsfeld, February 17, 2006. New York: Council of Foreign Relations.

Sharp, Jeremy M. 2005. *The Middle East Television Network: An Overview.* Congressional Research Service Report for Congress. Washington D.C.: Congressional Research Service.

Tiedeman, Anna. 2004. U.S. Public Diplomacy in the Middle East Lessons Learned from the Charlotte Beers Experience. University of South California Center on Public Diplomacy.

The White House. 2002. National Security Strategy of the United States of America of 2002.

Wolfson, Edyta. 2008. Dyplomacja publiczna z amerykańskiej perspektywy. In *Dyplomacja publiczna*, ed. B. Ociepka, 201-244. Wrocław: Wydawnictwo Uniwersytetu Wrocławskiego.

Part III – Politics

Paula S. Fass
University of California at Berkeley, USA

Children on the edges of history and historiography: confronting the New World

History as lived experience and the substance of the human past has no edges. It has many troughs and peaks, lulls and periods of rushed intensity, but just as the round sphere on which human history has been realized has no corners, the past has no edges. The history we study and create has edges of many kinds, and it is these edges and the ways in which studying children can allow us to transcend some of them and refashion how we study the past that I want to discuss here. In fact, in my paper I will engage three different kinds of edges: the boundaries created around disciplines; the borders inscribed by our imposition upon history and nature's geography of the nation and the state; the idea of a leading edge that governs what we study and how we study it. Bearing in mind that these edges are of our own making, I want to suggest that studying children and opening our sights to the possibilities of the history of children and childhood allows us to stretch beyond the limitations that our self-created boundaries have imposed on our visions of the past and to move toward a richer and more complete engagement with history in the twenty-first century. In this sense, the history of childhood and children is a truly vanguard enterprise, a cutting edge endeavor, a way of moving beyond earlier limits (Fass 2007).

Before I turn to these matters, I want to address one more boundary, but only to leave it behind completely: the belief that the history of childhood is not possible, that children are not appropriate historical subjects because they are not creators of history and do not leave sources behind them. I am not going to spend much time dwelling on this, since the best evidence against it is the flourishing enterprise that now exists as hundreds of historians actively (and successfully) pursue the study of children as historical agents in the economy and in the culture, as important figures in political imagery and rhetoric, as part of the literary canon and the popular culture, and as subjects of fundamental social policies and institutions. These investigations are considering all periods from the ancient world up to the present, within in all religious traditions, and regarding children on all the continents of the world. That children are a significant part of our history is beyond dispute; that they have become a vital component of contemporary scholarship demonstrates that we have moved into new and exciting territory. Instead of dwelling on what I take to be old news, I want to suggest how the history of children and childhood is becoming an active component of a potential global history that is beginning to challenge the limitations of conventional historiography.

It is not simply a coincidence that global or world history and the history of childhood have emerged together as exciting new fields of inquiry. They are natural companions and they signal a rethinking of national boundaries, intellectual categories, and personal identities in which historians and other scholars are currently engaged.

As the smallest and most impressionable constituents of every society and the subtext of all cultures, children encourage us to think globally – to ask what they share and how they become different. At birth, children are unmarked by most national and cultural boundaries. They are then at their most available to stimuli which until fully localized within a household, a community, and a nation, could as readily take one shape as another. Thus, children are by nature "citizens" of the world. How they become attached to specific identities is precisely one of the things that historians want to examine. Psychologists have taught us that they do this quite rapidly through attachment to a primary caregiver and language acquisition, but we also know that even after these initial attachments, it is only because of a long childhood (variously defined but always and everywhere extended and elaborate) that they become fully attached and identifiably members of a specific community.

A more global or transnational perspective encourages us to study this process by looking at how the boundaries of nations and cultures are formed from the children who are the fundamental units of social development. It can also suggest how identities can be remade in children who move across boundaries, and alerts us to their fungible nature. Children, far more than adults, make us aware of these possibilities today since more easily than at any time in the past, children today can travel physically or through their imaginations (and in their computer play) to other parts of the globe and into cultures other than those to which they were born. This flexibility also makes them ideal subjects for studying not just the present but the past.

Once we look at children as children, rather than as potential grownups in a particular nation, they share many things in common that historians can grasp only by looking beyond previously defined boundaries. On the other hand, the distinctions matter a lot, and these differences may be better understood cross-nationally. Children thus underscore the ways in which the global is a better vehicle than either the nation state, or social categories such as race, gender or ethnicity to help us understand the contemporary world. I do not want to be misunderstood. I do not believe that either the nation state as a form of historical analysis or gender or race are about to disappear from our commitments, and we would not want them to. I am suggesting that the present moment allows us to augment and resituate these studies as the new lenses of childhood and global history reveal aspects of the past that would otherwise be hidden and obscured. This is a fertile time when we can study children and youth in ways that unsettle conventional boundaries and thus move toward a more comparative, more holistic, and deeper set of inquiries into human behavior, cultural expression-, and the history of humankind.

At the same time, none of this is easy and none of it comes without resistance. Categories are created because they are convenient, not only for how we study the past but how they serve contemporary objectives, and there are still far fewer powerful stakeholders among children than adults, while the world perspective is hardly as well represented even today as national interests are. How then can we move beyond the edges created for us to launch new inquiries at this important moment? I begin my discussion about children at the edge of history by urging a more complete engagement beyond disciplinary boundaries something that students of American studies can well appreciate. We are, I believe, in a moment when disciplinary boundaries are becoming more and more obviously frayed and seem to be beckoning toward new resolutions. This has already happened in the physical sciences, and is happening in the humanities and social sciences. These reconfigurations will, I believe, require historical forms of thinking and knowledge of history more than ever before. History can help to open the way toward new disciplinary definitions in the twenty-first century, much as history was the source for the development of the social sciences in the late nineteenth and the early twentieth centuries. In the second part of my paper, I will draw upon elements of my own interests and work, specifically on migration, education, and youth culture to suggest how we can engage in analysis that is more fluid, and use children's history to begin to think in transnational ways.

I.

At an earlier moment of intellectual ferment and political redefinition in the West, when John Locke rethought the nature of government and claimed new ways to understand how we acquire our knowledge of the world, he recognized that children's cognition was the place to begin. John Dewey, three hundred years later, similarly turned to how children learn when he sought to anchor democracy in a new century while he redefined the epistemological project in the light of new scientific theories. Today, the world of cognition, that is to say the study of how children learn and how this learning functions at the level of the brain, is proceeding rapidly among brain scientists. Locke and Dewey were philosophers who contributed to the store of knowledge, but they were also products of their time. Historians understand that most such knowledge is not absolute but contingent; this is how we need to approach the science of the brain today. We must learn from it, but not adopt it unthinkingly. Nevertheless, at a time when the world's children are everywhere coming to our attention as the globe shrinks before our eyes, historians need to become familiar with some of this rapidly evolving literature that connects all children as learners and that follows in an important tradition of inquiry that influenced how adults think about children while telling us how children think. Just as Locke and Dewey fundamentally affected the West's view of childhood and then influenced how children were reared, so too is cognitive science currently affecting what we think children are like and affecting how they are being raised in societies all over the world.

Indeed, we may learn from current studies of childhood cognition those matters that will help us to see more clearly how children may be connected across the globe. As we update our understanding of early learning as a biosocial process, we should also understand that learning does not stop with infancy and early childhood. Contemporary neurologists are finding evidence that the brains of young persons even into their teen years (and beyond) continue to develop as new neural pathways grow and are then honed and pruned.[1] Thus brain science can open different parts of the life course to analysis and need not be limited to the earliest years of life. How children learn, the potentials and hazards of particular spurts of learning in infancy, childhood, adolescence and beyond are necessary foundations for historical understanding, and I therefore begin with this basic area of contemporary inquiry that does not often or obviously come into the historian's sights. From the global point of view, the science of the brain stimulates us to start to reconnect people everywhere whose distinctions of culture and language sometimes bewilder our sense of the fundamental similarities in physiological development and processes most apparent in children.

Historians of the last two or three generations have long sought insight from anthropology, which has often underwritten our social and cultural studies. Since it reveals both the variety and similarities among human societies, anthropology must remain an important source as we move beyond earlier boundaries. In the twentieth century anthropologists such as Margaret Mead understood that children are at or near the center of specific cultures because every human society assures its own continuity through the enculturation of the next generation. But, like historians, anthropologists have often acknowledged this and then turned to other matters. At this new global moment, however, anthropologists are once more turning to children, with visions modified by perspectives that endow children with greater autonomy and agency. Thus, the street children of Brazil and the A++ children of contemporary China are still a way to understand the culture in which they develop, but anthropologists now view them as actors in their own right. Anthropologists also increasingly appreciate how the local is connected to the global, how both the street children and the prodigies exist in an international commercial system and under the gaze of an international microscope. As self-conscious visitors from the West, anthropologists are well attuned to this global view and understand that the observer and the observed always stand in each other's sight. The West's dominant international position

---

[1] For a summary of this research aimed at a general audience, see Barbara Strauch, *The Primal Teen: What the New Discoveries About the Teenage Brain Tell Us About Our Kids* (New York: Doubleday, 2003).

since the sixteenth century age of exploration is a force that remains powerful and how local cultures have been known through and been affected by this force is an anthropological insight that is important for all historians, those who study children and those who do not. Anthropologists have often seen today's global world more quickly than historians, but they need historians in order to understand how it came into being.

And finally, in the midst of insights from the cognitive sciences and from anthropology, it would be too bad if we forgot economics. Today's world may require that we seek out common patterns of learning and the complex intersections of culture, but it also relies on powerful economic forces and reminds us that children are important economic actors. Once we think in globalizing terms, it is not possible to forget that economics is a fundamental contributor to the changes taking place today as we contemplate a world penetrated by corporations and their logos, where decisions are driven by global labor resources and underwritten by global capital.

For historians of childhood, this particular moment of globalization is useful because it allows us to observe the crucial role that children have played and continue to play in the world economy and to renew our investigations into their role in family decision-making.[2] Often today, children come to our economic attention as victims of human trafficking, but this journalistic understanding of children should encourage us to dig much deeper. Globalization refocuses our vision precisely because it challenges our usual image of Western children. In the West and in the United States especially, since the nineteenth century, children have been seen as belonging to the spheres of play and school, not work and not sexuality, and we insist on their protected innocence. We have learned over the course of the twentieth century to condemn the work of children where it is still found and to find their sexual exploitation heinous and even their sexual exposure as unnatural. Indeed, we have learned to divide the worlds of childhood and adulthood as firmly as Victorians once tried to divide the worlds of men and women. The new global perspective forces us to recognize that children have been a part of the social and economic life of most societies and deeply part of its sexual economy as well. For the global historian, a renewed understanding of the subtle and not so subtle consequences of money, investments, and work also reopens our history to new insights not only about children, but about economic choices registered in changing family patterns, and intergenerational relationships.

In all these ways, by attending to new insights into how brains function and minds develop, by examining how people, including children, negotiate between

---

[2] For a classic evaluation of children in the family economic calculations, see David Levine, *Family Formation in an Age of Nascent Capitalism* (New York: Academic Press, 1977) and *Reproducing Families: The Political Economy of English Population History* (Cambridge, UK: Cambridge University Press, 1987).

their own cultures and new global lures, and by watching how the global economy appeals to the young and incorporates them in its work as well as in its consumerism, sexuality, and play, global historians, including historians of children, can move to the forefront –cutting edge, so to speak – of a strong interdisciplinary research agenda.

II.

In our understanding of a more fluid world, migration is key. Migration is certainly not a new topic historically and American Studies scholars have viewed it as a fundamental feature of national experience, from Frederick Jackson Turner's moving frontier, through Perry Miller's Puritans on an errand into the wilderness, to Oscar Handlin's identification of the United States itself with the migrant experience. Migration has been so central to the experience of the United States as a nation that it is a truism to say that the society could not exist without it. But Americanists have often been blind to the degree to which migration has affected many other places and for long periods of time. Any scholar of American immigration knows that those who came to the United States left from somewhere—Poland and Italy, Greece and Sweden and many other places. And any scholar of Europe knows that people went not only to the United States but also to Canada and Australia, Chile and Argentina, among others. Today, the world is humming with mass migrations, and even countries like the Netherlands and Denmark, not to mention France and Italy, are made busy and anxious dealing with migrants in large numbers, while places that had previously not been the origin of important migrant streams now make significant contributions, such countries as Brazil, Thailand, and Guatemala. This new fluidity makes the North American experience, with its long history of migration an important basis for understanding the changes taking place all over the world and makes American studies a powerful resource. Europeans today are riveted by the American presidential campaign because the possibility that Barack Obama, a product of border crossings of many kinds, stands on the threshold of representing the American people. They are watching our experience, because world migrations are making Europe today more like the United States. By rethinking earlier migrations and specifically the intersection between childhood and migration in a new global way, those engaged in American Studies can provide insights useful to scholars eager to understand today's and tomorrow's world.

Let us begin with issues regarding family composition and childcare. Family migration has never been a process in which all members of the family necessarily moved together. Indeed, much migration history concerns the disassembling of families in order to underwrite a family process of survival and/or success (and sometimes failure). In Mexico today, 41% of all household heads have some migratory experience to the United States and 73% of all households have a social connection to someone living in the United States. This is obviously an extreme expression of cross national family interdependence, but people in the past also maintained bonds across borders, with relatives in far distant places. Today, in the context of instant communication and rapid transportation, this is becoming a normal way of life and it allows for a fluidity in family structure in many places around the world that is probably unprecedented. Globalization has not only made migration more possible, but has affected and reflects the family decisions that frame it. Thus, today many hundreds of thousands of Filipina women (some have estimated the total to be over six million) have traveled to Europe, the Middle East, and to the United States to clean other people's houses, take care of their elderly, their sick and their children (Salazar Parreñas 2001; Ehrenreich and Hochschild 2002). In most cases, these women leave their own children behind with grandmothers, aunts, fathers or unrelated caretakers as they send substantial parts of their wages back to improve the lives and prospects of their children and other family members. Most hope to return to better lives in the Philippines. Very often this lasts not for a few months, but for many years.

Historians are quite familiar with similar patterns of transient migrations. During the height of immigration to the Western hemisphere from Eastern and Southern Europe and China, in the late nineteenth and early twentieth centuries, hundreds of thousands of men left families, including children, behind and sent back their wages on a regular basis. Often they themselves returned after several years' absence. Sometimes, they went back and forth repeatedly. Italians and Poles did this regularly and Mexicans continue to do so into the twenty-first century (Massey in Rumbaut et al. 1999, 9). In the United States today, we are governed by ideals of family reunification, a policy enshrined in the Hart-Celler Act of 1965. But, international migrations, and international capital do not take issues of family preservation into account. And today, as in the past, particular families adapt and use the pressures and opportunities this presents.

Perhaps the most potentially destabilizing and historically unprecedented part of the modern version of transitory migration is related to *gender*. Rarely in the past did women leave children behind as they sought to raise their family's prospects, although single women could and did travel alone. Only in the context of the contemporary world in which female labor is often as valuable as, or more valuable than, male labor and where children no longer work in the countries to which their parents migrate has this become likely (Sassen 1984a and 1984b).[3] Globalization can pull children into new work contexts in many parts of the world, but this is very unlikely in Europe or North America precisely because Westerners view child labor as unnatural and abhorrent. We might want to recognize that by maintaining this posture toward children, a globalized twenty-

---

[3] For single – women who migrated early in the twentieth century see Susan A. Glenn, *Daughters of the Shtetl: Life and Labor in the Immigrant Generation* (Ithaca, N. Y.: Cornell, 1990).

first century makes it more likely that women will leave their children for long periods of their lives as they seek the work that is now available to them, but not to their children, work paid in valuable dollars and in euros. Today migrating women often have to depend on extended kin or strangers for child care arrangements. This dependence on intergenerational ties fundamentally contradicts the model of nuclear family mobility posited by Talcott Parsons in the 1950s when he argued that nuclear families, cut off from obligations to kin, could engage in the physical movement essential for social mobility in the modern world.

While it was highly unlikely (though hardly impossible) that mothers would leave their children behind as they do today, historians know that many children were left behind by hundreds of thousands of fathers in Europe as they sought better lives for themselves and their families in the new world, and we will want to revisit the consequences for family life, discipline, patterns of authority and intergenerational bonds. What affect did this "temporary" experience have once families were in fact reunited, either in the United States, in Europe, in China, or in Latin America. Historians should think hard also about the effect of unfettered male workers in American industries and Argentine cities on sexual life at the turn of the century and what abandoned women experienced sexually at home. The virus that causes HIV-AIDS today is frequently spread by migrating men –, just as migrating men in the early twentieth century carried syphilis and gonorrhea. Today's dangers can give us a more immediate and clearer sense of the feminist outrage at the contamination of women and children at home in that earlier context. And we will want to ask what kinds of marital discords may have been created or healed in that earlier migration from a Catholic Europe not yet accustomed to divorce.

Sociologist Rhacel Salazar Parreñas shows that women today use migration as an alternative to seeking divorce for an abusive marriage in the still deeply Catholic Philippines. In the nineteenth and early twentieth century, few Americans or Europeans divorced but many migrated. Were they too, like today's Filipinas, adopting a divorce alternative by disserting rather than divorcing? Migration can have many meanings and many consequences. The deep concern with abandoned women and their children in the early twentieth century among progressive reformers and social workers, the ease of common law marriage in American law of that period, provide us with clues to this fundamental migratory process; so do the campaign against baby farms, the drive to fund and expand orphanages in the early twentieth century, and the urgent emphasis on foster care guided by religion affiliation. These are all clues to the ways in which different groups whose members were involved in the migration process tried to maintain some continuity and control over children who had been abandoned by fathers of specific creeds and ethnicities. As in so many other arenas, the history of childhood (in this case of dependent children and the institutions created for them) provides us with an unusually effective vantage from which to observe a much broader process, one with cross boundary and cross national implications. By concentrating on the children, we come to understand much about the historical experience.

In the United States especially, migration is also identified with mobility of other kinds. American historians have developed a significant literature about the influence of schooling for social mobility and specifically on the differential mobility of ethnic groups. And their findings suggest that immigrant children are rarely as successful as those whose parents were native born. Marvin Lazerson and Michael Olneck (1978 and 1980), Joel Perlmann (1988), Reed Ueda (1987), and others, have investigated aspects of this matter. The contemporary literature on the schooling consequences of global migration is also large as sociologists, anthropologists and educators look at issues of great importance in contemporary policy. But what they have found can be profoundly challenging to those earlier conclusions, just as the new dependence on extended kin seriously challenges the Parsonian model of mobility. As two of the most highly regarded researchers in the field of immigrant education, Carola Suárez-Orozco and Marcelo M. Suárez-Orozco observe, "immigrant children are healthier, work harder in school, and have more positive social attitudes than their nonimmigrant peers. Every year, the children of immigrants are overrepresented in the rosters of high school valedictorians and receive more of their share of prestigious science awards … Immigrant children in general arrive with high aspirations and extremely positive attitudes toward education" (Suárez-Orozco, C. and M. Suárez-Orozco 2001, 2). Even Caribbean and other Latin American children (who usually lag behind in high school graduation rates and college attendance as compared to other immigrants) benefit educationally from migrating to the United States. Indeed, one of the most provocative findings of this contemporary literature is that children who themselves migrate are much more successful in school than their United States-born younger siblings. Thus, children born in the Caribbean and in Mexico are more academically successful, despite the apparent handicap of language, than their siblings born in the United States. The latter are more quickly and easily absorbed into local black and Latino peer cultures that often turn them against school. The drive to success of migrating children seems to be lodged in a self-conscious exploiting of opportunities while those born in the United States hope for acceptance in the peer culture of their usually poor inner city schools. The very "marginality" of those migrating children makes them more ambitious and better students. Anthropologist John Ogbu has shown that young migrants who know how much better their opportunities are as a result of migration than in their countries of origin, take advantage of the education they are offered, even if this is in poor neighborhoods with dilapidated schools (Gibson and Ogbu 1991).

As a historian who has worked on schooling, I find this data intriguing (Fass 1989). Since the requirement that children stay in school through their teen years was not in place at the time of the early twentieth century migrations, many of the comparable European children who migrated together with their parents earlier in the century would have been at work not in school, and their drive and ambition would never have shown itself academically. It may well have resulted in entrepreneurial inventiveness as David Nasaw's book on children at work in the city suggests or in underworld criminal activities that may also have grown from the thwarted ambitions of immigrant youth, a subject much less often studied in relation to children (or adults for that matter) (Nasaw 1985). In fact, their parents may have thought that because the younger, native born children had linguistic advantage, they should be kept in school longer, depriving the older ambitious siblings of real opportunities for academic success.

But there is another element here that historians will also want to grapple with: Why should the younger, technically *more* assimilated siblings today do *less well* in school? This finding challenges most of the historical literature that puts a premium on assimilation and its relationship to success. By interrogating the concept of assimilation and looking at schooling from the point of view of children who attend, rather than from that of school officials, this finding makes more sense. For what, exactly, are school children being assimilated to and who is doing the assimilating? Historians of education too frequently assume that they were assimilated to American standards by American teachers because this is how schooling is rationalized and planned, but contemporary data clearly confirm what historians of children more readily understand, that young people in schools usually assimilate within peer groups created by themselves. Historians of childhood understand that second generation students of European backgrounds, like those today, spent their time together, even at school, making similar choices in school and school-related activities. Their identities were not one or another, American or Italian, American or Polish, but both. This fluidity is confirmed by a new global perspective, and can be especially clear when we look at children and how they learn to identify as they grow. Without taking note of how young people operate independently of their elders in school, we would have no way of understanding this phenomenon either today or in the past. This is what an emphasis on children and youth and on interdisciplinary approaches can provide.

Today's globalization also forces Americanists to explore and rethink the very meaning of assimilation and mobility. Where blue-collar parents once produced white collar children or grandchildren, such a gradual ascent seems no longer necessarily predictable. In today's white–collar-dominant West, where a combination of schooling and youth culture determines children's lives and their future, the simple assimilation model may be altogether outdated and misleading, and as I have suggested it needs to be seriously qualified in the past as well. Today, many upper status and highly mobile students from around the world migrate to take advantage of American higher education, especially its graduate and professional schools. Assimilation may not apply to them at all. It is also possible to imagine that a parallel migration is taking place, one in which poorer young people migrate with their parents and strive for white-collar skills. In the United States today, high school attendance is required and some bilingual preparation has become an expected part of their integration into an age-defined curriculum. As a result, ambitious teenagers have far greater opportunities than in the past. It is also possible that we are seeing a situation in which the competitive educational success of migrants (from Russia and Asia, for example), may be displacing longer settled ethnic groups from routes of mobility in the United States.

Other effects of globalization for education in the United States are not hard to find. Over the past two decades, we have become familiar with recurrent educational "crises" as statistics on achievement at various school levels as compared to children in other societies reveal deficiencies among American school children. The schooling speed-up that has resulted as we try to cram more information into students earlier in their lives and measure them against international norms, culminating most recently in the "No Child Left Behind Policy" of the Bush Administration, is beginning to squeeze our definition of childhood and the role of play and a leisurely child-centered development in schooling, a hallmark of twentieth century childhood. At a time when the social placement and success of their offspring has become urgent to middle class families eager to maintain their status, the new globalized economy may be on the verge of redefining childhood in the West as Asian children and children from elsewhere displace those who had assumed they were at the head of the line. This insight can also serve to reopen historical investigations into subjects we somehow assumed were settled. In the mid nineteenth century, earlier migrations may also have altered the economic expectations of native born groups and their children. Indeed, as blue collar work became increasingly identified with immigrants, this helped to spur native groups toward using the schools, and inventing new forms of schooling, such as high schools, as routes to mobility. Michael Katz (Katz 1968) suggested this some time ago, but our understanding of displacement in school success today makes the subject newly significant. Indeed, I would argue, that the particular American idealization of childhood as a period spent in leisured, playful development at school and set safely apart from the market needs to be understood in this wider context. Childhood as a cultural ideal provided leverage to native groups, not only by controlling the children of newcomers, but by privileging those who could more easily access all its requirements.

III.

Youth and youth culture is another arena in which a new global awareness and children's history intersect in fruitful ways. The phenomenon of youth has become a powerful element in global politics and culture, and young people are beginning to alter their societies in far flung parts of the globe. Anthropologist Jennifer Cole is demonstrating that in Madagascar the desire for the identifying markers of youth is profoundly changing gender relations, sexual behaviors, and inverting generational hierarchies (Cole 2005). For many scholars, such as Joe Kincheloe corporate logos like Coca Cola, Nike, Little Kitty (a Japanese product) are rewriting the scripts of youth development and subverting the cultures of many developing societies as the young of the world look to commercial products to alter their identities and consciousness. But other scholars have seen some of these matters, especially for older youth, as more complicated, even as potentially liberating. For youth in highly structured traditional societies, the identification with consumer goods and with other young people who consume them elsewhere in the world provide a new sense of power and alternative identities. And they are liberating not just because globalization creates a market for goods, but also because globalization creates a market for the labor of those whom we in West would still describe as children.

Americans have developed a historical aversion to the work of children because starting in the late nineteenth century middle class reformers made child labor a taboo. By defining childhood as something to be freed from economic calculations and its contamination, child labor was redefined as a form of exploitation (Zelizer 1985). But labor can also provide the means to expand choices, as it has for women in the late twentieth century, for example. In many places in the world today, children work so that they can afford McDonalds and Nikes, but also so they can pay for more schooling. The older model of either school or work has never been a sufficient understanding of child life and is hardly sufficient from a global vantage point.

Nowhere is this truer than for older children who have never been entirely comfortable in their subordination to the family economy. Although what we usually mean by modern adolescence was attached in the early twentieth century US to childhood, and participated in its aims to protect children from the market place, youth soon became a distinct product in the arsenal of Western capitalism. Appeals to youthful sexuality helped to sell goods and the youth market became a special marketing niche. Over the past twenty years, *youth* has become a powerful and desirable international identity as the accoutrements of youth culture have spread everywhere through the very channels that bring globalization. Today the media spreads youth music through every corner of South America, Africa and Asia, connects young people through targeted television and movie programming, while the young become aware of each other through tee shirts and posters and connect on the internet. Youth has become a global force. Adolescents and young people into their twenties may actively pursue this identity – by working, by consuming, by rejecting parental authority, by networking with each other in ways that is sometimes political, and even by migrating to improve their chances in life. Thus, youth has itself become an active constituent of globalization, a potent instance of the intersection between global change and childhood that illustrates the relationship between them and how studying them can be linked.

Our contemporary awareness of this world-wide phenomenon should also reopen our historical inquiries as we examine how earlier periods of major changes in communications and consumption may have altered youth's experience of power inside families and outside families, as well as how this may have led to conflicts that were political as well as personal. While modern youth cultures are a product of the twentieth century, one should not discount the power of young adulthood in different settings and contexts. Thus, in the age of revolutions in the late eighteenth century and early nineteenth century, young people were similarly exposed to worldwide influences through new ideological fashions as a result of which they began to identify generationally. Historians of the US have not ignored the degree to which our revolutionaries were drawn disproportionately from the young people of the day but the international dimensions of this phenomenon has been less often noted by Americanists. Yet, a global perspective would encourage us to ask how young literati in the German states, Polish nationalists, political revolutionaries in the new French Republic and young Americans after the revolution may have imagined that they were sharing a powerful identity and an international connection. Youth even more obviously than children have the potential to remake how we think of the categorical boundaries we have created in our profession, since many of the history makers in the past were often what we would today define as youth, people still in formation.

This leads me to my final point. We historians in the West and of the West have come to understand childhood through certain lenses, fashioned from Enlightenment ideas, Victorian images, and modern childrearing beliefs.[4] We imagine that children are dependent, innocent, and need to be sheltered from adult institutions and experiences. We divide children sharply into age categories and

---

[4] For Enlightenment views, see especially Larry Wolf, "When I Imagine a Child: The Idea of Childhood and the Philosophy of Memory in the Enlightenment," *Eighteenth Century Studies*, 31 (1998), 377-401; for visual images, Marilyn Brown, "Images of Childhood," in the *Encyclopedia of Children and Childhood*, edited by Fass, vol. 2, 449-462, and Anne Higonnet, *Pictures of Innocence: The History and Crisis of Ideal Childhood* (London: Thams and Hudson, 1998); for the evolving experience of children's innocence and attraction, see Gary Cross, *The Cute and the Cool: Wondrous Innocence and Modern American Children's Culture* (New York: Oxford University Press, 2004).

impose hard-edged boundaries between children and adolescents and between both of these and adults. But these very boundaries are today being reconsidered and remade as preteens take on the characteristics (in dress, tastes, and lingo) of teens and twenty-somethings remain in school and unmarried. Seeing the children of the world before us should help us at this moment of rethinking. This is so, not only because many of the world's children and youth have joined classrooms in the West and are now OUR children as a result of migration, but because globalization is challenging the very carefully erected barriers of protection we have created around our children, now increasingly being forced to look forward to competing in a global marketplace. That marketplace is judging the educational preparation of young people across the globe just as vigorously as it does the material products produced by their parents. In the end, we cannot protect our children against a world that will soon be theirs and where they will become even more than today global citizens.

At this protean moment, we would do well to remember that childhood is itself categorically open to change, as indeed it has already changed when in the United States kindergarten students are tested on how well they read and not just how effectively they play with each other. More importantly, for historians childhood beckons us to look beyond former categories of analysis, to learn from other spheres of inquiry, and to engage in a serious rethinking of where exactly our children fit in our past as well as in our future. Children are always at the crossroads of these two, recipients of a past that they must negotiate in order to become successful citizens of the future. Today, as the future becomes ever more global, it is important to provide our children with both a history in which they play a part, and a history that has a more global prospective that prepares them for the future.

References

Brown, Marilyn. 2004. Images of Childhood. In *Encyclopedia of Children and Childhood*, ed. Paula S. Fass, vol. 2, 449-462. Farmington Hills, MI: Thomson Gale.

Cole, Jennifer. 2005. The Jaobilo of Tamatave (Madagascar), 1992-2004: Reflections on Youth and Globalization. *Journal of Social History*, 38 (Summer): 891-914.

Cross, Gary. 2004. *The Cute and the Cool: Wondrous Innocence and Modern American Children's Culture*. New York: Oxford University Press.

Ehrenreich, Barbara, and Arlie Russell Hochschild, eds. 2002. *Global Woman: Nannies, Maids, and Sex Workers in the New Economy*. New York: Metropolitan Books.

Fass, Paula S. 1989. Outside. In: *Minorities and the Transformation of American Education*. New York: Oxford University Press.

------. 2007. *Children of A New World: Society, Culture, and Globalization.* New York: New York University Press.

Gibson, Margaret A., and John U. Ogbu. 1991. *Minority Status and Schooling: A Comparative Study of Immigrant and Involuntary Minorities.* Westport, CT: Greenwood.

Glenn, Susan A. 1990. *Daughters of the Shtetl: Life and Labor in the Immigrant Generation.* Ithaca, New York: Cornell University Press.

Higonnet, Anne. 1998. *Pictures of Innocence: The History and Crisis of Ideal Childhood.* London: Thams and Hudson.

Katz, Michael B. 1968. *The Irony of Early School Reform: Educational Innovation in Mid-Nineteenth Century Massachusetts.* Cambridge, MA: Harvard University Press.

Levine, David. 1977. *Family Formation in an Age of Nascent Capitalism.* New York: Academic Press.

------. 1987. *Reproducing Families: The Political Economy of English Population History.* Cambridge, UK: Cambridge University Press.

Nasaw, David. 1985. *Children of the City: At Work and at Play.* New York: Oxford University Press.

Olneck, Michael R., and Marvin Lazerson. 1978. The School Achievement of Immigrant Children, 1890-1930. *History of Education Quarterly*, 18 (Fall): 227-70.

------. 1980. Education. In *Harvard Encyclopedia of American Ethnic Groups*, ed. Stephan Thernstrom, Ann Orlov and Oscar Handlin, 303-319. Cambridge, MA: Harvard University Press.

Perlmann, Joel. 1988. *Ethnic Differences: Schooling and Social Structure Among the Irish, Italians, Jews and Blacks in an American City, 1880-1935.* Cambridge, UK and New York: Cambridge University Press.

Rumbaut, Ruben G., Richard D. Alba, and Douglas S. Massey, ed. 1999. *The Immigrant Experience for Families and Children.* Washington, DC: Spivack Program in Applied Social Research and Social Policy, American Sociological Association.

Salazar Parreñas, Rhacel. 2001. *Servants of Globalization: Women, Migration and Domestic Work.* Stanford, CA: Stanford University Press.

Sassen, Saskia. 1984a. Notes on the Incorporation of Third World Women into Wage Labor through Immigration and Offshore Production. *International Migration Review*, 18: 1144-67.

------. 1984b. *The Mobility of Labor and Capital: A Study of International Investment and Labor.* Cambridge, UK and New York: Cambridge University Press.

Strauch, Barbara. 2003. *The Primal Teen: What the New Discoveries About the Teenage Brain Tell Us About Our Kids.* New York: Doubleday.

Suárez-Orozco, Carola, and Marcelo M. Suárez-Orozco. 2001. *Children of Immigration.* Cambridge, MA: Harvard University Press.

Ueda, Reed. 1987. *Avenues to Adulthood: The Origins of the High School and Social Mobility in an American Suburb.* Cambridge, UK and London: Cambridge University Press.

Wolf, Larry. 1998. When I Imagine a Child: The Idea of Childhood and the Philosophy of Memory in the Enlightenment. *Eighteenth Century Studies,* 31: 377-401.

Zelizer, Viviana A. 1985. *Pricing the Priceless Child: The Changing Social Value of Child.* New York: Basic Books.

Alfred Hornung
Johannes Gutenberg University, Mainz, Germany

The emergence of transnational American Studies from Ground Zero

The history of American studies in Europe consists of a series of transatlantic encounters between Americans and Europeans in the second half of the twentieth century. The ideological divide between East and West resulted in different models for setting up American studies programs, whose critical direction shifted according to political alliances, alternating between phases of agreement and disagreement with the politics of the United States. The voluntary embracement of American culture in many Eastern European countries after the collapse of the Communist world in 1989 contrasts with the enforced acceptance of American culture as part of the US reeducation program in West Germany after the war and the gradual acquaintance of most Western European countries with the American business world thanks to the economic recovery efforts of the Marshall plan. However, both the fall of the wall in Berlin and the fall of fascist Germany resulted in repercussions and revolutionary changes that in their dramatic nature resemble, to a certain degree, the collapse of the World Trade Center in New York in 2001. For the purpose of analysis I will argue that each of these three historical events generated a different kind of the engagement with the United States, which – taken together – form the concept of American studies for the twenty-first century.

The title of my contribution points to the similarity of *ground zero situations* at different times and in different parts of the world. These ground zero situations have been the result of devastating destructions caused variously by the systematic bombing of cities during the war, by the unexpected and abrupt collapse of political and economic systems in Eastern Europe, and by the implosion of skyscrapers after the terrorist attacks of 9/11. My application of the idea of ground zero to the proclaimed end of ideology in 1989 could also be extended to the collapse of the stock market in the current financial crisis of 2008, emanating from the United States with global repercussions (Hornung 2009a).

The term 'ground zero' was first coined with reference to the point of impact of nuclear bombs, the point where these explosives unfurl their most destructive potential. After the Second World War Germany and many European cities resembled such points of ground zero created by conventional bombs; the Japanese cities of Hiroshima and Nagasaki became the actual sites of nuclear destruction. In a metaphoric application of ground zero, historians called the capitulation of the German Empire on 8 May 1945 at midnight the "zero hour"

("Stunde Null") symbolizing the beginning of postwar Germany.[1] All of these ground zero situations became the starting point for a radical reorientation of culture and politics after the experience of human-made total destruction. Today it is a consensus among Americanists that the emergence and establishment of European American studies are closely connected to the Cold War and were intended as an ideological tool in lieu of military weapons. The initial efforts of instituting American studies programs in Western Europe centered on the ideas of democracy and freedom. Academic interests coincided with the political agenda of the United States of America. This is most obvious in the foundation of the Salzburg Seminar for American Studies, which was conceived as a "Marshall plan of the mind" (Ryback) by Harvard faculty for the promotion of human values represented by the United States of America. The first seminar in 1947, led by such distinguished Americans as anthropologist Margaret Mead and literary historians F.O. Matthiessen and Alfred Kazin, brought together ninety students from eighteen European countries to discuss American literature, politics, and economics. Liam Kennedy has recently criticized this idealized project in Schloss Leopoldskron by pointing to the brute reality outside of the ideal space of literature and culture, evoked in Margaret Mead's report "The Salzburg Seminar in American Civilization" (Kennedy 2006, 102-03).

> Salzburg with its bombed areas, its American MP's, in large bright tin helmets, its DP camps and its Jewish refugees, its population among whom there was not a single plump child … pulling the seminar members back to the real world and assuring them that Leopoldskron was not an escape but merely a setting within which it was possible to meet each other and breathe in new air for the months to come. (Mead 1947)

The original intention to introduce "American civilization to the young generation of post-war Europe" (Ryback) was part of the American plans to replace the ground zero of Europe, both in terms of its institutions and political culture. The American efforts were supported by German returnees from their American exile, like the political scientists Ernst Fraenkel and Arnold Bergsträsser, who had become familiar with the interdisciplinary American studies concept from their colleagues during their stays at American universities and saw it as a shield against the Fascist specter (Gassert 2003). Given their personal experiences of the Nazi past, these Americanized scholars were instrumental in establishing American studies programs at German universities and founding the German Association for American Studies in 1953, the year which also saw the foundation of the European Association for American Studies at Schloss Leopoldskron

---

[1] Roland Barthes's 1953 concept of "Writing Degree Zero," which abandons the so-called bourgeois notions of literature (i.e., traditional human and moral values) for the sake of an abstract and neutral form of analysis, can be seen as a structuralist equivalent of the ground zero situation. Cf. also Hornung, "Flying Planes."

(Grabbe 2003). What governed these academic postwar efforts were the rejection of undemocratic regimes and the intention to realize interdisciplinary cooperation between the social sciences and the humanities. There is no doubt that these activities launched the way for a successful Americanization of Germany that reached its culmination in John F. Kennedy's visit to Berlin in 1963. To what extent Kennedy's famous admission, "Ich bin ein Berliner," is a first instance of transnational American studies remains to be seen.

The critical edge of the original American studies concept as developed in the 1930s in the United States, i.e., its political opposition to conservative American politics, enters the European scene at the time of the Vietnam War in the 1960s. Inspired by the new ideas of American literature and popular culture, the 1960s generation applies the values of American civilization to a critique of American foreign politics, adding anti-American sentiments to the general mood of Americanization. The focus of European American studies from the sixties onward on African American literature and culture and aspects of race determined teaching and research. Members of the American studies departments at the University of Frankfurt and the John F. Kennedy Institute, especially Martin Christadler, Olaf Hansen, Günter H. Lenz, and Winfried Fluck, provide the theoretical basis for the postwar concept of American studies in Germany (Christadler/Lenz 1977). It consists of a radical application of the American value system in the classroom and critical dissent with American politics, often from the perspective of race. US American studies scholars, however, do not share this preoccupation of European scholarship at this time. Instead, the American Studies Association has adopted the role of the United States as the leader of the Free World for the classroom and scholarship and shapes American studies in analogy with the Cold War scenario of politics.

The second ground zero situation concerns the post-communist situation after the fall of the Berlin wall in 1989. The general belief that the United States emerged from the battles of the Cold War as the only remaining superpower in the world translated into President Clinton's vision of America "as the world's indispensable nation" (Clinton 1997). It is in the decade of the 1990s that white US Americanists gradually turn to and take up the issues of race, class and gender in American studies. Eric Sundquist's 1993 classic study *To Wake the Nation: Race in the Making of American Literature* acted as a sort of wake-up call for scholarship in the US, implicitly reconnecting with the research done in Europe. It became the association's equivalent to Toni Morrison's *Playing in the Dark: Whiteness and the Literary Imagination* of 1992. And at the end of the decade Mary Helen Washington posed the question in her presidential address at the ASA in Washington *"What* Happens to American Studies If You Put African American Studies at the Center?"* (Washington 1998). Around this time American studies scholars in the United States began to question the new role of exceptionalism resurfacing in political circles. Donald Pease edited a volume on

National Identities and Post-Americanist Narratives, whose contributors under-mined the assumption of an exceptional nation, and John Carlos Rowe tried to conceptualize the new turn in a volume called *Post-Nationalist American Stu-dies*. This new concept emerging from the post-communist ground zero links up with the changed situation in Europe and the practice of European American studies with its critical focus on race and the transgression of the nation state. In the altered political field, the European Association for American Studies was thrust into a new role of assisting Eastern European countries to reconnect to Europe, a process facilitated by the dynamic momentum of American culture. The foundation of new Eastern European American Studies Associations led to a realightent to the ASA and the EAAS. It is no surprise that the idea of a com-parative and dialogical concept of American studies first arose in the 1990s, convincingly formulated by Günter H. Lenz in 1999 (Lenz 1999). His ideas later enter into Donald Pease's series of engagements with the Re-Configurations of American Studies in the Futures of American Studies Institute at Dartmouth College. The stage was set for an internationalization of a post-ideological con-cept of American studies.

In the twenty-first century, 9/11 presents a third type of ground zero, specta-cularly visible in the media and on site in New York City, but also metaphorical-ly on a global scale. The ground zero caused by the terrorist attacks generated political and cultural reactions and led to the emergence of the transnational American studies concept. The war on terror and the institution of the Home Security Office with all its restrictive policies became the groundwork for Presi-dent Bush's unilateral actions. The global alliance of many nations in the wake of 9/11 collapsed in reaction to political measures implemented in the United States and military engagements in the Middle East, unlicensed by the United Nations. Instead, a new division arose between the alliance of the willing and the unwilling states, provoked by Donald Rumsfeld's opposition of New and Old Europe. The facile attribution of allegiance to and rejection of the United States in the years of the George W. Bush administrations seems to have faded for a more realistic assessment of friendly assistance and friendly critique. The triumphant reception of presidential candidate Barak Obama, drawing more than 200,000 people to a pre-election rally in Berlin in July of 2008, speaks a differ-ent kind of language in which the early European concern with race in America and global concerns of US Americanists come to fruition. This political practice reflects the nature of transnational American studies. Based on the cooperation of different national associations of American studies with the American Studies Association in the United States, the ASA launched a major campaign to inter-nationalize the organization and to create a global network. The dramatic events of 9/11 represented the decisive turning point for American studies scholars in the US and for the American Studies Association to link up with the concept of European American Studies and to open up to the new ideas. The annual conventions of the ASA in Hartford (2002), Houston (2003), and Atlanta (2004) were stages in the concerted efforts to counteract the unilateral politics of the United States with the multilateral forum of the American studies community for the discussion of different concepts of crisis resolution in the twenty-first century. European Americanists can bring to this discussion the historical dimension of global changes and the experience of the transformation of European nation-states into a European union, most evident in the acceptance of the Euro as a common currency in 2002.

It was Shelley Fisher Fishkin who – echoing Mary Helen Washington – asked in her 2004 presidential address in Atlanta "What would the field of American studies look like if the *trans*national rather than the national were at its center?" (21). Many answers have been given to this question since 2004.[2] They all thrive on the notion of superseding the national frame of reference with geographical boundaries, a uniform language and a monocultural identity. Beyond the borders of the continental United States, the topic of America and American cultures is everywhere where their influence is being felt. And instead of an international cooperation of scholars, which often privileges one partner over another, the transnational model does not know such a gradation of scholarship. It establishes in fact a form of multilateral cooperation of equal partners in research and teaching which ideally could become a model for political and cultural interactions worldwide, notwithstanding recent interventions which point to the self-deluding nature of European scholars (Kennedy 2006) or the romance aspect of the United States of America for European Americanists (Fluck 2009).

Much in contemporary American literature and culture seems to call for such a transnational American studies scholarship which arises from ground zero situations to chart a way for the future of American studies in the twenty-first century. Since September 2001, a great variety of reactions to ground zero, ranging from personal and political to religious and cultural expressions, have been in evidence. Most prominent in this series is former president Bush's political response, which evoked a Cold War scenario with the potential of a transnational perspective. In his early comments, Bush repeatedly designated the war on terror as a crusade to be fought against the forces of evil, apparently initially ignorant of the historical resonances of the term 'crusade,' especially to Muslim ears. Later he frequently drew an analogy between the American mission in the Second World War in Fascist Germany and the mission in Iraq. In both cases American troops liberated the repressed people from tyrannical forces and exported the American values of democracy and freedom to replace unbearable and deadly dictatorships. This rhetoric reinforced then secretary of Defense

---

[2] The foundation of the International American Studies Association (IASA) in 2003, which intends to provide a global umbrella for all American studies activities, is further evidence of this transnational cooperation.

Rumsfeld's demeaning division between Old and New Europe and became the guideline for the President's European visits in his second term. His one-day stay in Mainz and his subsequent visit to Bratislava the next day in February of 2005 were intended as demonstrations of the Cold War division, this time between the ungrateful Old Europe/Germany and the appreciative New Europe/Slovakia. Minus its ideological component, this transnational trajectory of the visit could have been used advantageously for a meaningful discussion of different perceptions of the role of the United States after 9/11 and of the acceptance of critical opinions concerning the deployment of American troops in the world.

The rhetorical flourishes and hasty actions in the world of politics contrast with a considerable silence in the realm of cultural production and reactions to ground zero after the events of 9/11. While first essays reflect the intellectuals politics of "dissent from the homeland" and comment on the tourist aspects of "Groundzeroland" (Lentricchia and McAuliffe 2003) or critically "reassess their subject matter" (Smith 2001), temporal and spatial distance seems to be needed for an adequate response, which always tends to combine the personal and the political on a transnational platform. The immensity of the televisional event often defies literary representation and calls for visual renditions (Whitlock 2006). My first example, which necessitates the practice of transnational American studies, is the work of Art Spiegelman, American comics artist born in Stockholm of Polish Jewish parents who had survived Auschwitz and emigrated to New York. In his Pulitzer Prize winning graphic novel *Maus* (1986, 1991) Spiegelman had first dared to address the topic of the holocaust. The comic strip series also seemed to be an appropriate genre for him to cope with the immensity of human destruction in which he was personally involved as the child of Auschwitz survivors. Given this history, he must have felt like a survivor after 9/11. Living near the Twin Towers, he had experienced the attack and the collapse of the towers directly while taking his daughter to school. To come to grips with 9/11 he again used the same genre of the graphic novel, which had worked for the representation of the holocaust. When he had finished his series *In the Shadow of No Towers* (2004), he could not find a publisher in the United States. Apparently the American public was not ready for such a "comic" response and there might have been cultural hazards. So it appeared first in the German weekly *Die Zeit*. The series consists of ten tabloid-sized strips and its pages are as thick as the cardboard covers of children's books. Each page is done in a large-page format, and the style of each page features a rather eclectic collage of original and inspired strips. The most potent image is one which Spiegelman calls "the glowing bones." It recurs throughout the series and represents the radiant outline of one of the towers, moments before it collapses.

Figure 1. Art Spiegelman, *In the Shadow of No Towers* (detail)

Rather than presenting a continuous storyline, the cartoonist presents single images and impressions of an event, which does not lend itself to easy representation. Spiegelman alternates images of destroyed buildings with those of shocked adults and frightened children. The smoke, dust and debris immediately evoke references to the Holocaust: "I remember my father trying to describe what the smoke in Auschwitz smelled like. The closest he got was telling me, it was 'indescribable.' That's exactly what the air in Lower Manhattan smelled like after September 11!" (3). Commenting on the reactions of the New Yorkers after 9/11, he draws a parallel between them and the Jews in Fascist Germany in 1938: "You know I've called myself a 'rootless cosmopolitan' equally homeless anywhere on the planet. I was wrong. … I finally understand why some Jews didn't leave Berlin right after the Kristallnacht" (4). The courageous stand of New Yorkers and the American people is set against the measures taken by the Bush Administration, which, for Spiegelman, "spent two years squandering chances to bring the community of nations together" (10) and instead moved in "Big Brother mode … into a colonialist adventure in Iraq – while doing very little to make America genuinely safer beyond confiscating nail clippers at airports" ("Introduction"). His anxiety over the effects of terrorism and his outrage over the handling of the crisis by the political United States take the form of comic strip images and sound bites. For Spiegelman, this comic representation of terror and human destruction is a way to recover from the post-traumatic stress and disorder he suffered after the attacks (see Orbán, Versluys, "Art Spiegelman's *In the Shadow of No Towers*").

In the Shadow of No Towers clearly transcends the frames of national art and transnationally connects the New York ground zero with the ground zero of World War II. The common concern is the suffering and destruction of human beings, the incineration of lives to ashes. The pictures of people of all ages and all classes in distress appeal to the universal commiseration of all humankind. The fact that Spiegelman's comic-strip representation of New York's much-publicized event was published in a German weekly rather than in an American newspaper points to the difficulties involved in the treatment of the topic comparable to the impossibility of writing about the holocaust immediately after the Second World War. In the final analysis, Spiegelman's graphic novel, which originates in New York, begins its cultural work in Germany to eventually return to its origin on a transnational trajectory. Transnational American studies scholars on both sides of the Atlantic will comprehend the author's representation of 9/11 as a form of global mediation between cultural differences for the sake of their peaceful resolution.

The difficulties in finding an adequate medium for the representation of the unrepresentable ground zero situation, and the resort to transnational areas of reference is also evident in 9/11 novels: "... the problem for the writer was how to write about events which seemed to defy the logic of traditional narrative realism and which presented a story that the whole world was already familiar with through an unending televisual loop" (Morley 2008, 295). While earlier responses by writers collected in *110 Stories: New York Writes after 9/11* (Baer 2002) self-reflexively comment on the inadequacy of the fictional craft and focus on the factual and emotional, later fiction uses the precarious status of American families to address the terrorist destruction on a transnational scale (Hornung 2009b).

The disruption of family relations and the problematic attempts to reunite family members after 9/11 is the topic of Jonathan Safran Foer's novel *Extremely Loud & Incredibly Close* (2005). The nine-year old protagonist and narrator Oskar Schell lost his father in the collapsing Twin Towers and tries to make sense of this loss in the company of his mother and grandmother. One form which this work of mourning takes is Oskar's search for the matching lock for a key that he finds in his father's closet after his death. In spite of the impossibility of this mission, Oskar sets out on this Sisyphus task throughout New York City and is eventually successful. The chance encounter with the former owner coincides with Oskar's unexpected encounter with his grandfather Thomas Schell, who links the action to the family's past in Dresden. The crucial event of this past is Thomas' experience of the bombing of Dresden in February 1945, when he loses his pregnant fiancée, Anna, in the catastrophic reduction of the city to ground zero.

> On my way to Anna's house, the second raid began, I threw myself into the nearest cellar, it was hit, it filled with pink smoke and gold flames, so I fled into the next cellar, it caught fire, I ran from cellar to cellar as each previous cellar was destroyed, burning monkeys screamed from the trees, birds with their wings on fire sang from the telephone wires over which desperate calls traveled, I found another shelter, it was filled to the walls, brown smoke pressed down from the ceiling like a hand, it became more and more difficult to breathe, my lungs were trying to pull the room in through my mouth, there was a silver explosion, all of us tried to leave the cellar at once, dead and dying people were trampled, I walked over an old man, I walked over children, everyone was losing everyone, the bombs were like a waterfall, ran through the streets, from cellar to cellar, and saw terrible things: legs and necks,

I saw a woman whose blond hair and green dress were on fire, running with a silent baby in her arms, I saw humans melted into thick pools of liquid, three or four feet deep in places, I saw bodies crackling like embers, laughing, and the remains of masses of people who had tried to escape the firestorm by jumping head first into the lakes and ponds, the parts of their bodies that were submerged in the water were still intact, while the parts that protruded above water charred beyond recognition, the bombs kept falling, purple, orange and white, I kept running, my hands kept bleeding, through the sounds of collapsing buildings I heard the roar of that baby's silence. (Foer 2006, 211-13)

Thomas Schell's flight from this scene of devastation takes him to New York, where he accidentally meets Anna's sister, whom he marries. He leaves her when she is pregnant with his son, Oskar's father, to return to Dresden. Here he writes letters to his son without sending them off. When Thomas Schell sees the implosion of the Twin Towers on television and learns about his son's death, he tries to reunite with his abandoned family, first as a secret boarder in his wife's apartment, then as a secret sharer of Oskar's plans to exhume his father's empty coffin. The nocturnal scene at the grave amounts to a ritualistic cleansing of both the grandfather's guilt at having ignored his son's existence and Oskar's guilt at not having answered the phone when his father called home shortly before his death on 9/11. In a liberating act, they deposit the grandfather's unsent letters from Dresden and Oskar's tape with his father's messages (recorded from the answering machine) in the coffin. This moment of spiritual union of the two family members relies on the transnational connection of the American ground zero to historical ground zero scenes of World War II. Thomas Schell's experience of the destruction of Dresden serves as a link to Oskar's experience of the destruction of the Twin Towers in New York; this is compounded by his school project on the nuclear destruction of human lives in Hiroshima, based on recorded interviews with a bereaved mother who mourns her lost child. The momentary crisis resolution for the grandfather and his grandson translates itself into Oskar's imagination about the reversal of time and action in which all things would be made undone like looking at the scenes in a flip book in reverse: the planes leaving the Twin Towers rather than entering them, his father rising from the ground into the air rather than falling to his death. Such a utopian turn is, however, counteracted by the grandfather's undecided plans for a future with or without his family, in New York or back in Dresden. Based on the novel's transnational perspective, it is left for the reader to mediate between the two positions, which are also mirrored in the formal rendition of the narrative. It varies from the inclusion of blank pages via colorful graffiti, partially legible and blackened script, and variations of numbers, to correction marks and single words on pages. These postmodern, unreadable features contrast with the family members' attempts to correspond with each other and bridge distances, including the grandfather's traditional, yet unsent letters to his son, the grandmother's occasional letters to her grandson, and Oskar's postmodern scrapbook entries.

These acts of writing represent efforts of communication in a ground zero situation, captured in the series of photographs of a body falling from the Twin Towers, which toward the end of the novel is repeated over several pages and becomes the final and dominant image.

This image at the end of Foer's novel is the topic of Don DeLillo's novel *Falling Man* (2007). It represents a powerful response to the ground zero situation and one with transnational resonances. In the course of his accomplished career as a novelist, DeLillo has repeatedly thematized dramatic events such as the toxic pollution of the environment in *White Noise* (1985), the assassination of John F. Kennedy in *Libra* (1988), or the nuclear arms' race in *Underworld* (1997). Immediately following 9/11, DeLillo published a critical article called "In the Ruins of the Future," in which he brand-marked the terrorist usage of modern technology for evil ends and evoked his earlier demand that art – after years of postmodern play and arbitrariness – be "grounded in reality" (DeCurtis 1991, 46). Six years later, he presents his version of coping with the reality of ground zero in *Falling Man*. Like Foer, DeLillo connects the topic of disintegration and destruction with family values and the transnational reach of terrorist persuasions. Unlike Oskar's father, the 39-year old lawyer Keith Neudecker survives the attack on the Twin Towers and manages to escape from the building before it collapses. Rather than returning to his own apartment he almost instinctively makes his way to his wife's and son's place from whom he had separated some years ago. Covered with debris and slightly injured, he moves back into his wife's household and intends to reconnect with his wife Liane and his son Justin. Yet this plan turns out to be futile because of alternate relations, which both partners pursue. Keith traces the owner of a suitcase, which he had saved from the debris, and begins a casual relationship with Florence Givens in the mutual endeavor to overcome their personal traumas suffered in the narrow escape from destruction. In addition, circles of friends substitute for the missing core of a family: both Keith and Liane intensify their relations to poker playing friends and a group of Alzheimer patients respectively, and their son Justin also seeks the company of friends. While Keith seeks playful diversion with his fellow 9/11 victim in New York and his poker friends in Las Vegas, Liane and Justin seem to be existentially concerned about their precarious situation. Fearful of future attacks Justin and his friends watch the sky for new terrorist planes. The personal experience of her father's Alzheimer case and suicide motivates Liane especially in her work as a copy editor and with Alzheimer patients, whom she encourages to write their life stories to cope with their disease as a form of mental ground zero.

The "fall of man," implicit in the dissolution of family relations and the disintegration of the human mind of Alzheimer patients, repeats itself on other levels. One of them is the playful mode of a performance artist called "Falling Man" who to the dismay of spectators jumps from elevations, buildings and bridges onto precipices. His performance takes on a new dimension after 9/11 with the televised images of figures falling from the Twin Towers.[3] Another level is the political dimension of falling man, contained in the structure of the novel. DeLillo uses a person's name to designate each of the three sections, which reveal the conscious or unconscious transformation of people in time. The first part titled "Bill Lawton" is the anglicized name of Osama bin Laden from the perspective of little Justin and his friends, the Siblings, who are incapable of measuring the event. In their helplessness, they search the sky with binoculars for new planes to fly into buildings. For them, 9/11 is reduced to the idea that flying planes can be dangerous. The second part refers to "Ernst Hechinger," which is the original name of Liane's mother's friend Martin Ridnour. While the real origin of Martin is left unclear, the text insinuates a connection with the Baader-Meinhoff terrorist group in 1970s Germany (Kaufman 2008), a group of radical leftists who planned to destroy the existing order of the country by terrorist means. The third part, "David Janiak," is titled for the real name of the performance artist "Falling Man," who dies in the course of his last stunt, planned as a conscious imitation of "the body posture of a particular man who was photographed falling from the north tower of the World Trade Center, headfirst, arms at his sides, one leg bent, a man set forever in free fall against the looming background of the column panels in the tower," making him into a "Brave New Chronicler of the Age of Terror" (DeLillo 2007, 221, 220; see also Raspe 2008, Drew 2001). In a final dimension, DeLillo incorporates in his system of "Falling Man" the 9/11 terrorists represented in the figure of Hammad or Mohammed Atta. In each of the three parts of the novel, DeLillo concentrates on one scene which traces the transformation of the nineteen terrorists from young Arabs who studied in Hamburg, Germany, went through training camps in Afghanistan, and took flight lessons in Florida until their hijacking of the planes on 9/11. What surfaces from this presentation are the analogies, which the novelist sees between the different groups and their actions. There is an evident analogy of human relations between family members and group behavior, of revolutionary actions between the German Baader Meinhoff group and the nineteen Arab terrorists, and of the political and religious dedication to the cause, as well as the artistic dedication to performance art. The common denominator seems to rely on the religious idea of the fall of man in paradise and hence the Puritan conception of the moral depravity of man, shared by all humankind. Yet in contradistinction to the Puritan worldview, which also determines the thinking of later politicians, Don DeLillo's position as well as that of his fellow writers is a humanistic one, which supersedes the ideological dichot-

---

[3] The fictional figure is modeled after the real-life artist Kerry Skarbakka, whose 9/11 imitations met with outrage among New Yorkers (see Versleuys, *Out of the Blue* 22).

omy of the political agenda. They represent transnational counterdiscourses to the nationalistic scripts (Versleuys 2009, 23).

Both Jonathan Safran Foer and Don DeLillo analyze the devastating destruction of the American ground zero on a personal level as the outcome of human failure. Rather than attributing guilt to one single person or group, they relate their actions to transnational events and historical forces, such as fascism, terrorist ideologies, and nuclear power, which have caused the ground zeros of the past. The long-range effects of World War I eventually led to the formulation of the American studies concept in the 1930s, whose scholarly activities included critical evaluations of American politics. European American Studies associations, especially the German Association of American Studies, emerged after the Second World War as part of a Western orientation but also as critical scholarship in the service of democratic practices in Europe and the United States. In the course of the internationalization of American Studies associations in the 1990s, the former imbalance between the dominant position of the ASA and other national associations gradually disappeared. The events of 9/11, which immediately created an international cooperation of most nations with the United States, also led to the creation of transnational American studies with a global resonance and a new *Journal of Transnational American Studies*. The forms of literature and culture, which have since appeared, indeed call for such a transnational approach. It could be a first programmatic step toward a worldwide humanistic approach advocated in Edward Said's posthumous work *Humanism and Democratic Criticism* (2005), and could eventually result in Jürgen Habermas' projection of a "cosmopolitan community of world citizens" and "global governance" (Habermas 2001, 109, 111).

References

"*Amerikastudien* / American *Studies* at 50." 2005. Anniversary issue of the journal of the German Association for American Studies. *Amst* 50.1-2.

Baer, Ulrich, ed. 2002. *110 Stories: New York Writes after September 11.* New York: New York University Press.

Barthes, Roland. 1977. *Writing Degree Zero.* Trans. Annette Lavers and Colin Smith. New York: Hill and Wang.

Christadler, Martin, and Günter H. Lenz, eds. 1977. Amerikastudien – Theorie, Geschichte, interpretatorische Praxis. Special Issue of *Amerikastudien / American Studies.* Stuttgart: Metzler Verlag.

Clinton, William J. 1997. Second Inaugural Address. January 20. http://bartelby.org/124/pres65.html.

DeCurtis, Anthony. 1991. An Outsider in this Society: An Interview with Don DeLillo. In *Introducting Don DeLillo*, ed. Frank Lentricchia, 43-66. Durham, ND: Duke University Press.

DeLillo, Don. 1986. *White Noise.* New York: Penguin Books.

------. 1988. *Libra.* New York: Viking Press.

------. 1997. *Underworld.* New York: Scribner.

------. 2001. In the Ruins of the Future: Reflections on terror and loss in the shadow of September. *Harper's Magazine,* December: 33-40.

------. 2007. *Falling Man.* New York: Scribner.

Drew, Richard. 2001. Photograph of "Falling Man."

Fishkin, Shelley Fisher. 2005. Crossroads of Cultures: The Transnational Turn in American Studies. Presidential Address to the American Studies Association, November 12, 2004. *American Quarterly* 57.1: 17-57.

Fluck, Winfried. 2009. American Studies and the Romance with America: Approaching America through Its Ideals. In *Romance with America?: Essays on Culture, Literature, and American Studies,* ed. Laura Bieger and Johannes Voelz, 87-104. Heidelberg: Universitätsverlag Winter.

Foer, Jonathan Safran. 2006. *Extremely Loud & Incredibly Close.* London: Penguin Books.

Gassert, Philipp. 2003. Between Political Reconnaisance [sic] Work and Democratizing Science: American Studies in Germany, 1917-53. *Bulletin of the German Historical Institute Washington, D.C.* 32: 33-50.

Grabbe, Hans-Jürgen. 2003. 50 Jahre Deutsche Gesellschaft für Amerikastudien. *Amerikastudien / American Studies* 48.2: 159-84.

Habermas, Jürgen. 2001. *The Postnational Constellation: Political Essays,* trans. Max Pensky. Cambridge: Polity Press.

Hornung, Alfred. 2004. Flying Planes Can Be Dangerous: Ground Zero Literature. In *Science, Technology, and the Humanities in Recent American Fiction,* ed. Peter Freese and Charles B. Harris, 383-403. Essen: Die Blaue Eule.

------. 2009a. Ground Zero: Cultural Repercussions of 9/11 [in Chinese]. In *Bianhua yu Yanxu: "9·11" hou de Meiguo [Changes and Continuities: The United States after 9.11],* ed. Mei Renyi and Fu Meirong, 426-433. Beijing: Shijie Zhishi Chubanshe [World Affairs Press].

------. 2009b. Terrorist Violence and Transnational Memory: Jonathan Safran Foer and Don DeLillo. In *Transnational American Memories,* ed. Udo Hebel, 171-83. Berlin: Walter de Gruyter.

Kaufman, Linda S. 2008. The Wake of Terror: Don DeLillo's 'In the Ruins of the Future,' 'Baader-Meinhof,' and 'Falling Man.' *Modern Fiction Studies* 54.2: 353-77.

Kennedy, Liam. 2006. Spectres of Comparison: American Studies and the United States of the West. *Comparative American Studies* 4.2: 135-50.

------. 2008. American Studies in Europe and the United States of the West. In *Transcultural Visions of Identities in Images and Texts: Transatlantic*

American Studies, ed. Wilfried Raussert and Reinhard Isensee, 94-109. Heidelberg: Universitätsverlag Winter.

Lentricchia, Frank and Jody McAuliffe. 2003. Groundzeroland. In *Dissent from the Homeland: Essays after September 11*, ed. Stanley Hauerwas and Frank Lentricchia, 95-105. Durham: Duke University Press.

Lenz, Günter. 1999. Toward a Dialogics of International American Culture Studies: Transnationality, Border Discourses, and Public Culture(s). *Amerikastudien / American Studies*, 44.1: 5-23.

Mead, Margaret. 1947. The Salzburg Seminar in American Civilization. www.salzburgseminar.org/reports/1947_MeadArticle.pdf

Morley, Catherine. 2008. Plotting Against America: 9/11 and the Spectacle of Terror in Contemporary American Fiction. Thematic Issue on "Revisiting Crisis / Reflecting on Conflict: American Literary Interpretations from World War II to Ground Zero." *Journal of Theory and Criticism*, 16: 293-312.

Morrison, Toni. 1992. *Playing in the Dark: Whiteness and the Literary Imagination*. Cambridge, MA: Harvard University Press.

Orbán, Katalin. 2007. Trauma and Visuality: Art Spiegelman's *Maus* and *In the Shadow of No Towers*. *Representations* 97 (Winter): 57-89.

Pease, Donald, ed. 1994. *National Identities and Post-Americanist Narratives*. Durham: Duke University Press.

Raspe, Martin. 2008. 'The Falling Man': Der 11. September in der Momentaufnahme. In *Nine Eleven: Ästhetische Verarbeitungen des 11. September 2001*, ed. Ingo Irsliger and Christoph Jürgensen, 369-82. Heidelberg: Universitätsverlag Winter.

Rowe, John Carlos. 2000. *Post-Nationalist American Studies*. Berkeley: University of California Press.

Ryback, T.W. No date. The Salzburg Seminar – A Community of Fellows. http://www.salzburgseminar.org/2005History.cfm

Said, Edward. 2005. *Humanism and Democratic Criticism*. New York: Columbia University Press.

Smith, Dinitia. 2001. Novelists Reassess Their Subject Matter. *New York Times,* September 20.

Spiegelman, Art. 1987. *Maus*. London: Penguin Books.

------. 2004. *In the Shadow of No Towers*. New York: Pantheon Books.

Sundquist, Eric J. 1993. *To Wake the Nation: Race in the Making of American Literature*. Cambridge, MA: Harvard University Press.

The Journal of Transnational American Studies. 2008 ff. Ed. Shelley Fisher Fishkin, Alfred Hornung, James L. Lee, Shirley Geok-Lin Lim, Takayuki Tatsumi, Greg Robinson, and Nina Morgan. eScholarship Repository. University of California.

Versluys, Kristiaan. 2006. Art Spiegelman's *In the Shadow of No Towers*: 9/11 and the Representation of Trauma. *Modern Fiction Studies* 52.4: 980-1004.

------. 2009. *Out Of The Blue: September 11 and the Novel*. New York: Columbia University Press.

Washington, Mary Helen. 1998. Disturbing the Peace: What Happens to American Studies If You Put African American Studies at the Center? Presidential Address to the American Studies Association, October 29, 1997. *American Quarterly* 50.1: 1-23.

Whitlock, Gillian. 2006. Autographics: The Seeing 'I' of the Comics. *Modern Fiction Studies* 52.4: 965-79.

Zbigniew Lewicki
Warsaw University, Poland
East is East, and West is West, and never the twain shall meet: or will they?

> Don't ask what you can do for American Studies, ask what American Studies has done to you.

Europeans who study America tend to see global politics, as well as culture, differently than their compatriots with a less immediate experience of that continent and its people. Moreover, not only our reaction to the idea of America, but also the way we research it is a good indication of who we are and what we believe it – as individuals, and as members of the two vast politico-cultural communities of Eastern and Western Europe.

During a recent meeting Christoph von Marschall, the author of a new book on Barack Obama, pointed out that while in Poland he is criticized for his overly enthusiastic approach to the candidate, in Germany the very same book has been blasted for not portraying Obama as an unblemished hero, presumably in the vein of Parson Weems' "life" of George Washington. Perhaps as many as 200,000 people gathered to see Obama in person in Berlin. If he came to an East European capital, say Warsaw, he would be likely to draw less than 5% of that crowd. Does this mean that Poles are incapable of appreciating the new beacon of hope? Or that Germans, like Americans, try to compensate for their own mistreatment of minorities by hurling themselves at the feet of the most prominent specimen of a visible minority?

One way or another, American politics functions as a catalyst, or as a lens that allows us to see our own problems in a new light. The upcoming American election, perhaps more than any other, is a mirror in which not only American voters but entire societies see themselves, their hopes, complexes, prejudices and predilections. In Europe this year's choice seems to define not only the contrasting views of interested observers, but also the division between East and West within the new, presumably unified, continent.

The Tehran-Yalta arrangements made one part of Europe subject to Uncle Joe while the other part found itself within the scope of interest and assistance of Uncle Sam. But the cultural division of Europe into two unequal parts is not simply a result of WWII. For centuries, the eastern part of the continent was perceived as the domain of snow, vodka, Asian mentalities and the ornately outdated Russian Orthodox Church, while the southwest portion was presumably that of sun, wine, the Enlightenment, and the dignified opposition between Protestantism and Roman Catholicism. Today, the West is routinely forgiven for what the East is frequently stigmatized. The pervasive corruption and blatant disregard for law by Italian politicians is considered an amusing, if perhaps slightly improper irritation, while similar phenomena are cause for contempt and economic sanctions in Bulgaria.

Still, after WWII the division was not a matter of intuition, of perceived and interpreted signals, but of borders, guards and the iron curtain, and it was onto such a divided Europe that the United States descended. For almost half a century the United States, with its funds, soldiers, and ideals, has been very much a part of the West European reality and was banned from Eastern Europe.

American presence in Western Europe was real, if for some too real, with the "overpaid, oversexed and over here" catchphrase expressing the European exasperation with hordes of young American barbarians. Their Mid-Western manners, their preference for the new and the mass-produced over the patina and historical significance, were unnerving and soon produced the battle-cry of "Yankee, go home." Or, to be more precise, stay within the confines of your bases from where you can protect us, but keep away from our streets – and our women. And so was born the post-war anti-Americanism, one of the strangest sociological phenomena in view of what West Europeans owed to American soldiers and to Marshall money.

The case of Eastern Europe was equally irrational, though in reverse. American soldiers chose not to make it over the Rein river, to say nothing of the Oder or the Vltava, and there was no Marshall Plan money here. And yet this abdication of responsibility produced a decisively positive, idealized concept of the United States, its might and its promise to the world. The imagined American soldiers were perfect, and life-saving UNRRA packages were stuffed with American goodies. And so was born an equally strange sociological phenomenon: instead of being resentful at the Yalta sellout, the populace of these countries nurtured their faith in the good American President who would surely annihilate Lords of the Kremlin to bring happiness and prosperity to all.

In other words Americans, who brought freedom to France and delivered Germany from its past, were perceived there as occupiers rather than liberators – while East Europeans, whom Americans had failed, perceived them as potential saviors in whom all hope was vested. While the French parliament debated the menace of Coca-Cola and there were serious warnings in Italy that this diabolical beverage would turn children's hair white, the other part of Europe could only hope for an opportunity to be exposed to the dangers of hamburgers, chewing gum and Rita Hayworth movies.

Still, there was progress. Even as anti-Americanism fed on misinformation and ignorance, the Marshall Plan paid Europeans to discover the New World – not as emigrants, but as observers and commentators. And if America was a little too distant or too expensive to visit, it was ready to oblige by presenting itself to Europe. There were crowds of Americans in Europe, Western Europe, which was no longer the domain of the New York elite out of Henry James' novels, but of good-natured "simple folk" straight from Sinclair Lewis' Main Street.

There were changes in Eastern Europe, too. The first Fulbright exchange in American Literature occurred around 1960, and a Polish-language, US-financed glossy monthly *Ameryka* entered the market at roughly the same time, bringing stories and color pictures about America's life and culture, if not about its politics.

During the same 1950s and 1960s at English Departments of several American universities the habit of reading the entire culture from inside literary texts was challenged by an academic heresy called American Studies. Their proponents (in those days one referred to American Studies in the plural) moved in the direction of cultural and intellectual history: not to reject literature, but to enlarge the field. The concept made its way across the Atlantic, and reached West Europeans, who had already been exposed to American values. It was particularly well received in Germany, where the established fields of *Kulturkunde* and *Auslandkunde* readily begot *Amerikakunde* – and somewhat less well in England. The late Tony Tanner of the *City of Words* fame used to quote his Cambridge colleagues: "American literature? Oh, yes, I suppose someone must be reading that stuff."

When American Studies reached Eastern Europe, the study of American literature also became its core, though for different reasons. To study American politics, economy or even history was possible only from the ideological perspective of unmitigated criticism, which for many was an unacceptable price. Consequently, the new, holistic approach to the field bypassed East Europeans at its inception. As catching up is rarely successful so, paradoxically, while Europe enlarges and unites, our respective positions on America and American Studies continue to keep apart Western and Eastern Europeans.

This is even truer for the fact that the nature of American Studies in Western Europe was transformed in tune not only with the growth of the field in the United States, but also with changes in American society. The self-satisfied conservatism of the Eisenhower era, the highly visible, if geographically limited, revolution of the Kennedy-Johnson-Nixon times, and the silly period of Carter and Reagan, all made an impact on how West Europeans perceived the current shape of the city upon a hill. Not so in Eastern Europe, where the American Dream retained its allure, untouched by either the Kent State abuses or by the ludicrous sight of President Carter's landing in Warsaw. For those of you who missed the occasion he brought with him his own interpreter who must have taken one of those "Polish in 30 days" courses and who announced to the stunned live TV audience that when the American president had decided that morning to emigrate to Poland, he felt sudden lust for its inhabitants.

East European scholars of American Studies missed the whole process of transformation from Women's Clubs and segregated military units in WWII to the empowerment of American minorities. But even more importantly, they re-connected with the American academia at a very advanced stage of its own transformation.

The field of American Studies in the United States had by that time shifted from being source-centered to being society-oriented. Scholars are not satisfied with describing America, they aim at being part of the force that changes it. Values are not only to be distilled and described, they are also to be improved upon, and there is only one direction for this improvement: to the left.

Soon after the 2004 election, I attended the annual American Studies Asso-ciation meeting. Just about every session included the ceremony, practiced far too frequently to be considered coincidental, of starting each paper by describing the presenter's despair at George W. Bush's victory, which led variously to de-pression, refusal to read newspapers, or bursts of energy expended at organizing recount drives in Ohio. To listen to all those comments, one would think that the president was elected by aliens, and not by a clear majority of American voters. American Studies academics clearly go beyond studying that society, they as-sume they have the right to know better, they believe, in fact, that they *are* better than the society they study.

At the same time I also visited several American Studies programs at US universities and was the only person at various meetings making a case for Bush. Being in the minority of one suits me fine, but I was much less prepared for what happened later, when on several occasions faculty members ap-proached me to say that they shared my views, but could not express them among colleagues for fear of being ostracized or worse.

This is, of course, when alarm bells start ringing for an East European. The frame of mind which chastises opinions considered inappropriate by the majori-ty is frightening. What's more, given enough time, professional intimidation leads, by slated hiring procedures, to full and real unanimity in the academia. The intentions may be, and presumably are, noble and worthy: to educate, to eradicate prejudices, to improve the world; as noble in fact as those held by hon-est, well-intentioned communist ideologues who had no other aim in mind but to make human existence better and just.

Noam Chomsky may speak freely on any campus and blame "reactionary" America for bringing on the 9/11 disaster, but when Shelby Steele, a conserva-tive African American academic, argued that the black people were not well served by the affirmative action, he was hounded out of academia. Such pro-gressive Diktat, by the way, is readily mimicked in Western Europe. To wit: the recent cancellation of the Pope's long-scheduled appearance at La Sapienza, Rome's main university, for his presumably conservative views on Galileo.

It is perhaps too banal to state that there is nothing to discover in the human-ities, but a lot to debate, and it is of utmost importance to admit and compare contradictory views. If there is something that scholars from East Europe realize so much better than their colleagues from the West, it is the danger resulting from enforced unanimity of ideological views at the university. Perhaps we should do more than pay lip service to the *Federalist Paper* No. 10 – which we like to teach to our students and too frequently disregard once the class is over: the rights of the minority need to be protected if democracy is to function.

We negotiate America "a la carte." We select what we believe is right, and reject what we believe is not, with West Europeans being much more interested in America's promise of progressivism, and East Europeans in its ideals of liberty. We project our hopes and fears onto America, we react to these projections, and we tend to disregard the less savory aspects of our choices. Is this studying America – or creating it for the occasion?

Another issue is that of relevance. Two hundred years ago, an English wit asked the oft-quoted question "In the four corners of the globe, who reads an American book?" Today we not only read American books, but keep on writing our own books about them. So the new question should be "what difference does it make?" Since the time of de Tocqueville (whom everybody knows and nobody has read) foreign interpretations of America matter very little to Americans, and even less so if they originate in such remote parts of the world as Eastern Europe. To give but one example, the three most recent American books on anti-Americanism (Hollander 2004; Revel 2003; Rubin and Rubin 2004) discuss at length such sentiments in Germany and in France, in Latin America and in Asia, in Canada and in Africa. In none of them there is even a single mention of Eastern Europe, or of any of its constituent countries. The French or German attitudes are presented as "European perspectives," with an occasional remark about Italian or Spanish views. One would think, for instance, that Poland's strong pro-American stand is sufficiently out of the ordinary to merit a least a brief comment, but it evidently matters less than an article by an obscure French essayist in some little magazine, given much prominence in these books.

Let's face it: European Americanists should recognize that the proper audience for their scholarly endeavors is at home, and not necessarily among their professional colleagues, but among people who could profit from the American experience. There are several fields where European Americanists, Eastern as well as Western, can formulate relevant and valuable insights on topical debates by providing the American context. One such issue, for example, is the American experience with immigration. How important was the insistence on one common set of values and a single language for the unity of a nation as diverse as the American people? How can American successes and failures be made useful for European nations as they try to deal with newcomers who refuse to conform to the norms of their new country? How to deal with immigrants who insist on maintaining their own value systems? European Americanists can render significant service to their communities if we partake in such discussions drawing on our knowledge of the American experience. More than anybody else, we should be capable of translating and explicating how such dilemmas have been handled, or mishandled, on the other side of the Atlantic, and how this experience can be of use for our own countries.

Yet I have seen quite a few historical studies of, say, German or Polish ethnic groups in the United States, but none of them even tried to apply the author's expertise to topical dilemmas. It is almost that we feel safer in the scholarly sanctuary (after all, who cares about the details of the XIX-century Polish community in Buffalo) than on the minefield of a highly relevant but controversial debate. To be fair, let me hasten to add that the late USIA funded at least one project aimed at comparing borderlands of Frankfurt on the Oder and Yuma, AZ – but the agency is gone now, and so are its projects.

Another topic for comparative studies could be xenophobia and various ethnic prejudices. Not so long ago, well into the 1960's, most European countries, both Eastern and Western, seemed to be models of tolerance, while anti-Semitism and anti-Catholicism, not to mention plain old racism, were very much present on the American landscape. A generation or so later, such prejudices have been banished from the public sphere in America, and they enjoy less and less acceptance in private. At the same time, there is sufficient daily evidence to conclude that we allow prejudices to grow in all corners of Europe. To jointly study these parallel yet reverse developments could provide not only scholarly observations, but also experience-based suggestions of how to best handle growing intolerance in Europe.

Unfortunately, European Americanists, Eastern as well as Western, shy away from undertaking such tasks, and thus significantly diminish their relevance for the environment they live in. Instead, they prefer to import wholesale context-bound American debates, such as political correctness, multiculturalism, or curriculum wars. The results are more often than not counterproductive. Political correctness becomes synonymous in Europe with imposing fanciful standards of behavior, multiculturalism with a disregard for rights of the native populace in favor of pushy newcomers, and curriculum wars with sacrificing quality for the sake of arbitrary equality.

Another belief, widely held among European Americanists, is that studying a culture from afar may add to the understanding of the American experience and to questioning assumptions taken for granted by Americans. But even if we avoid romanticizing this concept, it remains a fact that foreign Americanists are generally trained in the US and rely on permanent links with American academic institutions; as a result, their own intellectual contributions are less likely to be truly different, let alone "indigenous." This problem is shared by Eastern and Western Europeans.

One American theoretician of American Studies correctly notes that "it is the business of US Americanists to study ourselves – at home and abroad," and it is legitimate to ask what the business of European Americanists is. In my opinion, it should be critical internationalism, whereby through the comparative approach we strive to overcome the separation of domestic and international perspectives. Just as history is by nature comparative, so should be American Studies. Instead, we frequently allow ourselves to be satisfied with the easy task of producing yet another book on the American political system, which adds nothing to intellectual debates on either side of the Atlantic.

"A book on the American political system" and not "a book on American novels," for instance, even though the field of American Studies is dominated by scholars trained as language and literature specialists, adds nothing. The reason is simple enough: there are many more university chairs and positions in American language and literature than in any other component of American Studies. I have nothing against graduates of what is frequently referred to as "philological" faculties (in fact, I am one of them), but the field has an adverse and limiting quality, namely that unlike in other areas, its students and practitioners are confined to their own specialty. Other scholars, historians; economists, sociologists, and so on, are obliged to study different socio-geographical areas, including their own resident country, while graduates of European English Departments study only the Anglo-American culture. This limits their scope of research and makes cooperation with sociologists, anthropologists or political scientists sufficiently unequal to scare them away from American Studies. Consequently, American Studies has never become truly interdisciplinary, and runs the risk of becoming marginalized.

Prof. Werner Sollors analyzed this problem in the United States and found that even other area studies typically include significant contributions from disciplines such as political science or economics, and American Studies is unique in concentrating almost exclusively on the culture of one country. All this despite the fact that the original inspiration for American Studies was synthetic and integrative, aimed at comprehending American culture "as a whole." Even in Europe, American Studies at first was not "owned" by literary historians and philologists, who were initially in the minority in the EAAS. Nowadays, however, American Studies is being relegated to the shelf of "non-essential" subjects, pushed out not only by academic disciplines and fields that are perceived to be useful for intra-European relations, but also by fields such as Asian Studies, Japanese Studies, and so on. We are all an endangered species, faced with extinction.

But not all is lost yet and there are still ways to make ourselves useful. So, perhaps instead of joining the sufficiently large chorus chanting "Down with Bush," European Americanists should put more effort into trying to provide Eastern and Western European answers to, say, Robert Kagan's vision of valorous Americans and effeminate Europeans, or to Samuel Huntington's views on recent immigrants. I may have missed something, but I am yet to see a satisfactory European proposition of how to reconcile the need for America's presence in the world as the great equalizer (see Bosnia) with the European desire to limit America's freedom of action.

We should also put more effort into learning how to use to our joint advantage the fact that there is hardly an area today where East and West Europeans have a common perception of America, its arts, politics, security, or economy. Our respective attitudes towards the United States tell us a lot about how we, as Europeans, differ among ourselves. In politics, for instance, the once insecure Westerners fear now no danger from the outside, and are not only oblivious to the plight of their Eastern neighbors, but criticize us for doing what *they* had done only a few decades ago, i.e. turning to the United States. It is possible that Eastern Europe welcomes the American presence because it has not seen much of it yet, but our choice seems not that much different from what France, Germany, Italy, Greece, or Turkey faced half a century ago.

In societal issues, our respective visions of America inform much of the public political discourse, no matter how ill-conceived. When the famous XVIII-century naturalist, Comte de Buffon, great as a scholar, but truly diminutive as a man, wanted to score a point in a debate, he insisted to the gigantic Thomas Jefferson that humans and animals shrink when they remove to America. And in the 20th century, when José Bové wished to make known his opposition to genetically modified organisms, he was not satisfied with the destruction of transgenic crops, but he also had to thrash a McDonald franchise.

In Eastern Europe the issue of GMO is hotly debated, too, but McDonalds are doing fine. Granted, it may be a trivial point, but it is still a meaningful one. Unlike their Western counterparts, the rights of passage of East European boys does not necessarily include throwing a Molotov cocktail at the American embassy. There are several fine American concepts that many European societies would do well to adopt: professional integrity, proper work ethic, community spirit, charity, and we must not allow anti-Americanism to become Europe's common message, its unifying idea.

America has not turned out to be the Utopia Thomas Moore had envisioned, or the ideal it once was for enslaved Europeans. But that should not stop us from putting more effort into acting as intermediaries between the culture we were born into and the culture that has adopted us as professionals. In order to do so, European scholars of America should be more engaged in debates on issues that are of common interest to both cultures.

Is my diagnosis, and the suggested medicine, correct? I wish I could be more assertive about it, but I am reminded of Benjamin Franklin's comment on his own negative assessment of the American constitution: "The older I grow, the more apt I am to doubt my own judgment." But just in the case I am right, let me close by quoting my favorite passage from William Bradford's *Of Plymouth Plantation*:

But here I cannot but stay and make a pause, and stand half amazed at this poor people's present condition. Being thus passed the vast ocean, they had now no friends to welcome them nor inns to entertain or refresh their weather-beaten bodies; no houses or much less towns to repair to.

And yet they succeeded. They've come a long way, and so can we.

References

Hollander, Paul, ed. 2004. *Understanding anti-Americanism*. Chicago: I. R. Dee.
Revel, Jean-Francois. 2003. *Anti-Americanism*. San Francisco: Encounter Books.
Rubin, Barry, and Judith Colp Rubin. 2004. *Hating America*. Oxford: Oxford University Press.

Ulf Schulenberg
University of Vechta, Germany
Empire, theoretical practice, and postnational American Studies

From today's perspective, it is certainly tempting to state that since its inception as an academic field in the 1930s, American Studies has often been dominated by a certain antitheoretical bias. New Americanists, for instance, stress the importance of the fact that the inaugural texts in the field of American Studies should be considered both a radical critique of the New Critical formalism and of the traditional understanding of academic disciplines. At the same time, however, they underscore that the practitioners of American Studies have too often developed a narrowly nationalist model of their field and a consensualist ideology, and that they moreover have favored the idea of an American exceptionalism. Especially problematic has of course been the relation between American Studies and Marxism. At the center of Michael Denning's groundbreaking article "'The Special American Conditions': Marxism and American Studies," published in 1986, is the question: Why has there been so little engagement with Marxism by American Studies scholars? While Denning speaks of "the poverty of theory in American Studies" (Denning 1986, 372), John Carlos Rowe, in *The New American Studies*, emphasizes "that traditional American Studies has often been resistant to critical theory, especially of the philosophical cast taken by much Continental structuralism and poststructuralism" (Rowe 2002, 9). Undoubtedly, there had been interesting and fruitful theoretical discussions in American Studies before the full impact of theory could be felt in the US in the 1970s and 1980s. However, for our purposes it is crucial to understand that when American Studies did become more theoretically oriented in the 1980s, it was mostly poststructuralism, deconstruction, and New Historicism which had a strong impact on this field of study. The discussions which centered on the questions of identity politics, the culture wars, and multiculturalism were governed by theoretical approaches which used conceptual tools offered by Derrida, Foucault, Lacan, Deleuze and Guattari, Barthes, Spivak, and, maybe, Lyotard. Fredric Jameson's reading of the European dialectical tradition (Lukács, Adorno, Benjamin, and Sartre), for instance, as he had developed it since *Marxism and Form* (1971), hardly played a role in this context.

In his stimulating study *French Theory*, the French intellectual historian Francois Cusset seeks to elucidate what he calls the American invention of French theory. As he makes clear, the recomposition of French theory in the US led to the production of a new radical political discourse on the basis of these French texts. As Cusset maintains, many of these French philosophers would not have recognized themselves in the new American arguments and positions. In the second part of his book, "The Uses of Theory," Cusset discusses the use of French theory for radical political purposes in the 1980s, trying to explain the crucial role French theory played for identity politics, gender studies, cultural studies, and subaltern and postcolonial studies. What makes Cusset's study valuable, among other things, is that it calls attention to the fact that the American invention of French theory too often ignored the role Marx had played for many French philosophers. Following Cusset, Marx (still) plays an important role in the attempt to grasp the French theorists' significance. He contends that "their texts ... were neither pro-Marx nor anti-Marx. They were, rather, an endless confrontation with, discussion on, reinterpretation of Marxism" (Cusset 2008, xv). The last sentence of course reminds one of Derrida's comments on the relation between deconstruction and Marxism in *Specters of Marx*.[1] At the end of his study, Cusset formulates even more decidedly:

> Thus, everywhere except in France, Deleuze, Foucault, Lyotard, and even Derridean 'hypercriticism' incarnate the possibility of *continuing* a radical social critique beyond Marx, a critique that relative to Marx was finally detotalized, refined, diversified, opened up to the questions of desire and intensity, to flux and signs and the multiple subject – in a word, the tools of a social critique *for today*. (Cusset 2008, 330)

Although the insight is far from being new, it is worth repeating: even the notoriously dark tradition of French anti-Hegelianism, as Nietzscheanism, to which belong authors as varied as Artaud, Mallarmé, Bataille, Breton, Blanchot, and Foucault, not only cannot get rid of Marx, but it on the contrary does not want to end the conversation.

Does American Studies at the beginning of the twenty-first century wish to contribute to the reinterpretation of Marxism? What would be the function of American Studies for the development of what might be termed a postmodern Marxism?[2] This is one possibility of approaching this problem. In this paper,

---

[1] In *Specters of Marx*, Derrida declares that deconstruction "would have been impossible and unthinkable in a pre-Marxist space. Deconstruction has never had any sense or interest, in my view at least, except as a radicalization, which is to say also in the tradition of a certain Marxism, in a certain spirit of Marxism" (1994, 92). Furthermore, "a radicalization is always indebted to the very thing it radicalizes. That is why I spoke of the Marxist memory and tradition of deconstruction, of its Marxist 'spirit'" (1994, 92-3). In addition, see Derrida's "Marx & Sons," *Ghostly demarcations: A symposium on Jacques Derrida's Specters of Marx*, ed. Michael Sprinker (New York: Verso, 1999), 213-69.

[2] On the question of a postmodern Marxism, see Michael Ryan, *Marxism and deconstruction: A critical articulation* (Baltimore: Johns Hopkins UP, 1982); Douglas Kellner (ed.), Postmodernism/Jameson/Critique (Washington, D.C.: Maisonneuve Press, 1989); Antonio Callari, Stephen Cullenberg, and Carole Biewener (eds.), *Marxism in the postmodern age: Confronting the new world order* (New York: Guilford Press, 1995); Bernd Magnus and Stephen Cullenberg (eds.), *Whither Marxism?: Global crises in international perspective* (New York: Routledge, 1995); Michael Sprinker (ed.), *Ghostly demarcations: A symposium on Jacques Derrida's Specters of Marx* (New York: Verso, 1999); and J. K. Gibson-

I want to contribute to the discussion of the relation between American Studies and Marxism by focusing on two of the most important neo-Marxist texts of the last decades: Michael Hardt and Antonio Negri's *Empire* (2000) and *Multitude* (2004). Of primary concern in this context will be the following question: can these two Marxist manifestoes be useful for the development of a postnational American Studies? In my attempt to answer this question, I shall concentrate on two aspects. First, the meaning of the term 'theoretical practice' and its effectiveness in a field of immanence. Second, the contemporary significance of the concept of totality. After antifoundationalist, antirepresentationalist, antiessentialist, and nominalist attacks in the last three decades, at least since Richard Rorty's *Philosophy and the Mirror of Nature* (1979), *Empire* and *Multitude* urge us to confront those questions which many thought were long behind us: are there consequences of theory in history? Can theory be used for activist purposes? Is it possible, and necessary, to conceptually grasp late-capitalist totality? Whereas many texts by multiculturalists and scholars writing on identity politics in the 1980s and 1990s suffered from a hypostatization of difference, the books by Hardt and Negri force one to reconsider the importance of the tension between difference and totality (or singularity and commonality).

In the first part of my paper, I shall explain what Hardt and Negri mean by the term 'Empire.' Moreover, I shall elaborate on the significance of their notion of a 'theoretical practice' in a field of immanence. It is crucial to grasp the status of the following suggestions. I am not primarily interested in theory's 'real' relation with practice and political activism. Also, I shall not elaborate on theory's 'real' chances of connecting with and opening up toward historical reality and society, or its 'real' effectiveness in providing tools of resistance in the fight against Empire. It goes without saying that these are truly difficult and complex questions that ask for book-length studies. What I shall concentrate on instead is what I wish to call the gesture of holding on to the idea that there might be consequences of theory even under what is commonly referred to as postmodern conditions. *Empire* and *Multitude*, as we shall see, demonstrate the contemporary significance of this gesture. The second part of this paper will illustrate the meaning of what Hardt and Negri call 'the multitude,' as the power that confronts Empire. Furthermore, I shall illustrate their insistence on the importance of a global approach. Finally, I shall seek to elucidate why the results of my discussion of *Empire* and *Multitude* might be important for the development of a postnational American Studies.

Graham, Stephen Resnick, and Richard D. Wolff (eds.), *Re/Presenting class: Essays in postmodern Marxism* (Durham: Duke UP, 2001).

1. Empire and the idea of a theoretical practice

In his writings on postmodernity and its cultural logic, from *Postmodernism, or, The Cultural Logic of Late Capitalism* (1991) to *The Cultural Turn: Selected Writings on the Postmodern, 1983-1998* (1998), Fredric Jameson repeatedly advances the argument that globalized capitalism has penetrated hitherto uncommodified parts of the world. Capitalism in its third or multinational stage is characterized by the fact that the world market and imperialism have reached their limits. It is this static omnipresence of the capitalist market, which might also be interpreted as a capitalist fear of spatial limits, that makes it difficult to imagine genuine change. Michael Hardt and Antonio Negri's *Empire* (2000) offers a detailed and provocative analysis of late or multinational or postmodern capitalism. While Jameson has always concentrated on analyzing postmodernity and its cultural logic and has seemed somewhat reluctant to propose effective solutions to the complexity of the current dilemma, Hardt and Negri want their readers to believe in the possibility of change. They repeatedly underline in *Empire* that it has become increasingly difficult to name the enemy since capitalism has changed its form, the era of imperialism is over, and a new form of sovereignty and network power has emerged. Nonetheless, they also call attention to the possibility of imagining and finally establishing a new cartography, a new geography, or an alternative global society. Eventually, it will be the radical desires and creative forces of what they call the multitude that, by contesting and striving to subvert Empire, will construct a counter-Empire. On Hardt and Negri's account, the forces of liberation in form of the multitude have led to new struggles which have already begun to emerge. Through those struggles "the multitude will have to invent new democratic forms and a new constituent power that will one day take us through and beyond Empire" (Hardt and Negri 2000, xv).

What, then, is Empire? It is crucial to grasp that it has to be strictly differentiated from imperialism, and it is not synonymous with globalization. Moreover, it does not simply describe the effects of neoliberalism in its most aggressive form. All these are important aspects of Empire, yet the concept is much more complex. Hardt and Negri's contention is that along with globalization "has emerged a global order, a new logic and structure of rule – in short, a new form of sovereignty. Empire is the political subject that effectively regulates these global exchanges, the sovereign power that governs the world" (Hardt and Negri 2000, xi). Due to the processes of an ever-accelerated globalization, the sovereignty of nation-states has declined. They are no longer capable of regulating economic flows and cultural exchanges.[3] However, this does not signify that

---

[3] For a critique of Hardt and Negri's interpretation of the contemporary significance of the nation-state, see Stanley Aronowitz, *How class* works: *Power and social movement* (New Haven and London: Yale UP, 2003), 131-33.

sovereignty as such has declined or simply disappeared. Hardt and Negri's basic hypothesis is "that sovereignty has taken a new form, composed of a series of national and supranational organisms united under a single logic of rule. This new global form of sovereignty is what we call Empire" (Hardt and Negri 2000, xii). It is the primary characteristic of Empire that its power cannot be localized, that is, it has no actual or localizable terrain or center. Power in Empire is distributed in complex networks, through mobile, flexible, and nonhierarchical mechanisms of control. In contrast to imperialism, Empire does not seek to establish a territorial center of power which tries to increase its influence in as many parts of the world as possible. It does not need fixed boundaries or barriers in order to fulfill its mission. Empire can thus be described as "a *decentered* and *deterritorializing* apparatus of rule that progressively incorporates the entire global realm within its open, expanding frontiers. Empire manages hybrid identities, flexible hierarchies, and plural exchanges through modulating networks of command" (Hardt and Negri 2000, xii-xiii). With the passage from modernity to Empire, the idea of an outside to the capitalist system has become increasingly problematic. In the smooth space of Empire, where power is both everywhere and nowhere, traditional binary and spatial divisions lose their power. Empire is seemingly everywhere, in the Jamesonian sense a late-capitalist spatial totality, and nowhere since it cannot be grasped in its entirety. Thus, it "is an *ou-topia*, or really a *non-place*" (Hardt and Negri 2000, 190). Hardt and Negri elaborate on the complexity of the concept of Empire as follows:

> The concept of Empire is characterized fundamentally by a lack of boundaries: Empire's rule has no limits. First and foremost, then, the concept of Empire posits a regime that effectively encompasses the spatial totality, or really that rules over the entire "civilized" world. No territorial boundaries limit its reign. Second, the concept of Empire presents itself not as a historical regime originating in conquest, but rather as an order that effectively suspends history and thereby fixes the existing state of affairs for eternity. From the perspective of Empire, this is the way things will always be and the way they were always meant to be. In other words, Empire presents its rule not as a transitory moment in the movement of history, but as a regime with no temporal boundaries and in this sense outside of history or at the end of history. Third, the rule of Empire operates on all registers of the social order extending down to the depths of the social world. Empire not only manages a territory and a population but also creates the very world it inhabits. It not only regulates human interactions but also seeks directly to rule over human nature. The object of its rule is social life in its entirety, and thus Empire presents the paradigmatic form of biopower. Finally, although the practice of Empire is continually bathed in blood, the concept of Empire is always dedicated to peace – a perpetual and universal peace outside of history. (Hardt and Negri 2000, xiv-xv)

We have to face the end of the dialectic of modernity. The powerful networks of the capitalist market have reached most areas of the world, and nearly all of humanity is affected by the mechanisms of capitalist exploitation. However, we must not lose ourselves in feelings of nostalgia for a time when it was still possible to demarcate, or at least think, an outside to the system. A nostalgia for those power structures of modernity which still offered the possibility of establishing local identities and networks that were outside the increasingly global flows of capital, and could thus function as a kind of counterbalance, is misplaced. On the contrary, according to Hardt and Negri, we must confront Empire head-on, not attempt to resurrect the nation-state as a protection against global capital, and we ought to realize that Empire or the spectral reign of a globalized postmodern capitalism offers fascinating possibilities for a philosophy of liberation. The struggles against Empire, the desperate attempt to invent new democratic forms and a new constituent power, will have to take place on the imperial terrain itself. Since it is pointless to look for the purity of a political position outside this network power, one should rather engage in the task of discovering effective alternatives and potentialities for liberation, the forces of resistance, that exist within Empire. The power of the multitude exists within Empire, and the battle for social change has to be fought on this new imperial terrain. We must work through Empire in order to get beyond it. Hardt and Negri maintain: "We should be done once and for all with the search for an outside, a standpoint that imagines a purity for our politics. It is better both theoretically and practically to enter the terrain of Empire and confront its homogenizing and heterogenizing flows in all their complexity, grounding our analysis in the power of the global multitude" (Hardt and Negri 2000, 46).

The spatial reconfiguration of inside and outside in Empire, that is, the fact that there is progressively less distinction between the two in a globalized postmodern capitalism, does not only signify the disappearance of nature to which Jameson has already called attention, but it also concerns the relation between public and private in liberal political theory. The process of postmodernization also implies that public places are becoming more and more privatized. Following Hardt and Negri, "[t]he public spaces of modern society, which constitute the place of liberal politics, tend to disappear in the postmodern world" (Hardt and Negri 2000, 188). The privatization of public space in postmodernity, in the form of a shift from the common square, the (pre-capitalist) commons, and the public encounter and exchange of ideas to the closed spaces of malls, freeways, and gated communities in suburbs, forces one to admit that the modern dialectic between private and public spaces seems no longer useful. Although their analysis of this phenomenon is somewhat too totalizing, like Jameson's reading of postmodernity in many respects, they are right in stressing the severe problems for liberal politics in postmodern times: "The place of modern liberal politics has disappeared, and thus from this perspective our postmodern and imperial society is characterized by a deficit of the political. In effect, the place of politics has been de-actualized" (Hardt and Negri 2000, 188). What I would like to underline in this context is that if one is willing to grant some truth to Hardt and

Negri's suggestion that "[t]he end of the outside is the end of liberal politics" (Hardt and Negri 2000, 189), then this also leads to a reconsideration of Richard Rorty's notorious private-public split. So far as I can see, Rorty has not reflected upon this end of the outside. Consigning resistances, antagonisms, and dissent to the private sphere and seeking to create an atmosphere of harmony and consent in the public sphere, Rorty does not answer the question of what happens to reformist liberal politics and the consensus view of democracy when the outside is no longer the outside of modernity. The idea of a private-public split has to be radically questioned, of course. If we were to follow the notion of the disappearance of the outside and at the same time to hold on to the Rortyan private-public dichotomy, we would find ourselves in one of the worst situations imaginable, namely, alone with our private idiosyncratic fantasies, our playful theories, our new vocabularies, and our imaginative redescriptions. Strong poets and creative redescribers whose private theorizing eventually only confirms the end of history.

When the outside disappears in Empire, the question must be posed whether theory really ought to be relegated to the private sphere. Hardt and Negri make unequivocally clear in *Empire* that the idea of a theory which is utterly divorced from the world of practice and leftist politics must be radically dismissed. Following these two neo-Marxists, "political theory must deal with ontology," that is to say, "politics cannot be constructed from the outside. Politics is given immediately; it is a field of pure immanence" (Hardt and Negri 2000, 354). It is crucial to understand that, just like the desire of the multitude, theory has to become effective in this field of pure immanence. Theory here appears as practice, or critique as theoretical practice. In other words, theory does not seek to govern practice from an outside to practice, it is not a specter of transcendence which pretends to be capable of escaping the local, the historical, and the contingent, but it strives to be effective in the field of immanence which is the imperial terrain of Empire. Dialectics, mediation, transcendence, metaphysics – Hardt and Negri try to convince their readers that all this is behind them now. Consequently, they advocate "the definitive adoption of the field of immanence as the exclusive terrain of the theory and practice of politics" (Hardt and Negri 2000, 377). Within the framework of their "critical and materialist deconstructionism," Hardt and Negri offer "a toolbox of concepts for theorizing and acting in and against Empire" (Hardt and Negri 2000, 48, xvi). What this boils down to is that theoretical practice is supposed to serve as a tool or weapon in the struggle against Empire.

In an important passage, Hardt and Negri not only warn against the danger of 'theory in isolation,' but they also elaborate on the relation between modernity, revolution, immanence, and practice:

> Modernity's beginnings were revolutionary, and the old order was toppled by them. The constitution of modernity was not about theory in isolation but about theoretical

acts indissolubly tied to mutations of practice and reality. Bodies and brains were fundamentally transformed. This historical process of subjectivization was revolutionary in the sense that it determined a paradigmatic and irreversible change in the mode of life of the multitude. (Hardt and Negri 2000, 74)

Hardt and Negri see it as one of their main tasks to turn this modern story about the discovery of the fullness of the plane of immanence into a postmodern narrative.

Post-Cold War American Studies has been utterly incompatible with any kind of grand theory. Whereas Jameson, for instance, too often comes dangerously close to presenting himself as a paradigmatically grand theorist, Hardt and Negri's theoretical approach calls attention to the notion of a worldly and oppositional criticism. In other words, in Hardt and Negri, theory and activism do go together. Strongly influenced by Deleuze's idea of a theoretical practice, Hardt and Negri offer the possibility of recognizing the limitations of a neopragmatist essentialization of theory on the one hand and of an unreconstructed grand theory such as Hegelian Marxism on the other. What I wish to underline in this context is that this notion of a theoretical practice might be important if we seek to approach the role and function of American Studies at the beginning of the twenty-first century. American Studies is of course not the only field that has initiated a rethinking of the relation between theory and practice. In the last three decades approaches such as feminist studies, feminist legal studies, queer theory, postcolonial studies, and critical race theory, to name but a few, have drawn attention to the interrelation of theory and practice, that is, they have vehemently underscored that theory ought to be seen as critical or conceptual practice. To a certain degree, they argue, practice needs (provisional and heuristic) theoretical foundations, yet at the same time theory is dependent on practice. Theorist-activists have made sufficiently clear that political practice, that is, situatedness, contextuality, historicity, and contingency shapes our theory. In other words, theoretical work is viewed as contributing to social change, it has consequences in the practical world, the messy world of everyday life, and political activism is seen as shaping our theories. Since American Studies opened itself to theory, its practitioners have made clear that they desire for consequences of theory in history. So do Hardt and Negri.

A worldly and oppositional criticism (in the Saidian sense) inevitably finds itself in the aforementioned field of immanence. It is not only Hardt and Negri's work which can be useful for Americanists in order to realize the potential of this field of immanence and of the idea of a theoretical practice, but one could also, for instance, mention Cornel West's leftist version of neopragmatism, as he developed it in the 1980s, in this context. Although the themes of social change, (creative) democracy, freedom, and liberation lie at the core of West's cultural and social criticism, he does not advocate the idea that a radical dismissal of theory is necessary in order to reach these goals. He is thus highly critical of

Rorty's turn against theory and toward narrative. Rorty's distrust of theory is damaging to the idea of pragmatism; equally problematic is his "preoccupation with transient vocabularies" (West 1989, 209). West unequivocally states that pragmatism's antifoundationalism does not necessarily have to entail a resistance to theory. He convincingly differentiates between grand theory, which all pragmatists should, and do, reject, and provisional, tentative, heuristic, and revisable theories which carefully attempt to analyze differences and particularities and which aim at an understanding of experience within a historicist and genealogical framework. Abstract and totalizing theory must be criticized, because theory, trying to effect change, ought to be concerned with concrete political and social events. In "Theory, Pragmatisms, and Politics," West comments on his attitude toward theory as follows:

> On the level of theory, to be against theory *per se* is to be against inquiry into heuristic posits regarding the institutional and individual causes of alterable forms of human misery and human suffering, just as uncritical allegiance to grand theories can blind one from seeing and examining kinds of human oppression. Therefore I adopt strategic attitudes toward the use and deployment of theory, a position more charitable toward grand theory than are the ultratheorists and more suspicious of grand theory than are the grand theorists themselves. (West 1991, 36)

The subversive worldliness of West's thinking marks pragmatism as a discursive space in which theory is given the possibility of attacking nondiscursive operations of power and in which it thus contributes to the development of effective leftist strategies and tactics.

As *Empire* and *Multitude* make sufficiently clear, the theorist-activist (in our case: the practitioner of postnational American Studies) is not alone in the field of immanence which is the imperial terrain of Empire. On the contrary, he or she is surrounded by the various singularities acting against Empire. These creative and innovative singularities, as forces of resistance, form a new kind of commonality – the multitude.

2. The multitude, totality, and nomadism

Enter the New Barbarians. Faithful to their materialist approach, Hardt and Negri emphasize the importance of the shift from the realm of ideas to that of production in their analysis of Empire. It is in the realm of production that new forms of oppression, and new kinds of control, as well as a new kind of immaterial, cooperative, communicative, and affective labor, can be detected. However, this is also the realm where a new politics of refusal originates and where resistances and desires for liberation are vehemently articulated. The "Intermezzo: Counter-Empire" illustrates this shift in their analysis. In order to approach Hardt and Negri's understanding of the function of the multitude it is crucial to see that they maintain that Empire is a reaction to the force of the multitude. The construction of Empire and its global networks and mechanisms of control "is a *response* to the various struggles against the modern machines of power, and specifically to class struggle driven by the multitude's desire for liberation. The multitude called Empire into being" (Hardt and Negri 2000, 43). Because of the struggles of the multitude Empire is continually confronted with the task of systemic recomposition, it has to heighten its flexibility and mobility. Inevitably, this also leads to a change in the forms of resistance attacking Empire. The flexible force of the multitude in postmodernity brings Empire to change its structures and procedures, and this, in turn, leads to new forms of struggle and resistance: "New figures of struggle and new subjectivities are produced in the conjuncture of events, in the universal nomadism, in the general mixture and miscegenation of individuals and populations, and in the technological metamorphoses of the imperial biopolitical machine" (Hardt and Negri 2000, 61). The multitude is the productive force which through its labor sustains Empire, and at the same time it is the force that longs for its destruction. In their article "Globalization and Democracy," Hardt and Negri describe the flexibility and creativity of the multitude as follows:

> The multitude we are dealing with today is instead a multiplicity of bodies, each of which is crisscrossed by intellectual and material powers of reason and affect; they are cyborg bodies that move freely without regard to the old boundaries that separated the human from the machinic. These multiple bodies of the multitude enact a continuous invention of new forms of life, new languages, new intellectual and ethical powers. The bodies of the multitude are monstrous, irrecuperable in the capitalist logic that tries continually to control it in the organization of Empire. The bodies of the multitude, finally, are queer bodies that are insusceptible to the forces of discipline and normalization but sensitive only to their own powers of invention. (Hardt and Negri 2003, 120)

At the end of *Multitude*, in a somewhat messianic tone which is typical of both books, Hardt and Negri speak of "a new race" or "a new humanity" (Hardt and Negri 2004, 356) which the multitude should create. It is crucial to understand that the multitude as a multiplicity of singular differences, or as a social subject which is composed of a set of irreducible singularities, acts on what those singularities share in common. At the same time, the multitude produces "the common" (Hardt and Negri 2004, xv).

Hardt and Negri's concept of the common leads us to another important aspect of their work, namely, their refusal to consign the concept of totality to the dustbin of (a quasi-Stalinist) history. Following these two proponents of a postmodern Marxism, the creation of a new social body, a new postcapitalist mode of life, and a new community demands a global approach. In other words, an alternative that challenges, resists, and finally gets beyond Empire and the world market has to be posed at an equally global level. Isolated political movements operating on the level of local autonomy and seeking to establish a particular community based on race, religion, or region are not sufficient in order to oppose the power of Empire. Equally insufficient is the attempt to go back to former forms of resistance and protest. Referring to Deleuze and Guattari, one of the primary influences on *Empire* (especially their *A Thousand Plateaus*), Hardt and Negri suggest that instead of attempting to delink from capital's globalization one could try to accelerate the process:

> Empire can be effectively contested only on its own level of generality and by pushing the processes that it offers past their present limitations. We have to accept that challenge and learn to think globally and act globally. Globalization must be met with a counter-globalization. Empire with a counter-Empire. (Hardt and Negri 2000, 206-7)

I do not need to summarize the numerous attacks on the allegedly totalizing nature of American neo-Marxism here. The main target has of course been Jameson. From *The Political Unconscious*, where he speaks of "the necessity and priority of totalizing thought" (Jameson 1981, 21), to his texts on postmodernism, he has always unequivocally stated that the concept of totality is of utmost importance in the analysis of late capitalism.[4]

What makes Hardt and Negri's work valuable, among other things, is that it urges one to realize the potential usefulness of a thinking that is governed by a tension between the poles of difference and totality or singularity and commonality. This might be especially useful for Americanists because every time we enter the field of American Studies, we are confronted by exactly these dichotomies: difference and totality, particularity and universalism, singularity and commonality, or, maybe, Marxism and poststructuralism. On Hardt and Negri's account, "the challenge posed by the concept of the multitude is for a social multiplicity to manage to communicate and act in common while remaining internally different" (Hardt and Negri 2004, xiv). In connection with the 1999 Seattle protests they elaborate on the terms commonality-singularity as follows:

> In conceptual terms, the multitude replaces the contradictory couple identity-difference with the complementary couple commonality-singularity. In practice the multitude provides a model whereby our expressions of singularity are not reduced or diminished in our communication and collaboration with others in struggle, with our forming ever greater common habits, practices, conduct, and desires – with, in

---

[4] For a discussion of the question of Marxism and totality, see Martin Jay's by now classic study *Marxism and Totality: The adventures of a concept from Lukács to Habermas* (Cambridge: Polity Press, 1984). In addition, see Steven Best, "Jameson, Totality, and the Poststructuralist Critique," *Postmodernism/Jameson/Critique*, ed. Douglas Kellner (Washington, D.C.: Maisonneuve Press, 1989), 345-52. For the latest discussion of this question, see Judith Butler, Ernesto Laclau, and Slavoj Zizek, *Contingency, Hegemony, Universality: Contemporary dialogues on the left* (New York: Verso, 2000).

short, the global mobilization and extension of the common. (Hardt and Negri 2004, 218-9)

In his latest collection of essays, *Reflections on* Empire, Negri once again stresses that the main problem which has to be confronted under the postmodern conditions of Empire is, "how can one today conceive of democracy at a global level?" (Negri 2008, 166). And he also once again draws attention to the significance of the desire for the common and to its possible realization in the field of immanence: "Thus *the real problem is how to help to develop the subversive desire for the 'common'* which is currently being expressed in the multitude, balancing it against war, institutionalizing it, and transforming it into constituent *potenza*" (Negri 2008, 166). In his illuminating article "The Myth of the Multitude," Kam Shapiro correctly maintains that Hardt and Negri "advocate a new universalism grounded in not discrete demands but the creative power of human desire and activity. Moreover, they suggest that the multitude, so understood, is on the verge of a properly global manifestation" (Hardt and Negri 2004, 289). At the same time, however, Shapiro's contention is that Hardt and Negri discredit molecular or micropolitical struggles currently going on on the terrain of Empire "in favor of the genuine Revolution that is yet to be" (Shapiro 2004, 299). He also criticizes Hardt and Negri's "messianic gestures toward total revolution" (Shapiro 2004, 300). By contrast, Paul A. Passavant avers that after the countless attacks on allegedly 'totalizing theories' which have accompanied us at least since the time of identity politics, it is a merit of Hardt and Negri's neo-Marxist approach that revolution on a global scale, and thus the concept of totality, is no longer considered to belong to a dangerously old-fashioned and reactionary theoretical framework: "Today, revolution on a global scale against capital and on behalf of labor has reentered academic discourse with the publication of Hardt's and Negri's *Empire*, and this is an important contribution Hardt's and Negri's *Empire* makes" (Passavant 2004, 4).

As Hardt and Negri underscore in *Empire* and *Multitude*, although the social and productive capacities of the multitude can to a certain extent be controlled, by mechanisms of control which are more sophisticated and effective than those of modernity, the multitude can no longer be disciplined. In addition, throughout modernity attempts at the establishment of disciplinary conditions and situations for workers have always been disrupted by the labor force's mobility and migration. This mobility or mass worker nomadism, the mobility of labor power and the various migratory movements, characterize the multitude. Workers of all kinds, people seeking to escape from the Global South, political refugees, movements of intellectual labor power, movements of the agricultural, manufacturing, and service proletariat – these are the flows that constitute the postmodern multitude and that contribute to its power. "Desertion and exodus," if one follows Hardt and Negri, "are a powerful form of class struggle within and against imperial postmodernity" (Hardt and Negri 2000, 213).

In *The Will to Power*, Nietzsche posed the question of where the barbarians of the twentieth century were. This leads Hardt and Negri to the following characterization of the multitude: "A new nomad horde, a new race of barbarians, will arise to invade or evacuate Empire" (Hardt and Negri 2000, 213). In a Benjaminian sense, this is "a positive barbarism" typical of which is a "savage mobility" (Hardt and Negri 2000, 215, 214). These new barbarians "destroy with an affirmative violence and trace new paths of life through their own material existence" (Hardt and Negri 2000, 215). Crucially, near the end of *Empire* the authors contend that the being-against of the multitude must not be interpreted as a negative gesture since this being-against is actually a being-for, "a resistance that becomes love and community" (Hardt and Negri 2000, 361). The new vital and barbaric force of the laboring masses, the desire of the multitude, leads to new forms of resistance to exploitation, oppression, alienation, reification, as well as to a refusal to belong to a nation, an identity, and a people. Additionally, the desire of the multitude has no use for a body that submits to any kind of command (imperatives to adapt to family life, factory discipline, a traditional understanding of sexuality, gender roles, and morality). The positive connotation of the concept of resistance goes hand in hand with the proposal that nomadism and miscegenation are "figures of virtue" (Hardt and Negri 2000, 362).

Hardt and Negri's postmodern nomads, because of their mobility, creativity, and commonality, are a constant threat to late capitalism's global hierarchies and divisions. Hardt and Negri speak of "dangerous classes [which] continually disrupt the ontological constitution of Empire; at each intersection of lines of creativity or lines of flight the social subjectivities become more hybrid, mixed, and miscegenated, further escaping the fusional powers of control" (Hardt and Negri 2004, 137).[5] What ought to be of primary concern for our purposes is not Hardt and Negri's use of a Deleuzian vocabulary when discussing the phenomenon of a postmodern nomadism and its 'dangerous classes,' but rather the fact that the nomadic multitude, as a commonality comprised of creative and highly unpredictable singularities, can only be adequately theorized within a postnational framework. Hardt and Negri's contention is, to emphasize this once more, that we have to think globally and act globally in order to finally achieve a counter-Empire.

3. Romanticizing postnational American Studies

In his wide-ranging study *The Cultural Front: The Laboring of American Culture in the Twentieth Century* (1997), Michael Denning analyzes the cultural movement associated with the Popular Front of the 1930s. On his account, the

---

[5]   In this context, see Gilles Deleuze and Félix Guattari, *Nomadology: The war machine* (New York: Semiotext(e), 1986).

cultural front, that is, "the extraordinary flowering of arts, entertainment, and thought based on the broad social movement that came to be known as the Popular Front" (Denning 1997, xvi), had a deep and lasting impact on American culture. The cultural front reshaped American culture by transforming American modernism and mass culture. Denning even holds that what he has termed the laboring of American culture "connotes a birthing of a new American culture, a second American Renaissance" (Denning 1997, xvii). Illustrating the relation between Popular Front culture, leftist activism in the depression era, and the political culture of the 1930s, Denning underlines that while the Popular Front was defeated on the political terrain, its culture left behind a distinctive aesthetic, certain forms, and a leftist sensibility that had a strong impact on American culture. As examples of the literature and art of the cultural front Denning chooses, for instance, John Dos Passos's *U.S.A.*, proletarian writing, 'ghetto pastorals' (e.g., Michael Gold's *Jews without Money*), 'proletarian grotesques,' John Steinbeck's *The Grapes of Wrath*, the Popular Front musical theater, jazz, the cabaret blues, new theater and film (e.g., Orson Welles), and Disney cartoons.

I think George Lipsitz is right when he points out that Denning's book forces us to reconsider and retheorize "the relationship between politics and culture, between ethnic identity and class consciousness, between the myth of American exceptionalism and the always international identities of the US nation-state and its inhabitants, and between cultural practice and cultural theory" (Lipsitz 2001, 36). Denning has not only contributed to our changed understanding of the field of American Studies by connecting its origins to the social movements of the 1930s, but he has also demonstrated that from its inception this field has been governed by a highly productive tension between the poles of practice and theory. Theory and activism did go together in the 1930s. Furthermore, this kind of theoretical practice, that is, the desire for consequences of theory in history, forces us to develop a postnational framework which is adequate to the culture of the CIO. What this signifies is that, at least to a certain degree, the notion of a theoretical practice and the idea of postnationality came together at the inception of American Studies as an academic field in the 1930s.[6]

However, although theory and practice fruitfully came together in the American 1930s, one also has to see that practitioners of American Studies, as social

---

[6] On the program of a postnational(ist) American Studies, see Pease and Kaplan 1993; Donald E. Pease (ed.), *National identities and post-Americanist narratives* (Durham: Duke UP, 1994); John Carlos Rowe (ed.), *Post-nationalist American Studies* (Berkeley: University of California Press, 2000); Rowe 2002; Pease and Wiegman 2002; David W. Noble, *Death of a nation: American culture and the end of exceptionalism* (Minneapolis: University of Minnesota Press, 2002); Alan Wolfe, "Anti-American Studies," *The New Republic*, http://www.tnr.com/docprint.mhtml?i=20030210 &s=wolfe02100 (accessed June 03, 2003); and Wai Chee Dimock and Lawrence Buell (eds.), *Shades of the planet: American literature as world literature* (Princeton: Princeton UP, 2007).

activists, have often been reluctant as far as the acceptance of theory is concerned. In their opinion, theory was inadequate, if not damaging, to the task American Studies had to fulfill. As John Carlos Rowe points out:

> Since the 1930s and through many different dominant schools and movements, American Studies had preserved its purpose of social critique and intellectual activism, conveying this message quite effectively to several generations of students. One reason for the reluctance of many American Studies scholars of this period to embrace the 'politics of critical theory' may well have been their sense that theory's overt political goals were too modest, its social critique too restricted to academic politics, and its popularity in higher education decidedly too literary. (Rowe 2002, 38)

This antitheoretical bias, as I called it at the beginning of this paper, was unacceptable and ideologically suspect to the proponents of a New American Studies in the 1980s and 1990s. The New Americanists' *bête noire* was of course the idea of an American exceptionalism, primarily that of the members of the Myth and Symbol School, and any attempt to clearly separate the cultural sphere from the political sphere (from Lionel Trilling and Gene Wise to today's conservative literary scholars).[7] While the results of some of the New Americanists' books and articles were disenchantingly predictable, and while their theoretical approaches sometimes appeared somewhat standardized, their overall intent was to repoliticize this field of study in an innovative way. The power of theory and its conceptual tools, it seems, was hardly ever questioned in these texts. After 9/11, however, some critics have called attention to the necessity of rethinking the function of theory and its effectiveness. Discussing the role of theory in the context of the preemptive war on Iraq and the war on terrorism, W.J.T. Mitchell writes in his introduction to "The Future of Criticism – A *Critical Inquiry* Symposium":

> What can criticism and theory do to counteract the forces of militarism, unilateralism, and the perpetual state of emergency that is now the explicit policy of the US government? What good is intellectual work in the face of the deeply anti-intellectual ethos of American public life, not to mention the pervasive sense that a radical faction of the Republican party that is immune to persuasion, argument, reason, or even the flow of accurate information has established a stranglehold on political power? What can the relatively weak power of critical theory do in such a crisis? How can one take Edward Said's advice and speak the truth to power when power refuses to listen, when it actively suppresses and intimidates dissenters, when it systematically lies and exaggerates to mobilize popular support for its agenda,

---

[7] Donald Pease and Robyn Wiegman's introduction to *The futures of American Studies*, entitled "Futures," contains a harsh critique of Wise. In addition, see Donald E. Pease, "The Place of Theory in American Cultural Studies: The Case of Gene Wise," *Theories of American culture, theories of American Studies*, eds. Winfried Fluck and Thomas Claviez (Tübingen: Gunter Narr, 2003), 19-35.

when it uses slogans like the 'war on terrorism' to abrogate the civil liberties of its own citizens? (Mitchell 2004, 327)

Although Mitchell does of course not intend to radically dismiss the project of theory, he is right in drawing attention to these crucial questions. Critical theory, confined as it mostly is to academe, might indeed be weak in the confrontation with US belligerence, militarism, and unilateralism. A worldly and oppositional theoretical practice, by contrast, which strives to be effective in the field of immanence as the imperial terrain of Empire, does not necessarily have to be powerless. Although *Empire* and *Multitude* are so clearly directed against metaphysics and transcendence in their insistence that political theory must deal with ontology, maybe it is Hardt and Negri's messianism and romanticism, as a sort of return of the repressed, which are particularly useful for American Studies at the beginning of the twenty-first century. Hardt and Negri's materialist *and* romantic ontology, in its productively oxymoronic nature, suggests that the term 'theoretical practice' must not be regarded as strange, and it moreover demonstrates, by introducing a new way of speaking, a new set of metaphors or toolbox of concepts, and by holding on to the idea of change, that theory and activism might go together.[8] This, I submit, is one crucial aspect for the development of a contemporary postnational American Studies that seeks to critically and conceptually confront US hegemony in late capitalism and that at the same time tries not to forget about its activist roots.

Hardt and Negri's postmodern materialism as romanticism, inspired by the creativity and effectiveness of the anti-globalization protests from Seattle to summit meetings of major international or global institutions such as the World Bank, the IMF, and the G8, insists that "it is important always to remember that another world is possible, a better, more democratic world, and to foster our desire for such a world" (Hardt and Negri 2004, 227). Whereas *Empire* concentrated more on offering a conceptual toolbox for analyzing the new form of sovereignty, *Multitude*, since it was written after Seattle and some of the other protests, puts a stronger emphasis on questions such as activism, the organization of the Left, the multitude's biopolitical production of the common, and on the possibility of achieving democracy on a global scale. If one considers their discussion of the Bakhtinian notion of dialogical narration and polyphony, and if one remembers that *Mille Plateaux* serves as a kind of master text throughout *Empire* and *Multitude*, then it becomes obvious how fascinated Hardt and Negri

---

[8]   It should be obvious here that my understanding of romanticism is influenced by Richard Rorty's writings. See his *Contingency, irony, and solidarity* (New York: Cambridge UP, 1989); *Achieving our country: Leftist thought in twentieth-century America* (Cambridge, MA: Harvard UP, 1998), as well as "Pragmatism as Romantic Polytheism," "Grandeur, Profundity, and Finitude," and "Pragmatism and Romanticism" in *Philosophy as cultural politics: Philosophical papers*, volume 4 (New York: Cambridge UP, 2007).

are by "the performative, carnevalesque nature of the various protest movements that have arisen around questions of globalization" (Hardt and Negri 2004, 211). The carnevalesque, it seems, is a common reference point for both theory and practice. Furthermore, both theory and practice use the carnevalesque, in its creativity, polyphony, and unpredictability, for the production or invention of "new subjectivities and new languages" (Hardt and Negri 2004, 211), as well as for an illustration of the multitude's production of and desire for the common.

Does Hardt and Negri's 'new language,' the discourse of a postmodern Marxism which profoundly differs from other contemporary materialist discourses and which is romantic in a Rortyan sense, still need the concept of totality? I have suggested that it does, even if they prefer to speak about a 'global approach' and about 'commonality.' The potential use of this concept for the practitioners of a postnational American Studies is a highly stimulating question. For the purposes of this article, I shall concentrate on Amy Kaplan's piece "'Left Alone with America': The Absence of Empire in the Study of American Culture." At the beginning of her article, which is the introduction to the volume *Cultures of United States Imperialism* (which she coedited with Donald Pease), she gives a short summary of what the New Americanists as proponents of a postnational American Studies will concentrate on: "the multiple histories of continental and overseas expansion, conquest, conflict, and resistance which have shaped the cultures of the United States and the cultures of those it has dominated within and beyond its geopolitical boundaries" (Kaplan 1993, 4).[9] Although Kaplan clearly appreciates the field's orientation toward a multicultural critique of American society and culture, and the Americanists' emphasis on the notion of dissent, she also critiques what she terms "the new pluralistic model of diversity" (Kaplan 1993, 15) for its lack of a more global approach. In her opinion, this pluralistic model

> runs the risk of being bound by the old paradigm of unity if it concentrates its gaze only narrowly on the internal lineaments of American culture and leaves national borders intact instead of interrogating their formation. That is, American nationality can still be taken for granted as a monolithic and self-contained whole, no matter how diverse and conflicted, if it remains implicitly defined by its internal social relations, and not in political struggles for power with other cultures and nations, strug-

---

[9] In "What's in a Name?," Janice Radway describes the new understanding of American national identity as follows: "American national identity is thus constructed in and through relations of difference. As a conceptual entity, it is intricately intertwined with certain alterities that diacritically define it as something supposedly normative, normal, and central. As a material and social entity, it is brought into being through relations of dominance and oppression, through processes of super- and subordination. To take the measure of this national entity, it is necessary, then, to focus on these constitutive relationships, these intricate interdependencies, which ironically are figured as deep fissures and fractures in the national body. America is not an organically unified, homogeneous thing" (2002, 54).

gles which make America's conceptual and geographic borders fluid, contested, and historically changing. (Kaplan 1993, 15)

Kaplan confirms my aforementioned suggestion that while a multiculturalist critique of America, or an exclusive focus on identity politics, runs the danger of a hypostatization of difference and particularity within a national framework, the work of Hardt and Negri allows one to grasp the potential use of the tension between difference and totality, or singularity and commonality, within what might legitimately be termed a postnational theoretical framework. To put this somewhat differently, Hardt and Negri's work can be useful for the development of a postnational American Studies since it makes the practitioners of American Studies consider the necessity of what John Carlos Rowe calls "a revised conception of totality" (Rowe 2002, xxvi) or of what Eric Lott prefers to call "universalism" (Lott 2000, 665). In a time often designated as post-identity politics, Lott, basing his argumentation on Ernesto Laclau's *Emancipation(s)* (1996), warns us not to accept a "reactionary stand-in for old-fashioned totality" (Lott 2000, 669), yet at the same time he seems to regard universalism as the perfect tool for the task of dealing with the particularities of the new social movements after Seattle. Lott agrees with Laclau and others who have argued that "some kind of universalism is politically necessary to advance a politics of social movements beyond the recognition of pure difference; and for Laclau, is already logically entailed in any identity movement anyway. Just what this universalism is supposed to look like is the burning question" (Lott 2000, 668). A burning question, indeed. This is certainly not the place to discuss the question of whether the concept of totality is really as old-fashioned as Lott frivolously seems to insinuate, or why Laclau's notion of universalism in the 1990s differs so profoundly from the understanding of the universal as he developed it with Chantal Mouffe in *Hegemony and Socialist Strategy* in 1985. Rather, one should see that Kaplan holds that the lack of a postnational approach in the pluralist model of diversity might result in 'a renewed version of 'consensus'.' She elaborates on this point as follows: "By defining American culture as determined precisely by its diversity and multivocality, 'America' as a discrete identity can cohere independently of international confrontations with other national, local, and global cultural identities within and outside its borders. The critical force of multiculturalism thus may lay itself open to recuperation by a renewed version of 'consensus'" (Kaplan 1993, 15).

4. Conclusion

In this paper, I have sought to answer the question of whether Hardt and Negri's postmodern Marxism can be useful for the development of a postnational American Studies. Discussing their understanding of the relation between theory and

practice, or what I have termed their 'theoretical practice,' as well as their im-
perative to think globally and act globally, I have proposed that an analysis of
Empire and *Multitude* might be a fruitful endeavor for those Americanists who
hold that the project of a postnational American Studies is worth pursuing. What
has accompanied me throughout this piece is the question of whether it is possible, and desirable, to renew the dialogue between Marxism and the field of
American Studies.

Trying to clarify the new abstraction of finance capital or stock market investments (and land speculation), Fredric Jameson, in his piece "'End of Art' or
'End of History'?", names some of the main tasks Marxist theory has to confront
in a globalized late-capitalist world:

> Marxist theory needs to provide interpretations of all these things – of ideology and
> class struggle, of culture and the operation of the superstructures – on the vaster
> scale of contemporary globalization. The spirit of the analyses will have a continuity
> with the older ones, so triumphantly elaborated at the end of the modern period: but
> the terms will necessarily be new and fresh, given the novelties of the enlarged capi-
> talist world market which they are designed to explain. (Jameson 1998, 89)[10]

It is important to understand that Jameson himself has been very reluctant to
consider the necessity of what I have called a theoretical practice, since he sees
the task of 'theory,' or 'dialectical criticism,' as directly opposed to the attempt
to develop a theoretically informed activism in a field of immanence. The
last chapter of *Marxism and Form*, entitled "Towards Dialectical Criticism,"
offers a radical critique of Anglo-American philosophy, which for Jameson is
a thought-asphyxiating mixture of logical positivism, empiricism, and political
liberalism. Dialectical criticism is strongly opposed to this kind of thinking:
"Anglo-American philosophy has long since been shorn of its dangerous specul-
ative capacities, and as for political science, it suffices only to think of its distance from the great political and Utopian theories of the past to realize to what
degree thought asphyxiates in our culture, with its absolute inability to imagine
anything other than what is" (Jameson 1971, 416). In his recent response to Ian
Hunter's provocative essay "The History of Theory," published in 2006 in *Critical Inquiry*, Jameson makes clear that he sees Hunter as belonging "to the traditional Anglo-American empiricism that theory set out to demolish in the first
place" (Jameson 2008, 566).

---

[10] On Jameson's reading of globalization, see his "Notes on Globalization as a Philosophical
Issue," *The cultures of globalization*, eds. Fredric Jameson and Masao Miyoshi (Durham:
Duke UP, 1998), 54-77; "Globalization and Political Strategy," *New Left Review* 4.2000,
49-68. In addition, see Jameson's interview with Srinivas Aravamudan and Ranjana
Khanna in Ian Buchanan (ed.), *Jameson on Jameson: Conversations on cultural Marxism*
(Durham: Duke UP, 2007), 203-40; and Caren Irr and Ian Buchanan (eds.), *On Jameson:
From postmodernism to globalization* (Albany: SUNY Press, 2006).

In a truly Adornian manner, Jameson does not try to hide his aversion to (logical) positivism, empiricism, pragmatism, and nominalism. Consequently, he would presumably be inclined to think that Hardt and Negri's wish to offer a toolbox of concepts which might be used "for theorizing and acting in and against Empire" (Hardt and Negri 2000, xvi), or their desire to develop "a new science" (Hardt and Negri 2004, 353) for the democracy of the multitude, is too grounded in the field of immanence, too much a part of the world of practice, experience, and contingency where the power of (conceptual) mediation or tran-scoding is necessarily limited (or – the theorist's worst nightmare – not even needed). In his article "Symptoms of Theory or Symptoms for Theory?," Jame-son once more underscores the importance of the shift of our methodological practice from the analysis of individual texts to what he terms "mode-of-production analysis" (Jameson 2004, 408). This idea of an analysis of the re-spective mode of production has played a central role in the Jamesonian frame-work since *Marxism and Form*; it is a central component of the theory of inter-pretation which Jameson introduces in *The Political Unconscious*; and it is of course of utmost importance as regards his writings on the postmodern. A recent text like *A Singular Modernity: Essay on the Ontology of the Present* (2002) confirms our suggestion. In the aforementioned article, Jameson contends that to understand the cultural production of late capitalism today "is not the worst way of trying to understand that system and the possibilities it may offer for radical or even moderate change" (Jameson 2004, 408). Whereas Jameson for the past three decades has been concentrating on the task of conceptually grasping the multilayered complexity of late capitalism and its cultural logic, Hardt and Ne-gri, as we have seen, have argued that theory ought to strive to be effective in the field of immanence which is the imperial terrain of Empire. Calling attention to the fact that there might be consequences of theory in history, is a gesture, I think, that can (still) inspire those working in the field of American Studies.

References

Cusset, Francois. 2008. *French Theory: How Foucault, Derrida, Deleuze, & Co. Transformed the Intellectual Life of the United States*. Minneapolis: Uni-versity of Minnesota Press.

Denning, Michael. 1986. 'The Special American Conditions': Marxism and American Studies. *American Quarterly* 38.3: 356-80.

------. 1997. *The Cultural Front: The Laboring of American Culture in the Twentieth Century*. New York: Verso.

Derrida, Jacques. 1994. *Specters of Marx: The State of the Debt, the Work of Mourning, & the New International*. New York: Routledge.

Hardt, Michael, and Antonio Negri. 2000. *Empire*. Cambridge, MA: Harvard University Press.

------. 2003. Globalization and Democracy. In *Implicating Empire: Globaliza-tion and Resistance in the 21st Century World Order*, ed. Stanley Arono-witz and Heather Gautney, 109-21. New York: Basic Books.

------. 2004. *Multitude: War and Democracy in the Age of Empire*. New York: Penguin.

Jameson, Fredric. 1971. *Marxism and Form: Twentieth-Century Dialectical Theories of Literature*. Princeton: Princeton University Press.

------. 1981. *The Political Unconscious: Narrative as a Socially Symbolic Act*. New York: Routledge.

------. 1998. 'End of Art' or 'End of History'? In *The Cultural Turn: Selected Writings on the Postmodern, 1983-1998*, 73-92. New York: Verso.

------. 2004. Symptoms of Theory or Symptoms for Theory? *Critical Inquiry* 30.2: 403-8.

------. 2008. How Not to Historicize Theory. *Critical Inquiry* 34.3: 563-82.

Kaplan, Amy. 1993. 'Left Alone with America': The Absence of Empire in the Study of American Culture. In *Cultures of United States Imperialism*, ed. Donald E. Pease and Amy Kaplan, 3-21. Durham: Duke University Press.

Lipsitz, George. 2001. *American Studies in a Moment of Danger*. Minneapolis: University of Minnesota Press.

Lott, Eric. 2000. After Identity, Politics: The Return of Universalism. *New Lite-rary History* 31: 665-80.

Mitchell, W.J.T. 2004. Medium Theory: Preface to the 2003 *Critical Inquiry* Symposium. *Critical Inquiry* 30.2: 324-35.

Negri, Antonio. 2008. *Reflections on Empire*. Trans. Ed Emery. Cambridge: Pol-ity Press.

Passavant, Paul A. 2004. Introduction: Postmodern Republicanism. In *Empire's New Clothes: Reading Hardt and Negri,* ed. Paul A. Passavant and Jodi Dean, 1-20. New York: Routledge.

Pease, Donald E., and Amy Kaplan, eds. 1993. *Cultures of United States Impe-rialism*. Durham: Duke University Press.

Pease, Donald E., and Robyn Wiegman, eds. 2002. *The Futures of American Studies*. Durham: Duke University Press.

Radway, Janice. 2002. What's in a Name? In *The Futures of American Studies*, ed. Donald E. Pease and Robyn Wiegman, 45-75. Durham: Duke Univer-sity Press.

Rowe, John Carlos. 2002. *The New American Studies*. Minneapolis: University of Minnesota Press.

Shapiro, Kam. 2004. The Myth of the Multitude. In *Empire's New Clothes: Reading Hardt and Negri*, ed. Paul A. Passavant and Jodi Dean, 289-314. New York: Routledge.

West, Cornel. 1989. *The American Evasion of Philosophy: A Genealogy of Pragmatism*. Madison: University of Wisconsin Press.

232   Ulf Schulenberg

------. 1991. Theory, Pragmatisms, and Politics. In *Consequences of Theory*, ed. Jonathan Arac and Barbara Johnson, 22-38. Baltimore: Johns Hopkins University Press.

Sabine Sielke
University of Bonn, Germany
Memory, mediation, American Studies, or: challenging the division of a world before and after 9/11

Many recent critical enterprises in the field of American Studies have been informed by the specter of 9/11 and its aftermath. While such (re-) politicization of our discipline undoubtedly has its value, this perspective has also, first, blinded us to some of the tendencies of current American cultural practice, and secondly, redirected our critical attention. After all, the temporal trajectory of a world before and after 9/11 tends to reproduce in an inverted manner the world view projected by the Bush administration – a view that allowed legitimizing changes of policies, violations of international conventions, and the war in Iraq by insisting on a rupture imposed by the terrorist bombings of 11 September 2001. This trajectory relegates seriality and continuity between pre- and post-9/11 culture to the periphery of our attention – be it continuities in the foreign policy of Bill Clinton and George W. Bush, in the demonization of Islamic cultures in the early 1990s and after 9/11, or in the serial repercussions of aesthetic forms and effects.

Twenty-first century North American cultural practices resist such ahistorical views. Instead, films such as *Good Night, and Good Luck* or *Brokeback Mountain*, novels by Don DeLillo, Jonathan Safran Foer, Siri Hustvedt, and Philip Roth, and work by Art Spiegelman, to offer just a few examples, preoccupy themselves with intermediality and the history of their own genre and interrogate the interdependence of politics, memory, and mediation. In this way, cultural practices not only question dominant conceptions of (cultural) history which are guided by a sense of ruptures, turning points, or epoché (from the Greek word for "break" or "incision"). In foregrounding that practices and perceptions of politics are inseparable from processes of memory and mediation, film and fiction, in fact all texts and media, ponder the question how cultural practices (such as foreign policy or, again, film and fiction) interrelate – a question at the center of the American Studies agenda from its very beginning, my contribution also proposes directions for the transdisciplinary agenda of our field.

In order to make my claims more transparent, I will present a three-step argument. In step one I briefly reflect on the recent attraction to cultures of memory. In particular, I focus on trauma and its significance as a trope of both memory and rupture after 9/11. In a longer second step I move to matters of mediation proper. Taking a close look at Art Spiegelman's "comics" *In the Shadow of No*

I thank Ottilie Schmauss, David Schumacher, and Patrick Stärke for competent research assistance.

Towers (2004), I will argue that with regard to matters of representation, the 11th of September 2001 is a day when "nothing much changed," even if "the end of irony" (Sielke 2000) seemed to have suddenly come upon us. In step three I very briefly reflect on what the interdependence of memory and mediation may suggest for the future of American studies.

Step one: the ghosts of memory and the trope of trauma

To many critics and commentators twenty-first century US-American culture seems equal to post-9/11 culture. And many an author has been at pains to insist, as Philip Roth himself did, for instance, that Roth was not thinking of George W. Bush when imagining Charles Lindbergh ascending the presidency in the late 1930s and turning America from a bulwark of freedom and democracy into a fascist regime. In fact, while Roth's 2004 novel *The Plot Against America* quite ironically engages current memory cultures and their tendency to make the Holocaust an American memory, much of post-9/11 cultural critique appears like an exercise in forgetting and amnesia. Its very emphasis on rupture not only reinforces the short-sighted view that, after 11 September 2001, "nothing was ever going to be the same." For historian John Lewis Gaddis, even "the DNA of our minds" mutated (quoted in Kennedy-Pipe/Rengger 2006, 540). Implicitly, this insistence on, if not desire for, change also makes spiritual "rebirth" – the belief that one can completely disentangle oneself from a, perhaps disreputable, past and become anew and pure – into a politically valid agenda. Remember? George W. Bush claimed that hearing of the attack on the World Trade Towers had such a transformative effect on him.

As a consequence, our relentless "turning toward the past" and the emergence of memory as a key concept of cultural analysis not only stands "in stark contrast," as Huyssen argues, "to the privileging of the future so characteristic of earlier decades of twentieth-century modernity" (Huyssen 2000b, 21). Post-9/11, our preoccupation with issues of memory has – somewhat paradoxically – become closely entangled with a sense of sudden transformation. This sense of rupture, on the one hand, reinforces the fears of loss that have "accelerated" the production of memory discourses since the early 1980s (cf. Huyssen 2000b, 22). On the other hand, this rupture has, in the eyes of many a critic, retrospectively evolved new – personal as well as cultural – "identities."

Curiously enough, these new identities are frequently deemed a result of the "traumatic experiences" of 9/11. For E. Ann Kaplan, for instance, the "politics of terror and loss" have given rise to "trauma cultures," which forge new "subjectivities through the shocks, disruptions and confusions that accompany them"

(Kaplan 2005, 20).[1] This emergence of identity from trauma is curious because, after all, as trauma theory holds, trauma can neither be remembered nor forgotten, nor is it "compatible with the survival of the self"; it destabilizes rather than scaffolds identity (Assmann 2003, 26). Why then did trauma become so attractive as a cultural trope? There is, of course, no easy answer to this question. Yet part of its attraction is that, due to its metonymic proximity to the Holocaust, the term trauma not only allows all of us our share of "holocaustal experience" and thus a kind of "recognition" of substantial cultural currency. It also restores to the Holocaust an individual, personal dimension while retaining its "unrepresentability." As a trope, trauma moreover manages to re-member and thus, in a very literal sense: to partially restore the subjectivity of members of ethnic groups that, like African Americans, were never re-cognized as subjects in psychoanalytic terms.[2] Finally, the term (and trope) trauma reunites with his or her (albeit mutilated) body the very subject that poststructuralism reduced to an effect of discourse, thereby opening up new paths of cultural interpretation.

Particularly striking about this "obsession" with trauma (LaCapra 2001, x) is its significant shift in status. Like the Holocaust, once considered an experience that resists representation, trauma now frequently – and quite paradoxically – works as both a trope of the complexities of signification and its losses and as "sign of our times" (Kansteiner 2004, 194). While psychoanalysis holds that trauma resists representation, cultural trauma, we are made to believe, can be recollected, narrated, and visualized in multiple ways. Jeffrey C. Alexander even speaks of trauma as "a new master narrative" (Alexander 2004a, 10). Yet how can we relate what cannot be known? And what happened to the project of resisting, if not undoing, master narratives?

Step two: memory as mediation: the example of Art Spiegelman's *In the Shadow of No Towers*

In his introduction to the collection *110 Stories: New York Writes After 9/11*, Ulrich Baer speaks of "the need for narrative in the wake of disaster." Baer also insists, though, that unlike political discourses which – like Hollywood movies – aim for closure, "literature resists the call for closure" (quoted in Kaplan 2005, 137). While, in principle, we may want to agree, we may also need to accept that literature has long lost its status of exceptionality. And just as no walls get torn

---

[1] Kaplan even admits that her formerly leftist positions on US international politics did not seem to yield the appropriate perspective on the events of 11 September 2001 (Kaplan 2005, 15).

[2] Ron Eyerman, for instance, employs the term trauma to reconceptualise slavery as "a 'primal scene'" in "the formation of African American identity" "which could, potentially, unite all 'African Americans' in the United States, whether or not they had themselves been slaves or had any knowledge of or feeling for Africa" (Eyerman 2001, 1).

down without new ones being erected, there's no closure without new open vistas. For if there is one lesson we learned from deconstruction it is that all meaning – and thus all memory – is mediated, intermedial, and thus not to be contained – an insight flaunted in many, if not most, if not all, twenty-first century cultural practices. Let's look at one of them.[3]

As the work of the son of survivors (of the Holocaust) and of a survivor (of 9/11), Spiegelman's comic *In the Shadow of No Towers* reminds us – like any other attempt to "cope" with trauma in cultural discourse – that re-presentation is first of all a matter of mediation and remediation. In fact, its insistent self-referentiality and intermediality makes it hard, I think, to read *In the Shadow of No Towers* as "the record of a psychologically wounded survivor, trying to make sense of an event that overwhelmed and destroyed all his normal psychic devices" (Versluys 2006, 982). Such a reading attests more to the reader's desire to make trauma signify than to what the comic – as a transient genre "just right," as Spiegelman has it, "for an end-of-the-world moment" (quoted in Whitlock 2006, 967) – can manage to do. Thus, the very newspaper size of its colored plates (9.5 by 14 inches) rather embodies the media ecology in which the comic strip originally evolved. Moreover, throughout its fragmented narration *In the Shadow of No Towers* not only reanimates (and repeats with a difference) figures from Rudolph Dirk's *The Katzenjammer Kids* and George Herriman's *Krazy Kat*, among other pre-texts, and thus recalls the history of the comic as a genre central to US-American modernism and modernization, bound to new printing technologies and processes of serialization, as well as the rise of film as the central medium of the twentieth century and the status of "old comic strips" as "vital, unpretentious ephemera from the optimistic dawn of the 20th century" (Spiegelman quoted in Versluys 2006, 990).[4] Preceded by a two-page prose introduction by the artist, the ten pages of Spiegelman's comic book are even supplemented by a two-page "cameo history of newspaper comics in the US, illustrated by reprints of original cartoon strips and plates" (Versluys 2006, 981). Whether such strategies may amount to "healing through quotation," as Klaus Scherpe argues

---

[3] Another version of this analysis of Spiegelman's comix appears in my essays "Why '9/11 is [not] unique,' or: Troping Trauma," to be published in *Trauma's Continuum: September 11th Re-Considered*, ed. Andrew Gross and Mary Ann Snyder-Körber, *Amerikastudien/ American Studies* (2011), and "Troping the Holocaust, Globalizing Trauma," included in *The Holocaust, Art, and Taboo: Transatlantic Exchanges on the Ethics and Aesthetics of Representation*, ed. Sophia Komor and Susanne Rohr (Heidelberg: Winter, 2010), 227-47.

[4] The fact that Dirk's *Katzenjammer Kids*, as Ole Frahm's insightful close reading of *In the Shadow of No Towers* reminds us, are themselves inspired by Wilhelm Busch's *Max and Moritz* adds to the distance we travel in 'representations of trauma.' Evidently, these distancing effects also take place in what Gillian Whitlock calls "a global network of sequential art" (Whitlock 2006, 969) that involves transnational encounters and, in this context, the German intertext, of course, carries particular resonances.

in a different, though related context (quoted in Huyssen 2000a, 82), is yet another matter.

By presenting a drawing of the burning towers on the second and third page, the comic literally puts at its center a – comparably crude – reproduction, in graphic design, of the visual effects of digital imagery. I would resist, though, reading this image autobiographically, as does Karen Espiritu. Taking her cue from Spiegelman, who, by claiming that this image had been "burned into the inside of [his] eyelids" (quoted in Whitlock 2006, 188), offers to us a metaphor of traumatic memory at best, Espiritu sees this image lying "at the core of Spiegelman's traumatic experience" (Whitlock 2006, 188). However, other – less literal – interpretations may come to mind. Certainly, the recurrent image of the almost collapsing tower, on the one hand, acknowledges that, as Baudrillard has it, "the fascination with the attack is primarily a fascination with the image" (quoted in Wilson 2004, 105). Or as Slavoj Žižek argued in *Welcome to the Desert of the Real* (2002): "we were all forced to experience what 'the compulsion to repeat' and *jouissance* beyond the pleasure principle are: we wanted to see it again and again; the same shots were repeated ad nauseam, and the uncanny satisfaction we got from it was *jouissance* at its purest" (quoted in Wilson 2004, 109). On the other hand, the very porousness and simplicity of Spiegelman's image also foregrounds the limits of representation and the ways in which his "slow-motion diary" acknowledges these limits (Spiegelman 2004).

From the perspective of recent trauma discourse, the image of the tower which insistently recurs throughout the book may well read as a trace of a wound "that cannot be reduced to thematic content," a trace that "stubbornly persists in bearing witness" (Caruth quoted in Leys 2000, 269). At the same time, we may also see it foregrounding how human cognition necessarily reduces the technological complexities of mediation and crystallizes processes of perception and memory into iconic markers which trigger emotional responses (and how modernist aesthetics actually self-referentially enact and foreground these processes). In this way, Spiegelman's comic offers us kinds of afterimages which continue to appear in our vision after the exposure to the original image has ceased, and it thus stages – or mimics in slow motion – a "persistence of vision." At the same time, the artist engages what Leys calls "the pathos of the literal" cherished by a certain "school" of trauma discourse which holds that some violence and suffering bypasses representation, imprinting itself directly or "literally" on the mind. Assuming that "massive trauma precludes all representation . . .," Caruth, among others, argues, that "there occurs an undistorted, material, and – her [Caruth's] key term – *literal* registration of the traumatic event that, dissociated from normal mental processes of cognition, cannot be known or represented but returns belatedly in the form of 'flashbacks,' traumatic nightmares, and other repetitive phenomena" (Leys 2000, 266).

With reference to Spiegelman's *Maus* and its "modernist techniques of self-reflexivity, self-irony, ruptures in narrative time and highly complex sequencing and montaging" Andreas Huyssen, by contrast, speaks of "mimetic approximation" or "Angleichung" which, for Huyssen, "is precisely not identification or simple compassion" (Huyssen 2000a, 70, 72, 79). We may, of course, sympathize with Huyssen's attempt to make the "Adornean category of mimesis ... productive in a reading of Holocaust remembrance" (Huyssen 2000a, 80) and his resistance against what, in the year 2000, he considers "the recent revival of an aesthetic sublime and its dogmatic anti-representational stance" (Huyssen 2000a, 68-69). The question that remains, though, is whether it is modernist techniques – Versluys appropriately refers to *In the Shadow of No Towers* as a "modernist collage," Huyssen calls "irony, shock, black humor, even cynicism" "new narrative and figurative strategies" (Huyssen 2000a, 81) – which mimetically approximate trauma; or whether, due to the emergence of conceptions of trauma at a certain moment in cultural history, that is, during the nineteenth century, we have in fact come to correlate trauma with an aesthetics and style that emerged at the same time. And are the "urgency" and "formal excess" (Versluys 2006, 989) we detect in tales of trauma such as in Spiegelman's comics a property of the tales being told? Or are they rather projections of our own complicated desire for the telling of traumatic tales?

It is perhaps too simplistic to read, as Versluys does, "the broken-form of the narrative [as] a mirror image of [Spiegelman's] consternation." Versluys's claim that "[t]he fragmentary presentation serves as objective correlative for the author's scrambled state of mind," as "a direct, in-your-face impression of extreme confusion and perplexity" (Verslyus 2006, 989) reduces trauma to what Orbán calls "a convenient plot for structuring the representation ... of September 11" (Orbán 2007, 79). Instead, by foregrounding mediation and media history, Spiegelman's recent work on US-American "post-traumatic culture" (Kirby Farrell) acknowledges trauma's double status as an "experienced event" (Farrell quoted in Ball 2000, 18), on the one hand, and an "imaginary locus" (Ball 2000, 18), an "enabling fiction" (Farrell quoted in Ball 2000, 18), "a cultural trope that," as Ball has it, "structures public attention, even as it dissolves into a species of cliché" (Ball 2000, 16), on the other. "I live on the outskirts of Ground Zero," Spiegelman lets us know, "and first saw it all live – unmediated" while also confessing: "Disaster is my muse." Having "[n]ew traumas ... compet[e] with still-fresh wounds" (Spiegelman 2004) and "trauma pile ... over trauma" (Spiegelman 2004, 5), Spiegelman's panels in fact poke fun at the current obsession with trauma while also enacting the very hyperbole that LaCapra considers "the discursive symptom of, and perhaps necessary affective response to, the impact of trauma" (LaCapra 2001, xi). In some sense highly inadequate, the verb "pile" invests the term trauma with a spatial materiality and concreteness, suggesting that we could just "reach out and touch" trauma. Likewise the word "wound" fleshes out the abstract and bony concept of trauma, while being at the same time misleading, as Spiegelman himself seems to suggest. By reprinting on the flyleaf the 11 September 1901 front page of the New York newspaper *The World* with its headline "President's Wound Re-opened" the artist may certainly recall "another, now largely forgotten (but repeatedly re-enacted) collective trauma: the shooting of a president, in this case William McKinley" (Versluys 2006, 982). At the same time, though, focused on a surgical procedure which removed stitches in order to clean the bullet wound McKinley had suffered, this article also illuminates the limits of the wound metaphor: physical wounds can be attended to, psychical wounds are much less easily located. Thus Spiegelman certainly does not "interpret history as a concatenation of shocks, as a never-ending series of wounds that will not heal and keep festering," as Versluys claims (Versluys 2006, 981). Rather, his comic foregrounds how metaphors such as wound and trauma actually edit our sense of historical temporality by aligning highly distinct historical moments. Spiegelman's own strategy, throughout the comic, to relate, on the one hand, moments of his and his family's experiences on 11 September 2001 and, on the other, present a "savage satire" (Versluys 2006, 981) of the politics of the Bush administration until August 2003, may even suggest that metonymy is a more adequate figure to mark this particular moment in time.

Moreover, as Spiegelman's comics highlights the processes of remediation and intermediality it attests to the continuous shifts in our conceptions of trauma, to their function as "weapons of mass displacement," if I may appropriate Spiegelman's trope for the work of post-9/11 political rhetoric (fig. 1). In fact, Spiegelman quite literally acknowledges that, as Alexander puts it, "there is an interpretive grid through which all 'facts' about [cultural] trauma are mediated, emotionally, cognitively, and morally. This grid," Alexander holds, "has a supra-individual, cultural status; it is symbolically structured and sociologically determined. No [cultural] trauma interprets itself" (Alexander 2004b, 201). And Spiegelman offers us one such historically specific interpretatory grid that clearly calls into question the current paradigms of representing trauma.

More specifically, Spiegelman's grid makes much out of the fact that trauma as an experience escapes temporality, "is defined by temporal unlocability," as Leys puts it (Leys 2000, 271), translates into "time standing still" (Spiegelman 2004, 4), into "freeze frames," so to speak. Mediated by Spiegelman in part by a fragmentary aesthetics of collage and montage, this mode of temporality is aligned, albeit in a multiply mediated manner, with modernism and its attempt to create a "simultaneous order" (T. S. Eliot) and thus proximate to poetry (and poetics) rather than narrative (and narratology) or "counter-narrative," for that matter, as Kristiaan Versluys has it (Versluys 2006, 980). Inviting us, at times, to read and follow the images from right to left, thus evoking Arabic as well as

Hebrew, contributes to this irritation of traditional (Western) notions of narrative continuity.

Figure 1. Art Spiegelman, *In the Shadow of No Towers* (detail)

The very simplicity, iconicity, and seriality which characterizes the comic as a form of sequential visual art moreover makes it "well suited ... for dealing with abstractions" (Spiegelman 2004, 1) by images of embodiment. Physiologically, traumatic experiences cause stimulus satiation which blocks connections between the neocortex and other regions of the brain indispensable for information storage. The net effect of such overflow of stimulus is dissociative amnesia, a state of mind in which part of the past seems dead, yet may come back to life with a vengeance anytime, triggered by images, sounds, and smells. Or as LaCapra writes:

> Trauma brings about a dissociation of affect and representation: one disorientingly feels what one cannot represent; one numbingly represents what one cannot feel. Working through trauma involves the effort to articulate or rearticulate affect and representation in a manner that may never transcend, but may to some viable extent counteract, a reenactment, or acting out, of that disabling association. (LaCapra 2001, 42)

LaCapra therefore emphasizes the importance of the visual to account for "looks and gestures," "facial expressions," and the "body language" (LaCapra

2001, xiv) in survivor testimony. Spiegelman dares to mock such and similar claims, for instance, when he projects the "somatic imprint of trauma" (Orbán 2007, 81) as a kind of electric shock (fig. 2). Presenting a family (father, mother, kid, and cat) lounging in a ritualized position in front of the TV on September 10 (first panel), on September 11 (second panel), and on an unspecified day post-9/11, when the calendar (which marks time as a process) has been displaced by the American flag (a transhistorical sign), Spiegelman signals trauma by a clichéd, easily legible generic marker: having every family member move closer to the unbelievable images aired on September 11, their hairs frizzled and standing on end, everybody has already leaned back to their original position in the last panel, yet remains "on a permanent bad-hair day," as Orbán puts it (Orbán 2007, 80). Evidently, this sequence plays with generic conventions of repetition and difference to suggest that, on the one hand, September 11 was a "day nothing much changed" (Dobson 2006) while, on the other, emotionally everything did change, even if this transformation – the emotional shock following a stressful event – lacks adequate forms of representation. In this way, Spiegelman does not aim at representing trauma adequately, as some commentators claim. Rather, his images ironize the very notion that such appropriate mediation is possible in the first place.

Figure 2. Art Spiegelman, *In the Shadow of No Towers* (detail)

Thus Spiegelman's seeming attempts at mimesis come with an ironic distance. Even if the "haptic visuality and the materiality of the book" is, as Katalin Orbán argues, a central dimension of *In the Shadow of No Towers* (Orbán 2007, 72) which transports the physical impact of a deeply stressing experience, it does so in highly mediated manners. The same goes for the ways in which the comic foregrounds the olfactory dimensions of traumatic memory. Accordingly, like Auschwitz, 9/11, seen "all live – unmediated," is "indescribable," yet remembered as a disagreeable smell in Spiegelman's work and metonymically linked not to Auschwitz as the actual site of crime, but to how his father relates remembering Auschwitz. Similarly, in his novel *Extremely Loud and Incredibly Close* (2005) Jonathan Safran Foer does not simply create a link between the Dresden bombings, the nuclear destruction of Hiroshima, and the September 11 attacks. Rather he affiliates mediations of these events which in turn trigger processes of memory, including source confusion. Focusing on perception and cognition, both Spiegelman and Foer thus make an utterly significant distinction which is lacking, for instance, when Kaplan recalls that the gear of National Guard soldiers cordoning off Ground Zero reminded her of World War II: "The crush of people pressing around me made me feel as claustrophobic as did the crowds jamming into the underground shelters during my childhood" (Kaplan 2005, 7). Unlike the conjunction "as" that collapses one historical event into another, the focus on the mediation of memory in Spiegelman and Foer emphasizes the role of sense perception and the limits of representation. In other words: Unlike "[t]rauma theorists," who, according to Radstone, "associate trauma not with the effects of triggered associations but with the ontologically unbearable nature of the event itself" (quoted in Kaplan 2005, 35), artists focus on how these effects of (non-recoverable) traumatic experiences translate or, for that matter, do not translate into cultural practice. In fact, part of Spiegelman's "visual alternative" to the familiar loop of mediated images of the event is, as Orbán convincingly shows, to methodically work into his account of the events "a number of things he did not see," thus delineating how one can be haunted by images one did not witness (Orbán 2007, 73).

Ultimately, Spiegelman's comic pinpoints both the limits of representation and what Barbara Johnson, with reference to the primacy of trauma for psychoanalysis called "the trauma of interpretation." Psychoanalysis, as Johnson puts it in *Critical Difference*, "is the primal scene it seeks. It is the first occurrence of what has been repeating itself in the patient without ever having occurred. Psychoanalysis is not the interpretation of repetition; it is the repetition of a *trauma of interpretation* … the traumatic deferred interpretation not of an event, but *as* an event that never took place as such" (quoted in Belau 2001, 16-17). Like psychoanalysis itself, as Linda Belau underlines, any attempt to engage with trauma therefore engages in "a failed act of reading" (Belau 2001, 17). And it is this failure – acknowledged by some (e.g. Claude Lanzmann) and strategically ignored by others (e.g. E. Ann Kaplan, if I read her correctly) – which fires further repetition, or rather invites further interpretation. As Jacques Derrida wrote: "[W]hat is terrible about 'September 11,' what remains 'infinite' in this wound is that we do not know how to describe, identify, and even name it" (quoted in Versluys 2006, 987). Trauma thus is not so much "the impossibility of narration," as Aleida Assmann has it (Assmann 2003, 30). Our repeated acts of reading trauma are approximations that cannot but fail; that's why we keep reading, interpreting, repeating, producing a difference every time we do. The term trauma thus offered one meaning to the events of 11 September 2001 while at the same time resisting closure and suggesting that we will have to repeatedly return to the ruins of Ground Zero.

Part of the traumatic dimension of 9/11 may be just that: our failure to interpret "correctly," adequately what actually happened on 11 September 2001, locally as well as globally. However, Jean Baudrillard may still have been mistaken when he claimed that "[w]e try retrospectively to impose some meaning on it, to find some kind of interpretation. But there is none" (quoted in Wilson 2004, 101). After all, our approximations have produced a matrix in which trauma works as a model of identity that is ultimately exclusionary, ethnic, and closed-off. And where language ended, post-9/11 politics could easily have its way. This is why, ultimately, the rhetoric of the unrepresentable remains a risky business.[5] And yet, what has all this to do, you may wonder, with the business American studies?

Step three: 9/11 – "the day nothing much changed"? or: the futures of American Studies

William Dobson, in a 2006 issue of *Foreign Policy* provocatively speaks of 9/11 as "the day nothing much changed." Why then do we share the "*belief*," as Caroline Kennedy-Pipe and Nicholas Rengger put it, "that there has been a great change in the architecture of world politics"? (Kennedy-Pipe/Rengger 2006, 540). Partly because we like to keep things simple and easily fall for strong tropes. Reading 9/11 as "cultural trauma" certainly simplifies matters. Foregrounding that practices and perceptions of politics are inseparable from processes of memory and mediation, the work of Art Spiegelman just as that of Foer and filmmakers such as George Clooney, by contrast, makes us read very, very closely. As a consequence American studies as a discipline may want to be less concerned with self-reflexive revisions of its development and central terms – and instead reevaluate the significance of aesthetics, practice a new formalism, and, most important, create new alliances with media studies. And maybe American studies could also learn from the insights of the cognitive sciences and take into account that, as a physiological process, memory is quite indifferent to the past and in fact future-oriented. Only if we keep in mind the complex interdependencies of the processes of memory and mediation can American Studies as transdisciplinary cultural studies have a future.

References

Alexander, Jeffrey C. 2004a. Toward a Theory of Cultural Trauma. In *Cultural Trauma and Collective Identity*, ed. Jeffrey C. Alexander et al., 1-30. Berkeley: University of California Press.
------. 2004b. On the Social Construction of Moral Universals: The "Holocaust" from War Crime to Trauma Drama. In *Cultural Trauma and Collective Identity*, ed. Jeffrey C. Alexander et al., 196-263. Berkeley: University of California Press.

---

[5] I am indebted here to poignant comments by Andrew S. Gross.

Assmann, Aleida. 2003. Three Stabilizers of Memory: Affect-Symbol-Trauma. In *Sites of Memory in American Literatures and Cultures*, ed. Udo J. Hebel, 15-30. Heidelberg: Winter.

Ball, Karyn. 2000. Introduction: Trauma and Its Institutional Destinies. *Cultural Critique* 46: 1-44.

Belau, Linda. 2001. Trauma and the Material Signifier. *Postmodern Culture* 11.2, http://muse.jhu.edu/journals/pmc/v011/11.2belau.html (accessed April 28, 2009).

Bérubé, Micheal, ed. 2005. *The Aesthetics of Cultural Studies*. Oxford: Blackwell.

Dobson, William. 2006. The Day Nothing Much Changed. *Foreign Policy* (September/October): 22-25.

Espiritu, Karen. 2006. "Putting Grief into Boxes": Trauma and the Crisis of Democracy in Art Spiegelman's *In the Shadow of No Towers*. *Review of Education, Pedagogy, and Cultural Studies* 28.2: 179-201.

Eyerman, Ron. 2001. *Cultural Trauma: Slavery and the Formation of African American Identity*. Cambridge: Cambridge University Press.

Foer, Jonathan Safran. 2005. *Extremely Loud and Incredibly Close*. New York: Houghton Mifflin.

Frahm, Ole. 2004. Dreierlei Schwarz: Art Spiegelman's and Elein Fleiss' Interpretationen des 11. September '01. In *Narrative des Entsetzens: Künstlerische, mediale und intellektuelle Deutungen des 11. September 2001*, ed. Matthias N. Lorenz, 169-82. Würzburg: Könighausen und Neumann.

Huyssen, Andreas. 2000a. Of Mice and Mimesis: Reading Spiegelman with Adorno. *New German Critique* 81: 65-82.

------. 2000b. Present Pasts: Media, Politics, Amnesia. *Public Culture* 12.1: 21-38.

Kansteiner, Wulf. 2004. Genealogy of a Category Mistake: A Critical Intellectual History of the Cultural Trauma Metaphor. *Rethinking History* 8.2: 193-221.

Kaplan, E. Ann. 2005. *Trauma Culture: The Politics of Terror and Loss in Media and Literature*. New Brunswick: Rutgers University Press.

Kennedy-Pipe, Caroline, and Nicholas Rengger. 2006. Apocalypse Now? Continuities or Disjunctions in World Politics After 9/11. *International Affairs* 82.3: 539-52.

LaCapra, Dominick. 2001. *Writing History, Writing Trauma*. Baltimore: Johns Hopkins University Press.

Leys, Ruth. 2000. *Trauma: a Genealogy*. Chicago: University of Chicago Press.

Niday, Jackson A., II. 2004. A Rhetoric of Trauma in 9-11 Stories: A Critical Reading of Ulrich Baer's 110 Stories. *War, Literature, and the Arts* 16: 59-77.

Orbán, Katalin. 2007. Trauma and Visuality: Art Spiegelman's Maus and In the Shadow of No Towers. *Representations* 97.1: 57-89.

Radstone, Susannah. 2001. Trauma and Screen Studies: Opening the Debate. *Screen* 42.2: 188-93.

Sielke, Sabine, ed. 2002a. *Der 11. September 2001: Fragen, Folgen, Hintergründe.* Frankfurt: Lang.

------. 2002b. Das Ende der Ironie? Zum Verhältnis von Realem und Repräsentation zu Beginn des 21. Jahrhunderts. In *Der 11. September 2001: Fragen, Folgen, Hintergründe*, ed. Sabine Sielke, 255-73. Frankfurt: Lang.

------. 2004. The Politics of the Strong Trope: Rape and Feminist Debates in the United States. *Amerikastudien/American Studies* 49.3: 367-84.

Spiegelman, Art. 2004. *In the Shadow of No Towers.* New York: Pantheon.

Versluys, Kristiaan. 2006. Art Spiegelman's *In the Shadow of No Towers*: 9/11 and the Representation of Trauma. *Modern Fiction Studies* 52.4: 980-1003.

Whitlock, Gillian. 2006. Autographics: The Seeing "I" of the Comics. *Modern Fiction Studies* 52.4: 965-79.

Wilson, Emma. 2004. Europe's 9/11. *Paragraph: A Journal of Modern Critical Theory* 27.3: 100-12.

Žižek, Slavoj. 2003. Schatten der Neuen Weltordnung. *Der Tagesspiegel*, March 23.

Bohdan Szklarski
University of Warsaw, Poland
Presidential leadership as therapy

This essay has two principal goals, both predicated on one premise: political leadership needs legitimacy to maximize its potential. First, it offers the analysis of the conditions in which the presidents operate and discusses the choices of tactics they use in order to retain favorable evaluation of their leadership. Secondly, the conditions in which presidency functions are anarchic or, in other words, at any given moment numerous political actors exert often incompatible claims regarding the political outcomes.

Adding to the confusing character of politics is the fact that political opinions held by the public (ordinary people and the elites) are not consistent i.e. at any given moment people may hold views, articulate demands and embrace values which do not add up into a coherent system of opinions. That body of values and positions looks more like a cafeteria into which people enter and, based on their reading of a particular situation, select a matching standpoint.

Such a disjointed institutional and axiological context naturally produces tensions in actors and alleviates their perceptions of uncertainty, therefore, creating a favorable environment for those actors who can minimize the risks and provide security for other political actors. By bridging the gap between incongruent pressures in and around people, political leaders act as therapists.

It is the role of the President to manage these tensions and to convert them into a legitimate public policy. The incompatible nature of such demands creates a space in which leaders operate relatively freely, so long as they do not cross the imaginary line of accepted behavior. Those demands on presidents can be construed as leadership paradoxes and the latter part of the article is devoted to them.

The leadership situation

Most often, political leadership is defined through the prism of action and decisions and its success is measured by comparing intentions with tangible (legislative and legal) accomplishments. Such instances or emergencies when real leadership can be fully manifested are quite rare. Wars, economic and social crises, natural disasters come naturally to mind as "leadership moments." On daily basis "normal" politics comes closer to maneuvering among a multitude of actors with conflicting interests, each creating a rhetorical sense of urgency around their values and producing demands at various political institutions simultaneously.

In such circumstances leadership takes the form of a sequence of small steps, sometimes invisible for the public at large. Normal leadership consists of crafting alliances, overcoming resistance, taking stands on issues, managing personnel, and setting the tone of public debates all in an effort to define and control the flow of political developments. In everyday politics there is more deliberation than governance. Therefore, it is more appropriate to talk about "leadership opportunities" as those situations when leaders can actually step into the flow of things and make a difference.

The relationship between deliberation and governance is but one aspect of modern leadership that needs to be examined. The other one, no less important as the factor determining the range of power of contemporary presidents is their relationship with the media and their skill in controlling the coverage of the White House. This mediated aspect of leadership is most important for its success. In a fragmented, personalized and media dominated political sphere the consequences and causes of political phenomena i.e. events and decisions, have become decoupled. Neither their causes nor the consequences can be fully controlled by political leaders, therefore, in order to maintain high levels of support, they focus on the public procedures, which create the image of effective leadership in action.

Not only is the political process fragmented and disjointed, so is the media coverage of political events. Information and commentary become hard to separate. The entertainment aspect of mass media reporting only adds to the confusion. The multitude of news outlets (traditional media – printed press, television, talk radio, and new media – first of all internet) each hunt for stories and headlines. That rivalry makes reporting political events even more episodic and dramatic in character (Sheuer 2001). Political elites respond by creating staged and prefabricated events primarily for media consumption (Dayan and Katz 1994). Such an approach to mediated politics on both sides results in communication, on the one hand being routinized and ritualized (Campbell and Jamieson 1990), that is controlled by the politicians, and on the other hand highly sensationalistic and personalized: unpredictable and risky.

In plain language it might be said that modern leadership, rather than being a substantive and material distribution of goods and services, acquires a distinctly symbolic nature, sometimes equal to "going through the motions," political performance, or to signaling action (Szklarski 2006, 16-20). Leaders have in front of them a panel with switches and knobs activating gestures, moves, cues, clichés and catch-phrases that move the public. Thus, political leadership has become a virtual opportunity rather than a hard substance. It is up to individual leader's skills whether such moments are utilized to advance their position and agenda in order to achieve success in the public eye.

Ambiguous nature of public policy preferences

The institutional and axiological circumstances in which political leaders operate have a disjointed and competitive nature which makes it quite a complex reality. Paradoxically, the greater the complexity the more latitude a skillful leader may have in exercising his leadership due to a certain quality of human mind. Human beings possess "high plasticity" which enables them to respond to "variety and indeterminacy of the impulses" resulting in their lack of "instinctual specialization and world-openness [which allows them] to reduce the complexity of the environment through very free symbolic and manipulative activities which are not bound deterministically to refer to any immediate situation." Such psychological construction manifests in people's propensity to legitimize behaviors and attitudes of an "adaptive, ritual, risk free nature [in the *space*, emphasis mine] between the search for security and the need for freedom" (Zolo 1992, 38).

Thus, the world around us is complex and dynamic to the extent that makes it barely comprehensible for citizens. Yet there is no alternative, at least in America which has always rejected simplistic and all-encompassing ideological explanations of reality. Translated into the realm of politics, it means that what leaders need to do in order to achieve recognition and support is to locate their actions in that space of acquiescence. Sociological studies of public opinion lend support to the spatial model of leadership. They also see notice that actual policy preferences do not form a single line but are scattered between the liberal and conservative positions. That body of legitimate, though often incongruent expectations and opinions about current issues is referred to as "mainstream" or "zone of acceptance" by sociologists. They have us imagine two axes: vertical liberal and horizontal conservative, and opinions about current issues plotted between them. The distribution of opinions has certain variance which forms a clear pattern. Majority opinions form a broad winding stream with uneven borders. That is the zone of accepted opinions. The borderlines of the zone are defined in ideological terms as liberal and conservative. Policies which lie between them are accepted, those which lie outside are rejected as excessive. What lies within the zone constitutes a fluid mainstream, what lies outside is radical.

The liberal and conservative lines are not fixed. They are a reflection of current distribution of opinions and values by the public. For instance, in the 1940s and 50s the distance between them was fairly narrow and the whole stream was curved towards higher liberal loadings. In the 1960s the space between the ideological edges of the zone of acceptance widened. It narrowed down again in the 1970s and widened again in the 1980s, this time, however, the direction of the whole stream started decisively to move down closer to the conservative axis and continued the trend till 2008. From a distance, the zone of acceptance looks like a fat serpent.

If this is true, and we have no reasons to believe otherwise, it has repercussions for our understanding of the meaning of political success. Success need not be defined with regard to the achievement of concrete, specific goals (for instance electoral claims) but merely in terms of performing actions and taking positions that are perceived as locating consistently within the zone of acceptance or the space of acquiescence. The two terms, however are not exactly synonymous. They are both a product of actual distribution of opinions about concrete policies: liberal or conservative solutions to health care or social security reforms, welfare state extension, budget deficit reduction plans, subsidization of agricultural production, bailout of falling lending institutions, or interventionism in foreign affairs.

However, what differentiates them is the fact that the zone of acceptance is determined on daily basis and defined by opinions about issues of the day. Whereas the space of acquiescence has a longer time perspective in which it is observed. Its borderlines represent attitudes to long-term tendencies. It is more about values and orientations than about responses to current problems. In its magnitude, the space of acquiescence is a way of defining political culture (Stimson 1999, 22; Wilson 1992, 19-20). Nonetheless, it is the cumulative result of the attitudes to the issues of the day that produces long term trends, so the concepts of the zone (ideological and current) and space (axiological and extended in time) are related to one another.

The following list of incompatible expectations regarding the character and performance of presidency, or perhaps the whole political elite in Washington, reflects how unrealistic and confusing public perceptions are.

Not only does the complexity of Washington posed a challenge to the presidential leadership. The public serves as another check. In terms of resources – expectations relationship, the presidency is characterized by the awareness of the gap between the legitimate public expectations and the sytem's/presidency's ability to satisfy them (Rose 1991, 25-27). That is one of the paradoxes of American democracy: the presidency is becoming weaker and exposed to multilateral attacks, yet simultaneously, the public sees it as the best possible force that can overcome the crisis. The following list is a compilation of desired qualities of presidential power which reveals how ambiguous the public expectations may be.

Incoherent preferences regarding the character of the American Presidency:
1. People demand strong leadership but also feel uneasy about strong government
2. People want the President to be "one of them" but also want him to be charismatic and visionary
3. People want power to be held by "righteous" people but also admire shrewd and effective manipulators

4. People admire politicians who rise above ideological divisions (work both sides of the aisle) but also want the President to fulfill the electoral partisan mandate

5. People want their presidents to implement bold reform programs but also want them to follow the voice of the public (Cronin and Genovese 1998, 4-5; Hinckley 1990, 11; Hargrove 1998, 22-23)

This "post-modern presidency" operates permanently in the condition of "power deficit" (Szklarski 2006, 24). The list presented above of contradictions supports the following image of the presidency: "people expect that the man in the White House will do something in every sphere ... will bring peace, prosperity and security" (Edwards and Wayne 1997, 97). At the peak of presidential power, in the late 1960s, when the public still had fresh memories of Johnson's barrage of social reform programs such as civil and voting rights reform, war on poverty, social security, Medicaid and Medicare, affirmative action etc., Louis Brownlow concluded that "the public expects from the president more than he can accomplish, more that he could do in the present institutional context and with all the available resources" (Brownlow 1969, 35). Since that time the powers of the presidency have only declined while the expectations continue to exceed them.

The expectations regarding the presidency function as an important determinant of behavior and perceptions both in the current zone of acceptance and in the broader space of acquiescence. Zone of accepted opinions is constructed on daily basis as things happen, it changes with the flow of tangible political conflicts. Whereas the space of acquiescence consists of cultural symbols which anchor the political community to its past, tradition and beliefs. In practical terms the space of acquiescence consists of attitudes to founding institutions such as for instance: the Constitution, elections, terms and forms of discourse, behavioral articulation of demands and supports. At any given moment, that space is defined at many plains which reflect basic axiological disagreements in the American public. These incompatible demands made on American politics may be called paradoxes of American democracy and they are a subject of analysis in the latter parts of this essay together with the role that political leaders play in reconciling them.

Policy making in Washington as organized anarchy

Descriptions of the policy making process leave no doubt that even the ablest public orator and clear popular mandate holder faces a daunting task when it comes to prevailing in the legislative game (Penny and Garrett 1996, xii). Pushing an initiative through this maze of ambitious egos, intra-institutional rivalry and crisscrossing jurisdictions requires patience and skills not of a solitary hero but a supreme team-worker and bargainer. Persuasion not demand is the key to success, which often comes long after a measure has been proposed. When a non-controversial piece of legislation may take two years to pass through Congress, it is foolish to expect quick results.

The long temporal separation between policy initiative and policy outcome is standard and media often report only on one end of the journey. The policy process in Washington is incremental. Given the multitude of actors involved in it and multiple venues where at a given moment a said initiative may be deliberated it is also extremely fragmented. In the times when visibility is often key to success, much effort of the Washington actors goes to staging public performances which are supposed to promote an issue, not even any particular solution to it.

Moving issues through the Washington power maze requires great perseverance. Only few actors are capable of doing it: the President, naturally, and key leaders of Congress, and perhaps some efficient lobbyist whom we never hear about. For the general public, the presidency is the front office that must at least give the appearance of "holding the pieces together." Given the virtual impossibility of that task the Presidency has become an office that must be performed rather than exercised.

In the complex Washington political scene, given the disjointed nature of policy making process, where the initiation of the problem and a solution to it may be separated by many months if not years of hard, often invisible, work, success can be defined twofold. First, the very placement of an issue in the political agenda and forcing other key actors to deal with it is a success. It is measured by how well the problem is defined and how that definition is accepted by other actors and the public. A success at this stage means that President's concern was signaled and noticed and accepted as a sign of resolve. It is assumed that future actions will follow.

Secondly, success in and outside of Washington means that the public finds the President's actions fruitful, legitimate and sufficient. That may come from actual legislative outcomes but more often is achieved at the symbolic level. In order to reach that level of recognition, the President must appear as capable of prevailing over the fragmented, quarrelsome, egoistic and particularistic congressional actors and lobbyists. The best way to do it is by appearing to be a conciliatory consensus builder – a "healer" as Ford saw it in 1975 or as "a repairer of the breach" – as Bill Clinton said it in his 1997 state of the Union Address.

The symbolic nature of modern power and the elusive nature of presidential success

On a daily basis, it is logical to subscribe to the garbage can model of Washington as "organized anarchy" (Cohen et al. 1972, 1) that describes the policy making process as full of "fuzzy preferences, fuzzy boundaries, avoidance of conflict, unclear technology, fragmentary understanding/involvement of actors" (Lindblom 1959, 81). In this model federal government is "a collection of choices looking for problems, issues and feelings looking for decision situations in which they might be aired, solutions looking for issues in which they might be the answer, and decision makers looking for work" (Cohen et al. 1972, 2). This setting is disjointed (anarchic) and yields mostly incremental outcomes which is not what the public expects.

Overall, the situation of power fragmentation and dysfunctional polarization among major institutional actors affects the decision making process in Washington. It is hard to see it as driven by coherent, rational, goal oriented thinking. Instead, it assumes the form of "disjointed incrementalism" when decisions become a product of momentary opportunities, fleeting emotions, values and contextual factors (Lindblom 1968, 12). The cafeteria parallels used to describe the incoherent nature of public and elite beliefs applies as well to the policy making environment in which they function.

The disjointed character of the public sphere, both in the procedural and axiological sense, still calls for efficient ways of coping with them. Symbolic politics is one of them. When the success of presidential policies is less certain or more costly, the occupants of the White House seek alternative means to achieve their results. Today's success is measured more by how well one "moves in a certain direction" than by actually "getting there" (Szklarski 2006, 27). Success is a perception not a hard fact. Legitimate leaders are those who manage to convince their followers that they serve them well. With the wide dissemination of such terms as "gridlock" "deadlock" or "divided government" the public has been prepared for the lack of substantive effects of policies.

Consequently, the stage has been set for symbolic politics which puts premium on image, ceremony, and ritual. A public rally or a speech staged in front of a prison communicates the message: this president is tough on crime. A child-lifting-and-kissing media event set in a day care center says volumes about that presidents support for single mothers and though such images are "impermanent categories, malleable by definition, they leave lasting, sometimes painful imprints on the fabric of people's lives" (Ewen 1999, xvii) and perceptions we might add.

Modern leadership is communication of meaning that reinforces the legitimacy of the current policies. "Political forms come to symbolize what large masses of men need to believe about the state to reassure themselves" – says Edelman (Edelman 1985, 2). The hopes and anxieties of men determine the meaning they ascribe to the events they witness or experience via TV. The Presidency has extraordinary advantage in this competition for people's support. It is true that on the one hand it is burdened with the inflated expectations of a "single executive image," yet it also enjoys the center stage in the political theatre which gives it virtually unlimited access to the eyes and ears of Americans. Their position as the ones accorded "mythical legitimacy" (Nimmo and Combs 1980, 68) allows the presidents to use the symbolic aspects of leadership to command the hearts and souls of Americans. And this is what counts in politics today in a post-industrial world where economic differences lose significance and ideologies rise out of the grave where they were prematurely buried.

This is possible because the emotionally laden politics of symbols operates within a certain fairly clearly defined area bounded by shared memory, tradition, and belief system. This common public space in United States, according to Schlesinger is a product of uninterrupted development, remarkable for its absence of fundamentally divisive cleavages (Schlesinger 1993, 136). Social middle-classing and relative affluence also contribute to the absence of strong alternative value structures. In such a socio-economic context supported by exceptional constitutional-institutional stability it is easy to use symbolic politics. The chance of being misunderstood is very limited. Politicians in America (and their aides) have become experts in eliciting responses that serve their purpose. James MacGregor Burns calls such leadership when the goals and values of leaders and followers match a transforming leadership (Burns 1978, 4).

Such type of leadership might be misconstrued as "easy." Yet it requires constant reinforcement of existing orientations and affirmation of shared values. Successful construction of meaning which transforming (or transformative) leadership relies on passions and anxieties which makes it vulnerable to fluctuations and crises. Thus power is never constant. Mary Stuckey suggests that the president has become an "interpreter-in-chief ... a presenter" broadcasting for a "dramatized society" (Stuckey 1991, 5). Thanks to the use of rhetoric which is to reassure rather than convince or sway, political discourse is centered on engineering of consensus.

After Hume and Madison we might simply repeat that emotions drive human beings, not reason. Leadership requires a skilful management of emotions. Success comes to those who understand, not only that very premise, but who understand the emotional and symbolic and substantive borderlines which delineate the "space of acquiescence" for the public. Those who understand what lies inside and what outside of this space and successfully communicate it to the public win.

The communication process dominated by ceremony and symbolism contributes to consensus building not by "rationality and fact-finding" but by manipulation of existing beliefs and attitudes." Politics is "dramatic" not because of a clash of ideas in the public sphere but because it becomes grandiose and ceremonial. Presidential politics become more form than substance. In this context (public) image and style are two key components of presidential leadership. Symbolic politics may, though it does not have to, be a substitute of substantive politics. The use of symbolic appeals may be regarded as a supplement to other, more traditional tools at president's disposal. Their "popularity" is mandated by the TV dominated nature of politics.

Symbolic politics is an intangible power resource and belongs with "persuasive tools." It is tactics that serve long term goals rather than quick fixes. In a disjointed and incremental political setting, having an actor who gives the impression of coupling causes and consequences, and integrates the various stages of the policy making process and bestows on it a sense of direction must naturally be seen as a benevolent leader. Such psychological benefits must be counted among crucial aspects of presidential leadership today.

Therapeutic function of presidential leadership

Symbolic leadership and persuasion alone, are not enough to win and sustain successful leadership, yet they are an indispensable aspect of presidential leadership today. Symbolic leadership builds a climate favorable to compromises and prevents excessive disunity. It allows the presidents to play the role of consensual builders which further legitimizes their power. By reconciling differences and playing the role of an umpire presidents prove clearly that leadership is a two way street – presidents not only speak and persuade to solicit support but also listen to what the public says.

Therapeutic aspects of presidential leadership are likely to emerge in circumstances which are a particular blend of circumstances and tools. That leadership situation is characterized by the anarchic and disjointed character of the policy making process. A great multitude of actors make the political scene "congested" by formulating conflicting demands regarding the distribution of statuses, resources and uses of state power. Political conflict moves to the media where it is easier to shine and claim success than behind the scenes in the so called "corridors of power." Media presence and the ability to articulate interests become more important than much harder, sometimes impossible to achieve material political decision in Congress. Representation of interests and governance are separated.

Prevalence of media has two immediate consequences: on the one hand it brings up the emotional temperature of politics, contributing to anxiety and confusion among the public. On the other hand, politics presented through the media lends itself to rituals, celebrations and mass events in which everyone can be passively involved which reinforces the unity of the political community. So on one hand we have a disjointed and incremental, starved for success substantive policy making process on the institutional backstage and on the other in the foreground, on TV screens we have a constant parade of loud actors competing for highly particularistic rewards, principally in the form a piece of public attention and recognition.

Over that stage looms the president with central position both in the institutional and axiological order of things. With proper behavior and with the use of right words and gestures he can take advantage of that volatile and dynamic leadership situation to become a dominant actor that brings purpose, direction and cohesion to the realm of politics.

Table 1. How political leadership builds the "space of acquiescence" by reconciling contradictory tendencies in politics

CONTRADICTIONS	THERAPEUTIC FUNCTIONS OF SYMBOLIC POLITICAL LEADERSHIP
expectations vs. possibilities	Thanks to signaling activity in the substantive sphere of politics (creation of committees, task forces, public addresses) citizens are under the impression that White House decisions bring us closer to satisfying solutions to major problems. This way the "power deficit" is minimized
emotions vs. rational calculation	Signaling of activity towards the realization of electoral mandate and interactions with other actors create the impression of pragmatic drive towards a definite goal. At the same time, through rhetoric and participation in mass rituals the President bonds emotionally with the public. By using in political conflicts the special symbolic status of the White House to legitimize his positions the President creates positive anxiety among the public which results in them "rooting for" the presidency, particularly in sharp or lengthening crises (such as government shutdown over budget construction)
centralization vs. decentralization	The President speaks for many interests in his polyvalent and polysemic speeches and in briefings addressed to narrow audiences which make his politics multilateral. At the same time by making references to key constitutive creedal values of the society in public ceremonies, commemorative events and rituals he consolidates the diverse groups into a unified community.
continuity vs. change	Actions taken or signaled with specific goals in mind give the impression of dynamics and change. At the same time the impression of continuity is achieved in three ways: by defining political problems as inherited from the predecessors; by making references in discourse accompanying decisions haw these actions reflect ongoing commitment to key values of the community; by participating in mass political rituals
representation vs. governance	Signaling intent or taking action to realize electoral mandate reinforces the conviction that leaders represent interests and values of the public. Permanent presence in the media which are eager to report even minor presidential actions or comments gives the impression that the president is in charge of policy making institutions and processes
values vs. interests	By signaling intent or taking actions to realize electoral mandate the President caters to the demands of diverse interest groups, thus

	turning politics into a pragmatic competition of interests. By defining goals and interests in terms of their consistency with key creedal values and traditional aspirations of the community he manages to create the impression that there is room in politics for idealism and loyalty to traditional values that give the community its identity. Participation in mass rituals, celebrations and commemorations deprives politics of its materialism
now vs. future	Involvement in political competition with other actors over specific interests and distribution of goods anchor presidential politics in everyday current affairs and justify the slow pace in reaching the goals. On the other hand inaugural addresses, annual State of the Union messages and major televised speeches remind the public about the high minded, long term goals and visions which emanate from the White House and set the course of action for the coming years for the whole country. Often, concrete political goals are set beyond the time frame of his tenure.

The "contradictions" column reflects the major planes of competition always present in democratic politics. Unmitigated, such contradictions serve as centrifugal forces that have the potential of tearing the public sphere apart, by which I mean reaching such a degree of diversity that precludes constructive collaboration in solving major practical problems. Fortunately, as we may see, many of these contradictory tendencies are veiled behind "ordinary" mundane typical political behaviors. In each box on the right hands side of the table one finds quite normal political activities.

Average citizens may not be aware of their axiological incongruity. These paradoxes of presidential leadership exist at the subconscious level. Nevertheless, they are a source of anxiety and discomfort. As the only actors in the political system who can legitimately engage in actions representing each end one of the dyad, presidents bridge the gaps and bring the system to a state of equilibrium. Psychological research in emotional intelligence and cognitive psychology demonstrate that when people recognize their environment, understand basic terms of discourse and information provided by political actors, they are more inclined find satisfaction with their circumstances and are less inclined to question the words and actions of the elites or reason with them. In other words, under such conditions, people tend to "safely rely on unreflective abilities" which elicits routine and ritualized behavior and elevates the power of familiar and traditionally recognized institutions (Marcus et al. 2000, 47, 63). In political sense, equilibrium means a condition in which all key actors feel comfortable with the political process and are willing to accept its outcomes i.e. follow rather than challenge the leaders.

The presidency is capable of operating as a psychological backbone because it is simultaneously a cultural, political and social institution that embodies aspirations, values and emotions of the American people. It is a symbolic totem pole, a referent for all key actors, a centerpiece of the community. Its involvement in the public sphere which mitigates contradictions, transfers this sphere of competition and conflict, the scene of political (culture) wars into the space of acquiescence where actions, decisions and thoughts make sense. This transformative nature of presidential leadership definitely has a therapeutic function for Americans.

References

Boorstin, Daniel. 1964. *The Image. A Guide to Pseudo-Events in America*. New York: Harper & Row.

Brownlow, Louis. 1969. What We Expect the President to Do. In *The Presidency*, ed. Aaron Wildavsky, 35-43. Boston: Little Brown.

Burns, James MacGregor. 1978. *Leadership*. New York: Harper.

Campbell, Karlyn Kohrs, and Kathleen Hall Jamieson. 1990. *Deeds Done in Words. Presidential Rhetoric and the Genres of Governance*. Chicago: University of Chicago Press.

Cohen, Michael, James March, and Johan Olsen. 1972. A Garbage Can Model of Organizational Choice. *Administrative Science Quarterly*, 17, (March).

Cronin, Thomas, and Michael Genovese. 1998. *The Paradoxes of American Presidency*. New York: Oxford University Press.

Dayan, Daniel, and Elihu Katz. 1994. *Media Events. The Live Broadcasting of History*. Cambridge: Harvard University Press.

Edelman, Murray. 1985. *The Symbolic Uses of Politics*. Chicago: University of Illinois Press.

Edwards, George, III, and Stephen Wayne. 1997. *Presidential Leadership: Politics and Policy Making*. New York: St. Martin's Press.

Ewen, Stuart. 1999. *All Consuming Images. The Politics of Style in Contemporary Culture*. New York: Basic Books.

Hargrove, Erwin. 1998. *The President as Leader. Appealing to the Better Angels of Our Nature*. Lawrence: University Press of Kansas.

Hinckley, Barbara. 1990. *The Symbolic Presidency. How Presidents Portray Themselves*. New York: Routledge.

Lindblom, Charles. 1959. The Science of Muddling Through. *Public Administration Review*, 14, (Spring).

------. 1968. *The Policy-Making-Process*. Englewood Cliffs: Prentice Hall.

Marcus, George, Russell Neuman, and Michael MacKuen. 2000. *Affective Intelligence and Political Judgment*. Chicago: University of Chicago Press.

Nimmo, Dan, and James Combs. 1980. *Subliminal Politics. Myth & Mythmakers in America*. Englewood Cliffs: Prentice Hall.

Penny Timothy, and Major Garrett. 1996. *Common Cents. A Retiring Six-Term Congressman Reveals How Congress Really Works and What We Must Do to Fix It.* New York: Avon Books.

Rose, Richard. 1991. *The Postmodern President. George Bush Meets the World.* Chatham: Chatham House.

Scheuer, Daniel. 2001. *The Sound Bite Society. How Television Helps the Right and Hurts the Left.* New York: Routledge.

Schlesinger, Arthur M., Jr. 1993. *The Disuniting of America. Reflections on a Multicultural Society.* New York: W.W. Norton. & Company.

Stimson, James. 1999. *Public Opinion in America: Moods, Cycles, and Swings.* Boulder: Westview Press.

Stuckey, Mary. 1991. *The President as Interpreter-In-Chief.* Chatham: Chatham House Publishers.

Szklarski, Bohdan. 2006. *Przywództwo symboliczne; między rządzeniem a reprezentacją. Amerykańska prezydentura końca XX wieku* [Symbolic Leadership: between Governance and Representation. American Presidency in the End of the 20th Century] Warszawa: ISP PAN.

Wilson, Richard. 1992. *Compliance Ideologies. Rethinking Political Culture.* New York: Cambridge University Press.

Zolo, Danilo. 1992. *Democracy and Complexity. A Realist Approach.* Philadelphia: University of Pennsylvania Press.

Authors

Kacper Bartczak is Assistant Professor at the Department of American Literature and Culture, University of Łódź, Poland. He is author of *In Search of Communication and Community: the Poetry of John Ashbery* (Peter Lang, 2006) and *Świat nie scalony* (Biuro Literackie, 2009). He was a Visiting Fellow at Stanford University (2000-2001), a Kościuszko Foundation Visiting Fellow at Florida Atlantic University (2008). Currently he is a Visiting Fellow in Philosophy at Princeton University (2010-2011). He is working on a book on pragmatist poetics.

Alexander Brand holds a PhD in Political Science from Technische Universität Dresden (University of Dresden, Germany). His dissertation (2010) focused on the impact of mass media in international political relations thereby employing a discursive constructivist perspective. He currently works as a lecturer and post-doc researcher at the Chair for International Politics and as a lecturer at the School of International Studies (ZIS) at TU Dresden. His main research interests are: mediatization of international relations, US foreign and world policy, global development issues and sports/football and international politics.

Subarno Chattarji is Associate Professor in the Department of English, University of Delhi. He also taught in Japan and the UK. He has a BA, MA, and MPhil from the University of Delhi and a DPhil in American poetry of the Vietnam War from the University of Oxford. He was a Fulbright Senior Research Fellow at La Salle University, Philadelphia (2004-2005) and a recipient of Kluge Postdoctoral Fellowship at the Library of Congress in 2008-2009. His publications include: *Tracking the media: interpretations of mass media discourses in India and Pakistan* (Routledge, 2008); *Memories of a Lost War: American poetic responses to the Vietnam War* (Oxford University Press, 2001). He is co-editor of *Globalization in India: Contents and Discontents* (Pearson Education, 2009), and *An Anthology of Indian Prose Writings in English* (Penguin, 2004).

Katarzyna Dąbrowska is a PhD student in the Department of Epistemology and Philosophy of Science and an MA student in the Institute of Psychology, University of Łódź, Poland. Her research focuses on methodology and philosophy of science, especially on axiological aspects of science. Being an active member of the Philosophers' Scientific Association at the University of Łódź, she co-organized four conferences. She was a member of the Internet Philosophical Magazine Hybris' editorial team.

Luis E. Echarte, MD, PhD lives in Pamplona (Spain) where he teaches, as Profesor Contratado-Doctor, Medical Anthropology and Philosophy of Medicine in the School of Medicine at the University of Navarra. In 2002 Echarte defended his doctoral dissertation in Neuroscience in which he focused on the concept of the self through an analysis of three kinds of identity disorders: autism, schizophrenia and dissociative disorders. As visiting scholar in the Department of Philosophy, University of Berkeley, California he worked on neuroethics. In this research period he brought together his three major interests: philosophy of medicine, sociology and neuroscience, and currently his research focuses on moral neuropsychology. Echarte has published widely in English, Italian and Spanish, on consciousness and identity cosmetic psychopharmacology, psychiatrization of human condition and science-religion relations.

Paula S. Fass is Margaret Byrne Professor of History at the University of California at Berkeley and Distinguished Scholar in Residence at Rutgers University in New Brunswick Her books include *Children of a New World: Society, Culture, and Globalization* (2007), *Kidnapped: Child Abduction in America* (1997), *Outside In: Minorities and the Transformation of American Education* (1989), *The Damned and the Beautiful: American Youth in the 1920s* (1977). She is the editor of *Childhood in America* (2000) and of the award-winning *Encyclopedia of Children and Childhood in History and Society* (2004). Her most recent book is a family memoir, *Inheriting the Holocaust: A Second Generation Memoir* (2009). In 2008 she was awarded an honorary PhD degree from Linkoping University in Sweden.

William R. Glass is Professor of American Social History at the American Studies Center of the University of Warsaw. He is currently working a book length study of the image of the American military in Hollywood comedies.

Alfred Hornung is Professor and Chair of English and American Studies at the Johannes Gutenberg University of Mainz. He held guest professorships at various European, North American and Chinese universities. He was a fellow at Harvard, Yale, the National Humanities Center in North Carolina, and is a member of the Center for Cross-cultural studies at the University of Beijing. His publications are in the field of narratology, modernism, postmodernism, autobiography, postcolonialism and transcultural studies. He is on the editorial board of several journals (Amerikastudien / American Studies, American Studies Journal, Atlantic Studies, and the Journal of Transnational American Studies). He also served as a member of the International Committee of the ASA, as President of MESEA (the Society for Multi-Ethnic Studies: Europe and the Americas) and of the German Association for American Studies.

James Keller is Professor of English and Chair of English and Theatre at Eastern Kentucky University in Richmond Kentucky. He is author of nine books (most recently, *The Deep End of South Park*) and dozens of articles on topics such as early modern literature, film, theatre, gender and cultural studies.

Zbigniew Lewicki is Professor at Warsaw University (Institute for Interdisciplinary Research) and Cardinal Stefan Wyszynski University (Chair, American Studies). His past positions include Warsaw University English Department, and the American Studies Center (Director, 1999–2005). He held Fellowships from, i.a., the American Council of Learned Societies and Woodrow Wilson International Center for Scholars. He was assistant undersecretary for the Americas in the Ministry of Foreign Affairs (1991–1995) and Director for International Security at the EastWest Institute. He is currently at work on a multivolume History of American Civilization, two volumes of which have already been published.

Lars Lierow is a postdoctoral fellow at the Center for Research in Public History and Culture at the George Washington University. He received his PhD in American Studies in 2010 at GWU and holds a combined Master's degree from the Universität Leipzig in Communication and Media Studies and American Studies. His research combines the intellectual and institutional history of mass communication research with a cultural analysis of popular media narratives and of political movements. This work addresses questions of political power, ethnicity, and gender identities through the lens of changing interpretations of mass communication that are developed in academic settings as well as in popular culture, and which frequently circulate between these two domains. He is currently expanding and revising his dissertation *Gaps, Flows, and Networks: Social Space and the Cultural Work of Communication Theory in Social Science, Sci-Fi, and Political Movements, 1937-1980* for publication as a book.

Francesca de Lucia holds a Master's degree in English from the University of Geneva and a Diploma in American studies from Smith College. She received her PhD from the University of Oxford in March 2010. Her dissertation written under the supervision of Professor Paul Giles is entitled *Italian American Cultural Fictions: From Diaspora to Globalization*. She published articles on different aspects of ethnicity in American literature and film, including the representation of Italian American characters in Spike Lee's films, the novels of Anthony Giardina as a representative of the "renaissance" of Italian American writing and the combination of the African American and Italian American experience in Kym Ragusa's memoir *The Skin Between Us*.

Anna Mazurkiewicz, PhD, is Assistant Professor at the Institute of History, University of Gdańsk, Poland. Mazurkiewicz graduated summa cum laude from the University of Gdańsk in 1999. Ever since she has been teaching Cold War History, US and Polish History courses at her alma mater. In 2006 her doctoral dissertation received the main award of the Polish National Center for Culture. She published two books on the American response to the elections in Poland in 1947 and 1989; *Dyplomacja Stanów Zjednoczonych wobec wyborów w Polsce w latach 1947 i 1989* (Warsaw: Neriton, 2007) and *Prasa amerykańska wobec wyborów w Polsce w latach 1947 i 1989* (Gdańsk: University Press, 2009). She was a research fellow at the University of Notre Dame (Indiana), Immigration History Research Center (University of Minnesota), and the Open Society Archives in Budapest.

Grzegorz Nycz is a graduate of MA studies at the Institute of Political Science and International Relations (2005) and doctoral studies at the Institute of American Studies and Polish Diaspora at Jagiellonian University (2009). His PhD dissertation entitled *Between Persuasion and Intervention: American Democracy Promotion Policy after 1989*, defended at Jagiellonian University, aimed to analyze the significance of liberal internationalism in US foreign agenda after the Cold War. The author's research interests include contemporary US foreign policy, external factors of democratization processes and liberal theory of international relations, among others.

Elżbieta H. Oleksy is Full Professor of Humanities at the University of Łódź. She chairs the Department of Transatlantic and Media Studies and is Founding Director of Women's Studies Centre (2002), the first such institution in Central and Eastern Europe. She was Founding Dean of the Faculty of International and Political Studies (2000-2008). She authored/co-authored and edited/co-edited twenty-four books and over a hundred chapters and articles in the field of gender studies, visual culture, and literature. Her recent publications include three edited volumes: *The Limits of Gendered Citizenships. Contexts and Complexities* (Routledge, 2011), *Intimate Citizenships. Gender, Sexualities, Politics* (Routledge, 2009), *Teaching Visual Culture in an Interdisciplinary Classroom. Feminist (Re)interpretation of the Field* (Utrecht 2009). She holds Knight's Cross of the Republic of Poland. In 2007 she received Medal of Merit from the City Council of Lodz. She was a promotrix in the procedure of bestowing an honorary doctorate on President of the European Commission, José Manuel Durão Barroso.

Wiesław Oleksy is senior lecturer in the Department of Transatlantic and Media Studies, University of Łódź, Poland. He has edited and authored 10 volumes and numerous book chapters and articles on American Studies, contrastive linguistics, semantics and pragmatics, especially speech act theory, which appeared in Canada, Germany, Finland, the Netherlands, Poland, and the USA, e.g.: *Questions in English and Polish. Semantics and Pragmatics* (Edmonton:

Linguistic Research Inc.), *Contrastive Pragmatics* (Amsterdam & Philadelphia: J. Benjamins), *Language Function, Structure, and Change* (Frankfurt, New York: P. Lang), with P. Stalmaszczyk – *Cognitive Approaches to Language and Linguistic Data* (Frankfurt, Berlin: P. Lang). He was visiting professor at the University of Pittsburgh (1978-78, 1990-92, 2005) and SUNY at Buffalo (1990, 2001-2002). He is co-founder and co-editor of the American Studies and Media Series.

Ahti-Veikko Pietarinen is Professor of Semiotics at the University of Helsinki, Finland. He received the MPhil in Computer Science in 1997 and the DPhil in Philosophy in 2002. His scientific interests are in philosophy, theories of meaning, logic, Peirce and pragmatism. He has published logical and philosophical papers and edited several books, and is the author of *Signs of Logic: Peircean Themes on the Philosophy of Language, Games, and Communication* (Synthese Library, Springer, 2006).

Stefan Robel is Administrative Director of the School of International Studies (Zentrum für Internationale Studien - ZIS) at Technische Universität Dresden. His publications include articles on international hegemony and US foreign policy. In 2008, he co-edited the volume *Internationale Beziehungen - Aktuelle Forschungsfelder, Wissensorganisation und Berufsorientierung* (TUDpress). He is currently completing a monograph on US hegemony and theories of International Relations.

Ulf Schulenberg is a Visiting Chair of American Literature at the John-F.-Kennedy-Institute for Northamerican Studies, Free University of Berlin, Germany. He received his doctorate from the University of Bremen (Germany) in 1999, and in 2005 he finished his postdoctoral thesis ("Habilitation"). He has been a visiting scholar at Cornell University and at the New School for Social Research (Graduate Faculty, Department of Philosophy). His publications include *Zwischen Realismus und Avantgarde: Drei Paradigmen für die Aporien des Entweder-Oder* (2000), *Lovers and Knowers: Moments of the American Cultural Left* (2007), and *Americanization-Globalization-Education* (co-editor, 2003). His current book project, tentatively entitled *Romantic Redescribers: Pragmatism, Romanticism, and the Idea of a Poeticized Culture*, discusses the question of a romanticized pragmatism.

Sabine Sielke is Chair of North American Literature and Culture, Director of the North American Studies Program, the German-Canadian Centre, and the Forum Women and Gender Studies at Bonn University. Her publications include *Reading Rape* (Princeton 2002) and *Fashioning the Female Subject* (Ann Arbor 1997), the (co-)editions *Orient and Orientalisms in US-American Poetry and Poetics* (2009), *The Body as Interface* (2007), *Gender Talks* (2006), *Der 11.*

September 2001 (2002), *Making America* (2001), and *Engendering Manhood* (1998) as well as essays on poetry and poetics, modern, post-modern, and popular culture, literary and cultural theory, gender and African American studies, and the interfaces between cultural studies and the sciences.

Bohdan Szklarski is Professor of Political Science at the American Studies Center and in the Institute of Political Studies Polish Academy of Sciences. His research interests focus on political leadership, American politics and political culture and communication. He also serves as a director of the Institute for Leadership Studies in Collegium Civitas.

Barbara Tuchańska is Professor and Chair of the Department of Epistemology and Philosophy of Science at the University of Łódź, Poland. She held fellowships from, among others, St. Hilda's College, Oxford (1987), the Center for Philosophy of Science, University of Pittsburgh (1987, 1993, 1994-95), the Center National de la Recherche Scientifique, Equipe REHSEIS, Paris (1988); she was Visiting Professor at the Department of Philosophy, SUNY Buffalo (1990-91), and at the Cohn Institute of History and Philosophy of Science and Ideas, University of Tel Aviv (1996-97). Her last book *Science Unfettered. A Philosophical Study in Sociohistorical Ontology* (Ohio University Press, 2000) was co-authored with James E. McGuire. Her interests include philosophy and sociology of science, especially the problem of values in science, analysis of historical conceptions of analytic and a priori knowledge, the role of cognition and science in culture.

Index of names

Index of terms

American Studies and Media

Edited by Elżbieta H. Oleksy and Wiesław Oleksy

www.peterlang.de